TIBET-O-RAMA

Self and Other in a Tale from the Edge of Tibet

P. Christiaan Klieger

TIBET-O-RAMA

Self and Other in a Tale from the Edge of Tibet

Green Arrow Press   San Francisco

TIBET-O-RAMA. Copyright © 2002 by P. Christiaan Klieger. All rights reserved. Printed in Canada. No part of this book may be used or reproduced in any manner whatsoever without written permission except in the case of brief quotations embodied in critical articles or review. For information, contact Green Arrow Press, 584 Castro Street, #177, San Francisco, California 94114

Design by Eric

Library of Congress Cataloging Control Number 2001117919

Klieger, P. Christiaan
    Tibet-o-Rama: Self and Other in a Tale from the Edge of Tibet/
    P. Christiaan Klieger

ISBN 0-9711816-0-8

First Edition: January 2002
10 9 8 7 6 5 4 3 2 1

Printed in Canada

for Patrick Kho Sutomo Hermann

Contents

Preface...ix

Chapter 1. Coincidences..1

Chapter 2. Miniatures..21

Chapter 3. The Apotheosis of Captain Hook....................................45

Chapter 4. Frontiers of Experience..71

Chapter 5. On Dogmas and Cataclysms...105

Chapter 6. Götterdämmerung...139

Chapter 7. Knave of Hearts...177

Notes..199

Acknowledgements..201

Preface

This is a story about Tibet and some Tibetans, and Eric, an observer. I call it a type of reflexive ethnography as it attempts to locate meaning in an "interpretist" dialogue. There always has been at least some interaction between the ethnographer and those he or she studies--in this book the subject and object, Self and Other, become hopelessly blurred. I hope at least to convey some of the postmodern delight found in the position of an ethnographer working in the exotic corners of his or her imagination. In this book, I explore the developmental construction of the sense of the Other from Eric the child through the initiatory experience of anthropological fieldwork, and onwards. In a certain light, my work could be called post-feminist, as the classical feminist enterprise sometimes causes the investigator to disappear, "deconstructing the researcher as a whole human being, complete with biases and prejudices...an historic person who is engaged interactively with those being researched."[1] Through Eric's frequent entanglements, I attempt to break into one gender barrier that has yet to be crossed significantly in Western studies of Tibet: There are now and have been in the past many homosexual Tibetans and gay outsiders who have lived among them. Very few have bothered to note this fact let alone write about it. I hope to bring this ethnographic account closer to reality.

Since I like to think of myself as a complete being, this book is primarily about the blending of wild passions and professional interest in the exotic other, one of anthropology's last "taboos." Perhaps it is trivial, misrepresentative, and plain boring to continue promoting the cool paradigm that the "science" of other cultures can exist without emotional sentiment. The anthropological enterprise should be above all humanistic and enriching to civilization. Finally, my book is a post-colonial exercise, acknowledging fruitlessly the disparities of power and status, in this case between Eric and the largely marginalized, disenfranchised people he had studied for over 20 years.

This is a story about doing fieldwork in mythical and real Tibetan spaces. It examines the metaphorical image the "field" plays in the maintenance of the hierarchical relationships[2] between the anthropological undertaking and the world from which it derives its knowledge. In the process of depicting Tibetan culture, Eric is himself invented. In a series of small epiphanies, Eric's search for the Other makes a grand arc and falls back upon itself. The fertile matrix for these experiences is the amorphous realm of the field, which, as the ethnographer Hastrup suggests, has neither a firm past nor a distant future because its reality is intersubjectively constructed. The mystery of the field depends upon the ethnographer's presence there.[3] Thus Eric's story is an ethnographic reality, and only Eric can and his informants can tell it. As a work of non-fiction, everyone in this narrative is a real person and events actually happened in the sequence they are presented (Aha!--the claim to authority).

It is a curious irony that in historical discourse, all names should stay exactly as they were recorded; in ethnography, however, all names should change to protect the privacy of living people. Taking the hybrid route of the ethnohistorian, therefore, I have kept some names and changed others. In my own case, the author has chosen to maintain an all-too-transparent distance between himself and the narrator, Eric.

Perhaps because of particularly long history of myth building in the West and great expectations on both sides of the Sino-Tibetan political polemic, the nation of Tibet and the quest for Tibetan independence have always been profoundly conditioned by the literary, sociological, and artistic activities of distant outsiders. Eric and a thousand other *injis* (i.e. Western foreigners), as quixotic would-be heros and heroines for the cause of Tibet, may think of martyrdom of their Western selves, becoming "knights of Shangri-La" to serve the timeless utopian dream. In dogged pursuit of the Other, however, Shangri-La exists only as a moment lived.

P. Christiaan Klieger
San Francisco

1. Coincidences

It was late autumn, 1950. All around the northern hemisphere the leaves had turned orange and russet, and were leaving the trees as skeletons defying the icy wind. In China, the People's Liberation Army, flushed with the success of driving the forces of the corrupt Kuomingtang into the sea, invaded Tibet. Since World War II, China had been successful in recapturing some of the break-away territories of its former empire. In a bargain with the USSR, China received Manchuria back shortly after the war, despite Russia's domination of Mongolia and its successful 1945 invasion of the Manchu homeland. Mao's forces began not only consolidating their power in China proper, but expanded it to draw in regions that had gone their own way since the fall of the Ch'ing (Qing) dynasty. Tibet was one such country. Intermittently independent for centuries, the Buddhist pontificate had been, since the seventeenth century, bound to the Empire as a royal chaplain is bound to his king. Partly to insure the loyalty of devoutly Buddhist peoples of Inner Asia (mainly the followers of the Dalai Lama) and occasionally out of sincere piety, the Manchu emperors of China had patronized the Tibetan theocracy. However, by the early twentieth century, the weary Ch'ing dynasty finally threw in the towel and the child emperor Pu Yi was forced to abdicate.

The multi-national empire was finished. With no quasi-religious emperor to legitimize and counsel after 1912, and chafing at the abusive rule of Chinese overlords, the 13th Dalai Lama emerged two years later from the musty halls of the Potala in Lhasa and declared Tibet an independent nation. Although only marginally backed by the British empire, Tibet managed to hold its own against Chinese attempts at reabsorption until a stronger China under Mao was finally able to reassert its authority. On October 27, 1950, nearly 240,000 Chinese troops, imbued with a zealous mandate to redeem the Motherland, entered that forbidden land of Inner Asian antiquity.

Also on October 27, 1950, I was conceived in Kansas City, Missouri. My name is Eric Falkenberg. I am a German American who was born in Great Falls, Montana. My mother's parents were from Swedish Norway; my father was born in East Prussia. I come from a long line of square-jawed Nordics, tow-headed, with sea green eyes, who probably lived in their northern fastness since the end of the Pleistocene.

My story is about the quest for the absolute Other, about Orientalists and Occidentalists each battling windmills, individuals from the West and the East working in collusion to maintain their cherished myths about each other. It is a journey through time, both historical and lived, and a journey across continents and back again. It is about dogs chasing their tails.

Chapter 1

A string of molded, opalescent Christmas tree lights burned softly—a Zeus-like Santa's head, a pale blue bell, a snow-covered house. One light was of an inconceivable yet plainly human form. It was a little man: A softly glowing vitrine ivory face with painted cheeks of light rose…a long, jet black moustache and arched eyebrows framing curiously serpentine eyes. The glowing man wore an amber robe dashed in swirls of cherry red. A round hat was gathered to a topmost button of blue. The feet were tiny, the hands withdrawn in voluminous sleeves. In the eternity of a child's Christmas night, I reveled in these colors radiating from the man of unknown origins. This smooth form brought its own incandescence and warmth.

There is a major point of transformation in the developing minds of children. At first, ego literally creates the world—mother is materialized by one's pangs of hunger. Trees approach and recede to amuse you in dad's bouncing car. At some point, however, you realize that the isolated falling pine does make a sound. A child socialized in Western rationality soon learns that there is an external world, one frightfully indifferent to one's internal passions. But between such stages of mental development exists a transitional phase, a doorway wherein one can safely explore the external, dictatorial universe while enjoying the reassuring containment of the internal, self-engendered one. The boundaries between objective reality and self-projection are blurred. This is the child's magic.

My first experience with the excitement of radical otherness was catalyzed by a standard family Christmas, a time when the fantasies of childhood are usually granted freedom through the compassion of those serious rationalists known as adults. A light bulb became the agent, not merely the symbol, of a life-long inspiration. A Christmas decoration was my epiphany, an introduction to the Other, a kindling of a life-long quest to merge with it.

My mind had already developed to the point that I was assured the bulb was itself hardly animate. It just represented a real man from some mysterious realm. Does the man have a people with a history of glorious deeds? Each night that Christmas I blissfully gazed at the light, and each successive year my dreams of approaching the source of this mystery grew more concrete. Eventually I realized that this icon was but a mirror. The perceiver, the perceived, and the perception would be as one, and I would dissolve into the steady otherness.

It was one of those pure-blue spring mornings, turquoise and yellow, with the scent of white lilacs frosting the crisp air. I lay comfortably on my back in the neatly mown grass of my backyard. Clouds formed and disappeared—in the distance, a glint of silver. It grew into a gigantic Convair B-36, heralded by the haunting bass drone of six perfectly tuned piston engines. It was the earth's largest bomber, the vanguard of the Cold War, and was no doubt heading out over the Pacific to intimidate some Eastern enemy. It was the duck-and-cover time in America, full of dread and fear for us kids. The unearthly sound of the B-36! Its vibrations rattled the windows, effecting an ominous transcendence of sorts, carrying my essence with it. Six miles high, the lumbering bomber had captured me like Zeus' eagle. For that instant I had left the insane boredom of modest societal expectations. I projected myself beyond learning Miss Wing's silly songs about covered wagons and the mighty Columbia River and the dreadful anticipation of phys-ed class, high school proms, Lutheran marriage rituals, and carrying on the mindless chain of being. There is more beyond, and a means to reach it!

One went to Heaven in an airplane, I thought. Trains and planes were clearly the messengers of the gods. Appearing at one horizon, visiting mortals briefly, then moving off to some unknown world, such was the fascination in such objects. They were time machines, able to spirit you off to the antipodes.

Naturally, then, my first religious practice was building model airplanes. Model cement was a sacrament, paint and decals the gilding of the icon. No drug store, department store, or hobby shop was left unscoured for the rare Revell DC-7, Monogram Constellation, or Lindberg Comet. After hours of the most exacting construction, the styrene deity would be ceremoniously invested on the dresser/altar. Woe to the intruding mother or big sister who disturbed the sublime symmetry of this aeronautical pantheon.

Making graven images was augmented by actual pilgrimages to the airport. Sadly, the tiny municipal airport was graced by only two or three flights a day. One had to be content with soup and a sandwich at Mrs. Bosell's lunch counter at one end of the waiting room (Mildred Bosell had horrible bug-eyed, shivering chihuahuas at her home that were always flatulent).

As often as possible I would simply sit on my bike at the end of the runway, and relish the buffeting of the smoky wind of a landing propeller airliner. Avgas had a distinctive smell, a warm, comforting aroma completely different from the sharp, noxious fumes of the kerosene of the jet age. On occasion at this tiny airport, my favorite smothering aunt Minnie, redolent with cobalt colored "Evening in Paris" parfume and carrying a choice gift or two for me, would descend from a shiny Northwest DC-4 from Milwaukee.

The red-tailed Northwest Orient Airlines always signaled something special. The map on Aunt Minnie's ticket proved that it flew to Tokyo and Hong Kong. Perhaps this very aircraft had been there! It all became a big day in the community, too, when old Mayor Marian Erdman in mink coat and evening dress cut the ribbon on the gangway to welcome the first Northwest jetliner to service the milk run to Seattle. Jets were exciting, but dangerous: My fellow airplane cultists soon learned from the fat schoolyard know-it-all, Gordy Brown, that stewardesses were often sucked into the turbines.

Fair weather might herald enemy bombers. I had less fear on cloudy days and in the winter's darkness—so much more difficult to drop the A-bombs then. My home town was so near to a major SAC base for ICBMs. Unlike so many Kennedy-era adults, I didn't really believe we could successfully survive the Bomb under our little metal and wooden desks. I would hide in the restroom instead because it didn't have any windows. Is it true that radiation doesn't go around corners? We had a Third Grade teacher, the thin Miss Bean, a dead-ringer for the Grim Reaper.

My major vehicle of transcendence, trains, were something entirely benign, however. No one would ever deliver a hydrogen bomb by rail! As aircraft represented a young male's dreams of what could be, railroads were a link to a more complete past—a past with a father.

Dad and I shared a special trip from Montana to his original home in Milwaukee when I was a bright star at aged four. It seemed like traveling to Jupiter for me. Rail travel in America in the early 1960s forged a brilliant sunset to a wonderful era, a last valiant attempt to compete with advances in air and highway transport through the introduction of colorful streamliners. An image of sleekness, if not actual speed, had been applied by top industrial designers such as Brooke Stevens and Raymond Lowey to everything from Mixmasters to ocean liners.

Chapter 1

Most innovative of all the new passenger trains were the Chicago, Milwaukee, St. Paul & Pacific's *Hiawathas*. Cleverly combining an Indian motif suggested by Longfellow and Albert Speer's designs for Hitler's art deco super-train, Stevens created an orange, maroon, and chromium arrow that carried passengers from Chicago to the Pacific Northwest in innovative luxury. The new *Olympian Hiawatha*, stringing a Tip Top diner, Super Dome, and Pullmans, was terminated by a relentlessly phallic observation/solarium in tempered glass and a fluted band of red-trimmed stainless steel.

The train ride from Montana to Milwaukee and back would be the first, and only, experience of journey, excitement, and filial bonding ever shared with my father. Exotic Black porters proclaimed mysterious station names, and produced fluffy white pillows and an array of snacks from impossibly small spaces. Tucked securely with crisp sheets and warm olive-green blankets, night through the Pullman window brought the irony of an awake four-year old child rolling quietly through mysterious, empty city centers at 3 a.m. Day presented the spectacle of glimpses of the backyards of unknown families—blurred chickens scattering, laundry flapping in the wake of the train's rapid progress. The incongruous smell of diesel oil mingling with the smell of coffee and bacon in the diner—these impressions built upon the idea of "means" to achieve the goal of bodily escape.

Surely one of the most amazing travel experiences ever conceived was the bi-dimensional bomber's blister known as the Skytop Lounge at the back of the train. Gliding along at a moderate speed, sunk in a comfortable couch a few feet above the rails, it gave me the feeling of god-like omnipotence. More exhilarating than the flight of any bird, I was cocooned effortlessly in my own world of cushioned comfort, yet totally engaged in the other world of forest and brook drifting by, karmically immune from the outside world, but fully a part of it. I sped through the back roads like a soap bubble caught in the wind.

Dad had begun my initiation into the realm of the outside world. It was to be cut short two years later by his heart attack. Whatever remained of that early spark was subsequently smothered by an enveloping cloud of possessive maternalism. The Milwaukee Road and its *Hiawatha*, the colors maroon and orange, a day walking the rails—these were to become icons of interrupted initiation, symbols of lineage with the comforting Father and the archetype of the Great Other. The medium of the glass chrysalis lounge car became the ultimate vehicle of transcendence. I envisioned that it could carry me far, far to the east, to the lands where the mountains were twice as high and four times as beautiful as the Rockies. So I cried that day in May, 1961, when the bankrupt railroad discontinued its *Olympian Hiawatha* service across the Northwest. The Skytop Lounge cars disappeared, orange, maroon, and silver receeding. In 1980, it seemed a personal affront when the Milwaukee Road finally tore up its tracks. Now, whenever I look upon any railroad track, and note its disappearance beyond the horizon, I envision impossible feats. If I could travel fast enough along those steel rails, I would eventually come around to the past.

Similar, though darker imagery filled the most inner recesses of my consciousness. In a reoccurring nightmare, I walked along a railroad track. A menacing, inky black locomotive approached steadily, glistening in oil and grease and spraying voluminous clouds of acrid white steam. The stark, solarized midday landscape was as airless and disquieting as a De Chiraco painting. But the harder I ran, the more I was restrained. Powerful elastic bands suddenly attached themselves to my feet and to the ties. I was overwhelmed with a profound feeling of doom. Impact! And I would awaken in my little bed, hyperventilating, sometimes screaming.

How I fought to be delivered from Mother's social womb! I dreamt of running, breathlessly, silently from the widow's social matrix that aging Mother had created. I had a much older brother and sister, but they had departed for college when I was still very young. Being co-opted into matriarchal retirement is something ill-suited to most six-year olds, and potentially fatal to an adolescent. I was subject to a Donna Reed played by Queen Victoria.

The crushing confinement of the icy 1960s Betty Crocker kitchen was executed by the routine of sitting at home and being polite when the panoply of Mother's priggish woman friends came to call. There was the faintly mustached Midge Pfaffenburg, a thin, choleric polio victim married to a Dürer-like Lutheran carpenter. The diminutive Midge would moor up the driveway every couple of weeks in her huge bullet-finned Dodge Dart to cluck about her older son, perm my mother's hair and be preened in return. Pink rollers snapping, the sweet-sulfurous stench of developer would choke the house for hours while her big boy Stephen groped me on my bedroom floor. A luncheon of tuna fish sandwiches and frigid celery sticks would follow in the chrome and Formica kitchen. I was a dutiful son.

Then there was Mother's "Masonic" phase. Ever the patriot for the Old Country, she would visit the Sons of Norway Ladies Auxiliary, housed in a granite, Egyptian art-deco Valhalla from the 1930s. Here I passively listened to feminine war stories of the evil Quisling and the handsome hero-king Haakon VII. I'd hear about the ancient King Gustaf V, a spry tennis star at age 90. Bound to a chair at these Scandinavian tete-a-tetes, I sat rock still during the torture. A diorite Chephren enthroned, my impassivity would usually be betrayed by a display of inflamed, red ears. Similarly, the visits to the dowager Sena Schwabe, who was wealthy enough to serve boiled lobster on little rosemaling trays, was made claustrophobic by her obsessive devotion to the "Lawrence Welk Show" and its Norwegian accordionist, Myron Florin. "What a nice boy, Charlotte! Eric is always so quiet and reserved."

Prometheus bound to the girdle counter at Fliegelman's, I occasionally sneaked off down the block to Woolworth's pet department, to be found gazing at the caged birds or fiddling with the exotic Indian wisteria incense boxes in housewares.

Most adults presumed that I would rather be playing baseball or marbles, but I was actually complacent to my mother's wish for companionship. Realistic alternatives did not exist. I had no desire to play with my peers, as there were no peers. No one had bothered to teach me how to be a little anything, except as a footnote to my mother's being. The child's world became an arena of ridicule and taunting, a pack of wolves spotting and destroying the weak or inept. My response was not to implode into some sort of autism, but to ignore the affronts rather studiously. After all, I was going to live in the Taj Mahal, or in the Tartar prince's pagoda, swathed in the blue smoke of wisteria incense and lit by fireflies. Not only would I discover lost tribes in Central Asia, I'd join them and disappear forever. Rather than merely refusing to eat my broccoli, I choked on Beefaroni too. Escape the nurtured body! To the mother-fed matter that holds one down, let the gross body evaporate.

My universe became self-created, a solipsism fabricated upon the knowledge gleaned from distant others—books, maps, documentary films, and above all,

Chapter 1

National Geographic. Non-fiction only—the imminent world was too fantastic already, the neighborhood unfathomable, its society impure. A real world of excitement and freedom existed deep in Asia, where I would find the initiating father, the king, the philadelphic brother, and the compassionate companion. Male warmth had been terminated abruptly on September 7, 1957, the day my chameleon turned brown and stopped moving, and my father died.

My mother's sororal universe of WWII war brides brought with it the usual anti-Asian prejudice. "They were all japs!" they would say, a phrase that grated on my soul. Kaiser Wilhelm's jingoistic "Yellow Peril" reached a delayed apogee among these provincial, feminine American victors of the Pacific war. The Valkyries of Siegfried perpetually relived their triumph over the little brown Niebelungens. The few Orientals in town were relegated to the margins of society, and were mostly held in subdermal contempt. I felt especially sad for this.

I saw a beautiful photograph in the latest Time-Life Book of the Month that arrived one day. The book, entitled *Mountains*, dealt with both the geology and cultural geography of mountain peoples. In it was a documentary photograph of two intriguing, handsome looking young men on an airport tarmac, both wearing magnificent brocaded silk robes and holding bouquets of flowers. They were walking away from an old Soviet airliner. Older men in baggy fatigues were walking with them. The young men were the ruling lamas of Tibet, the caption read. The engaging, smiling monk on the right wore spectacles, which gave him a stately grandeur despite his teenaged years. Mesmerized, I read about this man, the Dalai Lama. Together with the Panchen Lama, the youth were being officially entertained in Beijing as guests of Mao Tse-tung. These awesome figures seemed to have jumped out of a legendary past, yet here they were in the flesh. What seemed astonishing was that these two archaic symbols still survived in the modern world! What wonders life beheld. I began to visit the library, reading everything I could find about Tibet. The little library contained very little, but I kept looking. Northern India, Siberia, Manchuria—a very ancient civilization was there as the heart of Asia. The Other was Truth itself.

Compared to the reality of books, my mother and her friends seemed illusory and hypocritical. Caroline Clary represented the converse of Midge—obese, with an eye for Civil War antiques and married to a Hungarian tax auditor. Perhaps she was descended from Napoleon's family, I fancied. Caroline drove an old, stately black Packard. When feeling adventurous, Mom and Mrs. Clary would head to the local Chinese restaurant. Caroline would look suspiciously at the vermiform noodles and bean sprouts at Wong's. She picked at her pork. "But they have such beautiful black hair, don't they?" my mom would apologize as the waitress receded, "You know, they helped build the railroads." Laughing silently at the debacle, I wondered why the Chinese who settled in the West had run away from their own Tartar prince. For this sort of future?

When not attempting to mollify the excesses of her friends, Mother had pointed observations about Asians herself, usually about the evil dwarfish Hirohito and his proud horse named White Snow. But one unintendedly became a prophetic suggestion to me. "There's nothing as handsome as a young Japanese man, you know," she proclaimed, "and nothing as ugly as an old one."

She maintained a odd vigil to a precious artifact from my father's war days—a Japanese officer's sword. For Mother it represented the humiliation and defeat of an enemy and was symbolic of the agents that had kept her husband away during the war. For me, it eventually became a phallic symbol of the warrior/lover. I became aware of its existence, though, only when my older brother took the sword away to Philadelphia after one of his more thorough lootings of my dead father's possessions. I appealed to Mother, who demanded, and achieved, the return of the sacred artifacts to her care. It was an ancient blade. What an idea, to seek initiation from a young Samurai, I thought--the golden boy at the gate of Asia.

National Geographic taught me much about the Tartar prince, from some unfathomable region deep within that continent. Young boys' fiction and Rimsky-Korsakov's music also hinted of a Central Asian hero who lived in the Jade Pagoda and hunted stags by moonlight. Phoenixes and dragons cavorted in his rock gardens, and wisteria draped from his bow. I will be this, I dreamt.

But formidable obstacles presented their chlothonian selves through my unfortunate natal circumstances and pubescent biology. This, my own Eric-self, discovered that adolescence brought an unacceptable hirsuitness. Stiff yellow flax could never match the satin black mane of my own Asia. A furry, lymphatic countenance would be no equal to a silken, caramel skin. Ambiguous, efflorescent beryl eyes are surely outclassed by the pharonic-onyx almonds of the Other. What sublime contrast!

But there is great danger with the absolute Other. The old journals I read were explicit about the eastern hordes that invaded the West:

> Towards other people, the Tartars are most insolent, and they scorn other persons, noble and ignoble. Moreover they are angry and of a disdainful nature unto other people, and beyond all measure deceitful, and treacherous towards them. Whatsoever mischief they intend to practice against a man, they keep it wonderfully secret, so that he may by no means provide for himself, nor find a remedy against their conspiracies.
>
> They are unmannerly also and unclean in taking their meat and their drink, and in other actions. Drunkenness is honorable among them, and when any of them has taken more drink than his stomach can well bear, calls it up and falls to drinking again. They are most intolerable extractors, most covetous possessors, and most niggardly givers.[4]

Were these the same people as those written about by the Victorian scholar Austine Waddell who encouraged Tibet to "herald the rise of a new star in the East, which may for long, perhaps for centuries, diffuse its mild radiance over this charming land and interesting people"?[5] Well, these were the Tartars—close, but really not the same people as the Tibetans. I read an account from a thirteenth-century Catholic cleric, Frater William:

> Beyond these are the people of Tibet, men which are in the habit of eating the carcasses of their deceased parents...However, of late they have left off this custom, as they became abominable and odious to all other nations on account of it. But they still to this day make fine cups out of them.[6]

In the fourteenth century, Friar Odoric commented on the white land of snows:

> Going on further, I came to a certain kingdom called Tibet, which is in subjection to the great Khan also...Many other vile and abominable things

> does this nation commit, which I mean not to write, because men neither can nor will believe, except they should have sight of them.[7]

It was clear that to survive, one had to become one of them, to join the tribe and proclaim loyalty to that chieftain. Maybe that is why they are still on this planet.

Throughout adolescence I had few intimates, no one with whom I could compare my changing body. The horrible seventh and eighth-grade gym classes – the typical scene of the more developed boys teasing the late ones, while a paedophillic instructor looked out from his picture-windowed office in sadistic glee. Luckily, being about in the middle of the development curve, I escaped the more severe taunts. Mystifyingly, however, adults changed their attitude to straight-laced Eric as puberty hit. Mother became visibly uneasy, and oddly forbade me from going out with girls. Aunt Mamie no longer let my female cousin and me play in her house unattended. Mrs. Hoell dissuaded her teenaged daughters from keeping up their long-standing, innocent friendship. People's anticipations of what the polite boy will now become changed as my body did. Internally, however, I was constant. In protest, I always refused to become what was somehow expected of my biology. I would revenge this miscalculation: instead of marrying the girl next door, I would marry a boy on the other side of the earth.

Puberty announced Eros, and with him a deeper probing into the nature of my prototypical Asian man, and further resignation to the realities of difference. The symmetrical axillary whorls and other subtle suggestions of indigo silk on ivory, elegantly accentuating, foiled this wooly, glacial-bred Caucasian. The Asian being no doubt possessed an ethereal violet scent with a hint of deepening. In comparison, I felt myself a musky trumpet, a burlap bag with stiff straw for hair.

My life of dedicated perpetual adolescence evoked Marie-Louise von Franz's *Puer Aeternus* and Antoine de Saint-Exupery's *The Little Prince*. The problem with Peter Pan was that he could not find initiation to the adult world, and therefore remained a boy. He remained the immortal *ephebe*, a gilded cup-bearer for the all-male pirate society dominated by Captain Hook. Decades later, Robert Bly brought it home:

> In any case these flying people, giddily spiritual, do not inhabit their own bodies well, and are open to terrible shocks of abandonment; they are unable to accept limitations, and are averse to a certain boring quality native to human life.[8]

All forms of nutrition were abhorrent to me. I became anorexic in an attempt to free spirit from matter. Voluptuaries and hedonists revolted me. My natural initiator had deserted me senselessly.

My male cohort went from ignoring me to showing a certain "fraternal" locker room interest that was just short of rape. This conditioned me to avoid all sports, becoming ill just before gym class, and holding my bladder all day. After school, I would quickly ran home, recommitted to building model airplanes, walking the tracks, and reading about Eskimos. Most special, though, was steeping myself in images of the Tartar clans and the Tibetans of the high plateaux. The visualized Other was Transcendence.

No one would take me to the den of male sponsorship in repressive, Republican Great Falls. While the girls in high school were pre-occupied in sampling the strawberry flavored frosted lipstick, and gossiping about who is doing what to whom, the boys went off in their packs, talking about sports, boobs, or the anguish of groundings. Mom, meanwhile, kept burning the rice. But there remained occasional glimpses of the sun-dappled forest, if only someone could help guide me there.

The Greeks, it seemed, had been responsive to the needs of their young men. Sadly, the modern West has only remembered the Law—not the sacred emancipatory drama of initiation. St. Augustine and other Doctors of the Church threw the young bloods out in the transformation of pagan baths into baptistries. Classical Greek society provided for a continuum of male life-stage initiation, with recognizable places and styles for its developing youth. As childhood faded, young boys were separated from their mothers and placed under the care of older youths who were bound to their charges' education and holistic well-being. As boys blossomed into young men, they would in turn secure a boy to nurture. In time, many young adult men transferred their attentions towards women—thus completing the cycle. What we call culture was the essence of this intense, intimate, age-graded transmission of extra-somatic knowledge.

The Greek model was evident in the actions of the gods. Even Apollo, locked in perpetual battles against the chthonian earth-mother Python, had time for beautiful Hyacinthus. Apollo was the prototype *kouros*, the "just-grown son" who becomes the master initiator.[9] Hesiod refers to him as the "epitome of that turning-point in the flower of youth, *telos hebes*, which the *ephebos* has attained and which he also leaves behind with the festival which gains him admittance to the society of men."[10] It is appropriate that Apollo is the patron of young men's rites of passage, for he himself is eternally a youth in transition. Apollo exists just on the inside side of the doorway, in that powerful state know as liminality.

The Church fathers, in concentrating on sodomy, missed the value of affection. There had been the blessing of male love throughout this process of turning a child into a man. The process of male bonding for the transferal of knowledge, common in other traditional societies, has been further and further buried in our own, the inheritor of Greek civilization. The nurturing male largely absent, many modern western boys are simply thrown from Mother's kitchen into the streets.

For me, self-empowerment and self-initiation were possibilities, but self-testing difficult. One could glean rational knowledge from books, but something or someone else was needed for proving intuitive awareness.

The summer of my first year in high school was a time that many of my generation felt the potentiality of great change. In one year the Beatles would change from preppie mod rockers to furry Sgt. Peppers and Grace Slick stopped ironing her hair, grew a double chin, and proclaimed her town of San Francisco the free-love acid bower of the world. The internal revolution began to quiver that special summer.

On an electric day during that summer we were slowly driving in Aunt Mamie's Ford Fairlane—mom and her two old-lady sisters, Mamie and Alma, with young teen Eric in the back. Riding along on a clear June 27, we paralleled the eastern front of the still snow-capped Rockies out on the high plains of central Montana. Our destination: the little farming town of Choteau, to visit cousins—raw-boned Luke, wife Edith, and their only boy Frankie. (Frankie used to play an odd game called "apartment" in the combine cab, but being eighteen, was now compelled to amuse himself by purchasing his high school friends' affections with the help of a generous allowance).

Chapter 1

The desiccated air was tinged with the smell of alfalfa, the fields in green wheat and yellow mustard. It was mid-afternoon, hot and dusty in the car. Mother's tackle box began emitting its reminder of last week's trout trip to Bean Lake. Elderly Aunt Alma, in dark glasses and straw hat, had dozed off. Suddenly I was struck by an impulse to remember that instant, that time, that day—to circle the calendar and stop my watch. Mark it!

Throughout the weekend of eating Edith's insipid ham and scalloped potato casserole and passively listening to Luke's Mancini records, I managed to keep fresh that lucid sensation. It gave me the motivation to avoid Frankie's groping hands during Disney's "Dumbo" at the Choteau Roxy.

The message had been from my significantly older sister. The year before, Judy had met a tall airman from Malstrom Air Force Base, was swept off her feet by his corn-fed Nebraska charm, and landed pregnant in the U.S. base in Izmir, Turkey. The encyclopedia entry read: "Izmir—near the Ephesis of the ancients, home to the great Temple of Artemis/Diana, an important fertility goddess of Asia Minor." About two weeks after visiting the barnyard cousins, a letter arrived announcing the birth of her first son. She had been thoughtful enough to provide the exact time of her delivery. With great confidence I checked time zones in the atlas. Sure enough, I had perceived the exact moment of birth.

No great feat in this changing world of imminent social upheaval, but it was a glimpse of my mind's potential to be receptive to non-rationality. It was also perhaps a means to escape the walls of monotony. For awhile I kept that channel dangerously open, often with the non sophistication of forcing the consciousness, straining Kreskin-style, with squinty eyes and furrowed forehead, to receive further clairvoyance. With nothing more forthcoming, I quickly went back to building airplanes and other self-absorbed diversions.

My own very special sixteenth birthday followed on July 27. I spent that morning at home in my very own sunny garden of ornamental gourds. Pollinating the flowers with a cheap artist brush, I had become intrigued with the varied shapes and colors of the bright squashes, their substantiality and weight. Yellow and green stripes. Meanwhile, my lazy cat scratched in the warm dirt at the edge of the plot. A Northwest 727 with a sooty tail flew close overhead on its final descent into the airport on Gore Hill. Further above, I watched the contrail progress of a distant jet. Like a blow to the head, I encountered an unmistakably recognizable sensation of "mindful significance"—an accute appreciation for the moment. It struck hard, ecstatic and frightening, as if a low-voltage current had begun in my feet and spread upwards throughout my body. The next recollection was of soft warm soil pressed on my nose, vines pricking my arms. For some unknown reason, I had lost consciousness. I picked myself up and brushed the crushed gourd flowers and pollen off my jeans. Moving out of the miasma, the dark swirls, I had the lucidity to go immediately to the calendar, circle the date, and jot down the time.

There were many significant referents to this incidence. Sixteen was the common iconographic age of Prince Siddartha Gotama Shakya, the Buddha, and the perpetual age of the god Apollo. It was the moment of the most transitory flowering of all *ephebe*, and coincidentally the apogee of the Summer of Love in San Francisco. In Beijing, the Emperor Hsuang T'ung, Henry P'u Yi, had dropped dead. Despite my agitated anticipation, no conformation of anything of personal significance was forthcoming in the weeks that followed—no letter arrived, no calls. Nothing unusual on t.v. It would be 21 years later, in a place 10,000 miles away, before I discovered the most compelling coincidence.

In high school, I saw a few Olympian gods. Contemporary Brian Lynch was the classic *ephebe* at sixteen, a true Apollo, frozen for a moment in a young male's bloom. He was a fleeting efflorescence of subtle physical beauty to grace the world, who would fade as the darker hormones added their adult gravity. Straight-A scholar, an athlete, Brian unfortunately gave nothing more of himself to others except the iconography of his outer visage. Like the unflinching sun itself, smoothly-chiseled Brian stood immobilized, unapproachable, as unmalleable as his marble jaw. However, locked into his own Narcissistic gaze, the sky-boy himself had not been fully initiated. He remained so—away to college on a full scholarship, Brian became a fabulous experimenter of drugs. And he became a Robin Hood for all sorts of activism. The government finally caught him sneaking on to Malstrom Air Force Base in Great Falls. He was arrested, tried, and shipped off to a god-forsaken prison named Boron in the middle of the Mojave desert in California, where smoothly muscled forearms turned into Popeye hams and his cool green eyes turned a dull grey.

The search continued. I signed up for an experimental class in Russian studies at school. Russia had Tartar princes. "Tartar" was really a Russian catch-all term for various Mongol, Turkish, and Uighur people, even the Tibetans. I reckoned the study of the language and history of the great Eurasian empire would be a way to find my past as possibly my future. Young Miss Palo was the teacher. We began with the alphabet, followed by simple phrases. Two weeks in, we were paired off to demonstrate our primitive dialogues. My partner was a boy named Karl.

Karl Folker Weiss was a golden German—one year younger than myself. While I was the lithe Prussian whippet, he was raw-boned and Afghan hound-like. Karl Folker was lightly bronzed from summer's farm work—and lanky, with big feet and hands that were comically at war with the general elan of his torso. He was exactly my height—that was important. Behind heavy tortoise shell glasses, mischievous brown eyes were framed by distinctive epicanthic folds. He was well-stamped with the legacy of the Mongol invasion of Europe. Bounding up to me at that first meeting, Karl boldly caught me off-guard with a quick sexual joke, then surprisingly stuck out his tongue, Tibetan-style, panting a greeting like a friendly panther. Irreverent as I was conventional, we quickly became good friends.

Karl and I learned about the gossamer Byzantine veneer of Russian culture, and of the absolute power of the Germanic Romanovs. We studied the Scythians, Kalmucks, Don Cossacks, and the people of Tamerlane. Together we discovered a world of holy icons and Gregorian chants, piroshki and samovars. We soon could speak to each other Russian, which became our secret language. We built St. Basil's Cathedral out of toilet rolls and golden Christmas bulbs. And we confidently tried to send ourselves to Moscow through Russian Club donut sales at school lunch. I continued reading everything I could find about the Russian experience with the Tartars. This golden race...

> the Tartars, broke loose from its mountain-environed home, and piercing the solid rocks (of the Caucasus), poured forth like devils from the Tartarus... Swarming like locusts over the face of the earth... For they are inhuman and beastly, rather

Chapter 1

> monsters than men, thirsting for and drinking blood, tearing and devouring the flesh of dogs and men, dressed in ox-hides, armed with plates of iron, short and stout, thickset, strong, invincible, indefatigable...[11]

But then, the Tibetans seemed to shine far above. I read:

> The Thibetians are of middle height; and combine, with the agility and suppleness of the Chinese, the force and vigour of the Tartars. Gymnastic exercises of all sorts and dancing are very popular with them, and their movements are cadenced and easy.[12]

We thought that the old Russians were astonishing, having finally thrown off the Mongol yoke.

Karl and I dressed up in Russian embroidered clothes and had the greatest of times, but our friendship existed only within the context of Russian class at school. There was little Rheingelt for me outside of this pedantic exploration. Pitifully unaware of his radiant splendor, Karl fumbled in half-hearted attempts to seduce buck-toothed Sheila MacConnell. His father took him hunting; he went camping with older friends; he joined the carnival! I went off to college.

I knew nothing about the social world around me. I was completely incompetent at university social life. Freshman boys would begin an acquaintanceship, then mysteriously abandon me. Cloistered in the dorms at the other end of campus, girls did not exist. All there was were monotonous core courses, libraries, and homework. Worse yet, Mother decided to move to town. A cost-cutting move, she rationalized. Besides, she could be closer to her sister Alma. She bought a trailer at the edge of town, and I had to live there.

I buried myself in Russian studies, Russian culture, the closest thing to the Tartar East that I could experience. I joined the Russian folk dancing club. In my father's riding boots, and in satin tunic, I could execute the most demanding steps for hours. My Russian professors were old emigres, who would hold intimate gatherings with vodka and *blini*.

On the other side, Karl had run off to work on his cousins' farm in Missouri after high school. Then he joined Strain Brothers carnival touring the upper Midwest. He ran the Zipper, and slept under the flat-beds, if he wasn't with some barker's young daughter. Aunt Mamie, returned in a pique from the State Fair the summer of 1971, announced his return to Montana:

"The fair was grubby as usual," she sneered, "and the carnival people were despicable. There was this greasy blond man that ran this ride...you should have seen him picking up the coins that fell from them. Those awful carnies are the *lowest!*" I knew then that Karl would be my fast pal.

Karl wandered onto campus one late winter's evening, and right into my path. He was soft-spoken, timorous, perhaps a bit intimidated by the august university. Karl had returned, and I had the upper hand on college experience. By now I had immersed myself in this thing called anthropology. For me, it was a safe means for an outsider to safely view the exotic Other from the comfort of the Lodge fireside, the quiet library, and Mom's trailer. I would try to bring him to these new discoveries.

Karl now was a boy of the world, the immediate world of the flesh and the pharmaceutically stimulated mind. He entered a state that bore the imprint of a sacred chrism. Girls lined up for his blessings. He seemed almost Christ-like, bearing fools and injustices with warm compassion. His golden hair was shoulder-length, he wore matching gold-rimmed glasses. He dressed in faded jeans and supple flannel shirts. His feet padded softly on winter-worn leaves.

Karl had a special girlfriend, living in the redwoods in California. I had a car. So I thought, until Mother decided she couldn't part with shopping at Safeway for two weeks. Then, at least I had the time—it was spring break. We found a ride to Chico, out on the flatlands of California's Central Valley. Then the work began—hitchhiking across California to Humboldt County.

"We have to split up. We'll have better chances getting picked up that way," Karl intoned. Protesting, I walked a hundred feet away and watched while a car door opened for Karl. It seemed like a Steinbeck novel. Eventually, through harrowing rides with drunken high school kids, single businessmen, and even with an odd gold prospector or two, I arrived at Arcata. Karl, who had arrived that morning seemed proud.

I met Molly, his passion, and her mother, an actress. An all woman household. Here were five daughters, all playing bit parts in "Playboy of the Western World" at the village theater. That night, while Karl disappeared into a bedroom, the other muses prepared a magnolia bower for me on the porch. Bridget, a Garbo-esque younger daughter, lingered, presenting me with an unexpected kiss while tucking me in. The scenario was all wrong. We were drones in a hive.

In a few days Karl and I were off to San Francisco. The southbound bus from Arcata depot was an old Greyhound Scenicruiser, the 1950s type with a glass enclosed upstairs in imitation of the railroad streamliners. We camped out the front row of the empty dome, sitting up all night talking. We shared secrets as stars and mysterious little towns on U.S. 101 drifted past. It was cool and I felt Karl's warmth, arms brushing. He told me his shortcomings—I asked him to instruct me with the things that I knew. We both became quiet, the whine of tires on asphalt. I drew inward, imagining a coyote howling. Headlights caught the dust-frosted windows, turbulent semis strained to pass. An eon of silence smoldered dull red with the eastern horizon. Whether in sleep or its pretense, Karl's blond head found support upon my shoulder.

There had been a heavy night of drinking and marijuana in the dorm. The holidays were over, and we were glad to return to the social rounds. I had become the dorm paramedic—something in my genes, perhaps. I enjoyed patching up my male colleagues. Andrew had taken a nasty tumble on his cycle. It took quite some time to carefully wipe off the blood and clean up the abrasions from his arms and forehead. Brad and Tim had retched their guts on cheap vodka, so out came the chamomile tea and saltines in intervals throughout the day.

The late Saturday afternoon was dark with winter. A few new students had arrived, and those of us with tenure stood around in the corridor gossiping about the neophytes.

"Faggots moved in down the hall," recovering Tim chuckled, "the R.A. found them sleeping in one bed last night."

"Do you mean the guy with fuzzy hair and that goon in 724?" I laughed, but Karl turned away.

"I s'pose we can deal with them—but there's my new roommate who's a real interesting character," Andrew suggested. "You've got to meet him, Eric—sort of spacy."

I peered into Andrew's room, and shot a quick salute to a young man

Chapter 1

named Ross. After dinner, Karl began to groom himself for Saturday night's one-night stand. I didn't care — I needed a respite from the usual tension. Suddenly Andrew and Ross entered the small room. Karl slipped out for his date.

Ross had been a football jock — now he was a serious biology major. Naturally a big guy, with nearly inaccessible, beady eyes and walrus mustache. Ross Howard was the son of a wealthy family that nearly owned an entire county in the rangelands of eastern Montana, between Roundup and Ingomar. The Milwaukee Road ran through it. I found the mark and looked at him squarely: I seemed oddly mindful of my life playing through at that moment. My life, my stage.

"What are you doing here?" I unexpectedly blurted out to this complete stranger, as if I had known him all my life.

"What?...nice to meet you too," Ross flinched.

"So...what?" I continued, "Let me guess. You're from Flathead Lake and have just transferred from Bozeman. You have something to do with bugs, or something?"

"Yeah, sort of. You've been talking to Andrew, I bet. You guys!"

"No, let me finish. You have a lady friend named Cheryl or Shari. And she has long blonde hair and a small nose. This is a difficult relationship. And I think your family has a lot of property somewhere."

I would have continued, but Ross reached into his wallet and showed me a photo of a Sharleen with features identical to those I had described.

"You've just told me the story of my life, too," Ross flushed.

I maintained my stare. "Right," I growled. I could not believe the strange discourse, yet it continued the entire evening.

I built upon the confidence of that first meeting. While I uncannily knew everything about the events in Ross' life, I never could probe the workings of his enigmatic mind. At some level I always hit a brick wall. Furthermore, while trying to plumb the depths, he methodically noted the structure of my own mental machinery. Soon he knew all the switches of my personality, as I had known Karl's. One false step, one betrayal of trust, I would be in serious trouble.

Nothing ouija-board about this encounter. It was merely a demonstration of power that I had no idea was contained within. Ross had simply made me aware of it. This had been, unknown to me at the time, my first empowerment. And Ross was no Apollo — straight as an arrow, bespectacled, with a Dionysian pot-belly at 21. I didn't expect the initiator to come in such an incredulous package.

Poor Karl was dismissed as a would-be mentor, a warm but simple Ozark boy. He was relegated to the status of an unattainable grown-up Ganymede. The gods of the intellect were at play — let the games begin.

Imagine visiting a party in the women's dorm lounge with your male friend, not being seen or heard, gliding silently like St. Elmo's fire, recording all the details of conversation, the girls clothes, and the sequence of events. The next day we would confirm the details with the women party-goers who had never seen us. "Someone must have told them," sniped Louise, "and why would they want to know — it was nothing anyway, just a little get-together." It seemed like Ross and I had been without material form.

I would never know if Ross led and I followed, or if we merely inspired each another to seek out the unknown through the power of will. A manifestation of this will created a shared reality. Without this counterpoint, it would be easy for one to dismiss such dealings as hallucinations. Without Ross, I could easily console myself that these ventures were merely the dreams of a stressed-out student during exam week.

At school, I began a serious study of the peoples and cultures of Asia. Best of all, an undergraduate seminar called the Peoples of Inner Asia. The professor talked mystically about the Tartars, Mongols, Manchus, and Tibetans, the shamans of the Yakut, and the Dalai Lama. Dr. Frank Bessac had been "there," a footnote to the times of the great Heinrich Harrer, the Dalai Lama's Austrian tutor. Soon, I found myself painting Chinese landscapes and writing *sutra*—on both accounts I was unfortunately accused of plagiarism.

My focus grew sharper. The word "Tibet" turned all the lights green. The remotest of possibilities was attaining a certain gravity—Tibet might be a real place after all. Despite the Chinese, despite the borders sealed since 1950, it may someday be possible to visit. And if that was not a Sisyphian task, perhaps in this long-forgotten mountain fastness, the living Grail breathed—the perfect Tartar prince, with jet eyes and a black stallion's mane. I would endeavor to be prepared for those impossible occurrences. Ross' "teachings" and our experimentation with time and space, were understood within the context of prosaic purpose. *Tantus labor non sit cassus.*

With mouth agape, like Alexander Ammon with the ram's horns, I was on the path. Certain colors, textures, and perspectives would sometimes bring on vivid images of a different world. I set off on my own. I read further from the journals of Abbé Huc:

> There is lamentable licentiousness amongst [the Tibetans], and we are disposed to believe that the blackest and ugliest varnish is powerless to make corrupt people virtuous.[13]

Unusually cold for early spring, nearly eight inches of dry-powder snow muffled the streets. The blue shadows grew darker. At 6 p.m. Ross and I were walking home from Safeway. Soft fuchsia and green pillows of neon-tinted snow lined the path through the parking lot. Sealskin footfalls were the crunch of bone-dry marshmallows. My Air Force parka became a snug sheepskin. My ski cap grew fur-lined lappets framing conical, embroidered felt. The shopping bag became a leather lead—two small ponies followed. I hesitated to look at Ross. I let the image develop and sharpen. Missoula, Montana had disappeared. Looking outward, I saw yurts girding the eastern horizon on a vast expanse of snowy steppe. I was as warm and as shaggy as experience had told. Footfall following footfall, we crunched ourselves homeward. Approaching the village, we passed the long, grey and maroon lamasery, windows stenciled with the dull orange reflection of countless golden Buddhas contained within. Slowly, flickering butter lamps became streetlights again. Conical felt tents dissolved into split-levels with picket fences, maple trees lining the sidewalks. I had fallen through the White Rabbit's burrow and Ross hadn't flinched!

Two months passed. I was up to the usual patching up of my buddies. Drugs were becoming a major recreational toy on campus, and I was often sought out as "navigator" to steer my friends back to normal reality. Bomber jacket, white scarf, compass, and astrolabe became symbols of my profession. A precise chronometer was needed to propitiate the Zeitgeist, and to ground oneself in real time for the voyages of my colleagues and myself. Quartz crystal technology was just coming out and Ross and I rushed to build the most accurate clocks possible.

Chapter 1

Two Heath M100 kits were ordered, built, and calibrated (over the dorm phone) by a tone from the National Bureau of Standards atomic clock in Ft. Collins, Colorado. I found rub-on letters in a futuristic font, and inscribed the letters "LTV" from the aerospace company on the face plate of the clock. It sounded so high tech. We didn't know what to expect of the awesomely precise chronograph—perhaps the clock would serve as a flight controller for exploring the frontier of mind and body.

It became evident that as "scientists" Ross and I needed to develop our technique beyond that of parlor tricks—something to prove beyond doubt that apparent manipulation of time and space could reveal itself with empirical evidence. No one really believed in the English plumber's son turned Tibetan scholar known as T. Lobsang Rampa, who wrote such spurious tomes as *The Third Eye*; we were working on something altogether different.

Outside of the famous dorm room where so many experiential firsts had occurred, spring had begun to melt the blue ice. I had been suffering cycles of fever, brought on perhaps by the usual cold or flu. At night, as my temperature rose beyond 102 degrees, my consciousness hovered a few feet over the physical inferno below. In the early morning, as the body temperature dropped, I would return. This occurred repeatedly, until the out-of-body phenomenon became accepted, predictable, and eventually enjoyable.

Clocks installed, experience gained—Ross and I waited. Nothing remarkable about this evening. Ross returned at 9:00 pm from the library. I had spent those hours doodling in my notebook on Central Asian nomadic life for a term paper due in a few days. I was anticipating finals week and another spring break sojourn to California with Karl. Sleep came easily—then morning. I awoke to a splitting headache, my bed damp with perspiration. My entire body trembled, as if I had run the marathon. Ross awoke with a start. We both stood up and began instinctively to investigate the room.

"Something weird happened here last night," I suggested to Ross.

"Moroccan leather and candles," Ross sputtered. "What?"

"Why are the windows open?" I asked, the sharp wind blowing melting ice crystals onto my desk. We always kept the windows shut in the winter. "You're not going to believe this. Look at the furniture!" The chairs, the stereo, the draperies, the books on the floor, the beds themselves—their long axes were oriented to a point just outside the southwest window. Papers were scattered on the floor. It was as if a great blast had forced the window open and blown the objects into alignment. Or perhaps the opposite: A tremendous pressure had emanated from the room itself, propelling objects towards the window like a ruptured aircraft in explosive decompression.

"What the hell," my roommate sputtered while closely examining the pens, pencils, coins, and coffee mugs strewn on the floor.

"Ross, I think we did this," I cautiously suggested.

"Moroccan leather and candles!"

"Yes, and it was dinner somewhere," I added, "somewhere exciting and expensive."

"Lights. There were candles on the table, and lights outside."

"They were city lights. We were in a tall building. On the top of a tall building."

"In San Francisco. The Mark Hopkins Hotel—last night," Ross added.

"Green Moroccan leather upholstery" I elaborated. "There were two women with us."

"Two brunettes. One was short," Ross suggested. "We were there about two hours. You had shrimp and I ate steak."

We continued to feed each other details in counter-point. The image became more lucid. I recalled the words on the menu, the dinner conversation. Then our talk abruptly stopped; a chill ran up my spine. San Francisco is 1,000 miles away. We had left late one night and returned early the next morning. Tiny Missoula had no flights to the West Coast at that hour. Even with a Concorde, it would have been impossible to have visited San Francisco that night.

There were really only two possible explanations. Ross and I could have shared a dream, or we had mutually experienced astral travel. Not even the finest Hollywood stagecraft expert could have aligned the objects in room in such a convincing manner. This was not artifice — a Tungusian comet had imploded just outside the window. We had empirical proof of the dissipation of energy that had carried our aetherial bodies out the window and 1,000 miles to the West Coast. Static electricity still filled the room. Tiny arcs crackled from fingertips; body hair stood outwards. By slender silver cords, we had been tethered to our sleeping bodies under the steady glow of the quartz chronometers. Very dangerous business, this. Had anything disturbed our sleeping bodies, the umbilicus might have snapped. That would be certain death, according to my dog-eared Tibetan *Book of the Dead*. And for the matter of hubris, *miserere nostri Domine*!

Adepts? For me, the title was easier to accept — my Asian interests, my prophetic childhood. But Ross was an empiricist. Spring break began two weeks after the profound explosion in Room 325. Ross took off, by conventional flight, to San Francisco. A visit to the top floor lounge at the Mark Hopkins Hotel dispelled any remaining doubt he had. Ross drank a cocktail, sitting on green Moroccan leather.

Initiation is non-cyclical — it runs a course as straight as an arrow, as vectored as time. Ross and I remained roommates the following year, but no amount of contrivance could replicate the experience. Nor would we ever discern the initiator from the initiated. Ross denied having any capacity for instruction of this nature. I certainly knew my limitations.

"You will eventually forget all of this," Ross pontificated, "and you will fall to the ground as surely as a tower built on quicksand." He was mistaken.

While Ross went off to make a fortune in Saudi oil fields, and Karl fell deeper into various indulgences, I departed to search for the source of knowledge fleetingly glimpsed from childhood. Coincidence was not a good answer.

Since I had begun to master some of the empirical knowledge of my own Western culture, it seemed logical that intuitive, non-empirical knowledge might be gathered at the antipodes of the West. To do this, I would have to remain the fly-boy, Pan, or King of Sea Otters.

That third year of college, when I read the *Bardo Thodol* and Baba Ram Das, and began to learn of reincarnating *tulkus* and other forms of Tibetan metempsychosis, I completely convinced myself of a proximate past life as a fallen Khampa warrior in the Chinese invasion of Tibet in 1950.

I lived a fractual life in the West. Roles that significant others played in my life had become increasingly specialized, as Weber's theories of individual propriety suggest. As socialization progresses for Western children, there are teachers teaching ever more narrow subjects. As adults, our employers offer work for highly specialized tasks over carefully defined time limits. We have specialists to advise us on our finances, taxes, insurance, our unhealthy habits—doctors for every part of our bodies. Many have different people providing sex, social standing, and companionship. In the development of Western industrialization, our family structure has moved steadily from the extended family, through the nuclear family, to a point of social cohesiveness which exists only at the individual level, if not beneath. EuroAmerican identity is particularly subnuclear; the social aggregate is thoroughly dead.

If there is a thread of ego that provides a degree of relationship between the multifarious roles that we play, it is usually buried by layer upon layer of accreted, contractual role expectations. The statement "I will" becomes a hollow cry of self-determination as the tidal forces of modern society tear the individual into smaller and smaller units.

I wanted to rejoin the tribe. I was living then, miserably, in Chicago, full of *anomie* and frostbite. Except for the harsh weather, there was nothing remotely Central Asian here, just a down-and-out Chinatown on the scary South Side. I stayed with the Logan family, that all-female household from Arcata, California via Great Falls who moved to the big city. They were all teaching or studying drama, or acting in the theater. We all lived with two other young males reaching out to the acting profession; but we were all distinctly non-sexual in this matriarchy. We were as eunuchs brought into the household for amusement, it seemed. Rob played the brooding Hamlet, Danny was a cartoonist, I acted the scholar. But there was no wholeness in this highly artificial family. My complete lack of integration fueled the long-standing quest for the absolute Other. The consumption of exotica became my passion.

Of course, the quest for atonement has many other manifestations. The appeal for the foreign is manifest in the tension between "traditional" and modern societies. Traditional societies are those whose religious, vocational, procreative, economic, and political activities are embedded in a highly integrated social network. An older, less complex way of dealing with the vicissitudes of every day life.

The exotic, defined as being supramundane and beyond the realm of everyday experience, may have either a spacial or temporal aspect. Some seeking integrative therapy wax nostalgic for the past, or the idealized past: Donna Reed's nuclear family kitchen of the 1950s, the neo-pioneer survivalists of the American Northwest, Art Deco collectors and Model T buffs. Being in control of a simpler world—this is why pot bellied middle-aged men wear choo-choo hats and play with toy trains. In the recent past, Marxism no doubt appealed to many with visions of bringing an ideal, egalitarian past to the foreground of present experience.

Yet others seek the exotic by roaming the world, experiencing glimpses of apparently integrated traditional societies through plastic bubbles provided by the international tourism industry. Still others dabble in Eastern religions, pan-African revitalistic movements, the vanilla religions of the New Age, and the darker realms of the Occult. Characteristic of all is that both spacial and chronological dimensions are distanced from the position of the seeker. There is repressed knowledge careening backwards in time and space to the ancient Greeks, perhaps also thecohens of the Jewish Temple, sun-worshipping priests of Pharonic Egypt, and even to the nebulous inhabitants of the violet-hued halls of mythical Atlantis.

With the failure of science to provide self-integration, post-modernists seek atonement in institutions with deep historical or exotic spacial referents. Sending men to the moon was done not so much out of practicable scientific concern but for the social power gained through knowledge of a different world. Such also motivated Alexander of Macedon and Captain Cook.

Having lost the tribal chieftain, we in the modern West still search for the archetype, the Father of the Country or the Great She-elephant. What great symbol do we have, that transcends all time in our historical legacy and is still a presence in our everyday thoughts?

Powerful symbols of this sort do not drop from the sky, but rather are invented concepts charged with meaning through human thought, acceptance, and action. Key symbols are over-layered with manifold meaning as they transit the experience of human history. There is a diversity of meaning inherent in this sort of symbol, establishing a "reservoir of historical potential waiting as it were for its own pragmatic clues."[14] Although apparently fixed at any given point of time (a historic document, for example), symbols are always meaningfully negotiable. Contextual changes, however small, continually affect the interpretation of symbols.

Powerful symbols tend to be contradictory, simultaneously revealing and concealing themselves. I kept thinking of the Dalai Lama, finding it hard to believe that such an institution was still present in my lifetime, the god Chenrezi, the sacred teacher of the Manchu emperors. But in the 1970s, few people knew anything about him. He was tantalizing, and mysteries and secrets partly revealed are powerful. Ironically, the Dalai Lama institution would become a core symbol in the modern world over the next 30 years. The ability of the present Dalai Lama to skillfully manipulate a complex of indigenous Tibetan and Western meaning demonstrates his success as a leader.

All kings and queens regnant, then, are divine—even modern ones. What a precious resource so few in the contemporary world appreciate. These beings are generators of immense stores of rich mythology. The twenty-first century West, with its obsession with secularism, has tended to dismiss thoughts of the continuing, and very real power of living symbols and their religious indices. We still have a need for them. Perhaps Wagner was right when he explained the ancient story of the Götterdämmerung, the "twilight of the gods":

> European men and women gradually stopped feeding the abundant gods and goddesses with their imaginative energy. The inner heaven collapsed, and [all] we see around our feet is broken glass.[15]

The inherent dualism of kings is further demonstrated by the existence of a "body politic" and a "body natural." Not only do kings represent deeply imbedded mythohistorical ideals representing society as a whole, they possess a human body that is in no way different from other individuals in society. It generates a paradox, and power arises in the tension between apparently contradictory references: worldly/otherworldly and mortal/ immortal.

Through religious ideology, spiritual inheritance as well as biological ancestry tie the Tibetan people to the symbol of the Dalai Lama. As stated repeatedly by the present Tibetan leader, however, the role of the Dalai Lama is determined by the will of his people. This must be a magical democracy, then, and his people must be as sacred and pure as the snows of the High Himalaya.

Chapter 1

The question compels: who are these people?

I had read all I could about the legendary Dalai Lama and the mythical Tibetans. It was now time to discover the reality, my own colonial experience:

> The unknown is at once an enticement and a challenge; it awakens in us both the lover and the would-be conqueror...Each projects his romantic hopes on the stranger, as well as his designs; and each pursues both his illusions and his vested interests with a curious mix of innocence and calculation that shifts with every step.[16]

2. Miniatures

Despite several recent, gallant attempts to demystify Tibet and to pull it unabashedly into the glare of the twentieth century, most of the West refuses to budge from an imaginative hold on its last terrestrial fantasy. Even the august halls of the National Geographic Society, purportedly a fortress of scientific objectivity, pines away like a sensitive school girl over Tibet. A while back, the Society ran an advertisement for its exhibition, "Shadows of a Lost Civilization":

> The remote Tibetan-border regions of western China, whose forbidding beauty has drawn adventurous travelers for centuries, was home to a dwindling culture when famed National Geographic photographer [Rock]...first ventured there in 1922.[17]

While written in 1992, the style could have easily been 1792. Tibet the Sacred is ageless.

There would be many others seeking the same from Shangri-La, but I thought I stood among the first. Thinking you've made a great discovery is a peculiar characteristic of the Tibetan subject matter in the West, regardless of the age. Having long lost our familiarity with the principle of divine right, many Westerners set forth to the Himalayas for their god, their divine king.

I sought to find redemption through the exotic Other from these great mountains. Eric with his aquamarine eyes and mouth agape, sought no less than the Golden Fleece. Over the years, many Tibetan refugees living in exile would become victims of the exotic hunger born in the West. Other Tibetans were motivated into action by their own "occidentalist" fantasies of the West.

For many alienated Westerners, Tibet-in-Exile formed a viable court around a holy king, the Dalai Lama. He came to be a shared king, a divine king for the West and the traditional leader of the Tibetan exile community. The popular culture image of the Dalai Lama is generated though ideological convergence. Tibet is deeply embedded in the collective Western memory[18] as the paragon of Otherness. It lingers still, for its roots are nearly as old as western civilization itself.

Having glimpsed the realm of spiritual possibilities by peering over the edge of consensual reality, I plunged headlong to the antipodes of my own existence, heedless of college buddy Ross's stern warning and even the needs of my own body. Temporary jobs were merely generators of funds to fuel intellectual endeavors in the pursuit of exotic redemption. Casual relationships were tolerated only as they contributed to mundane expediency in the quest for the distant Other.

I had never thought much about Hawai`i. It's just a place where pineapple comes from, I gathered, having never been there. Yet I was troubled by a reoccurring dream about the islands. I simply conjured up a ideal setting; I never

Chapter 2

did anything in it. My mind just formed an image of a bay, with a tiny island in the middle. There were mountains on either side of a turquoise inlet, a landscape framed by two coconut trees in full bloom. I did not know why I was there, but it felt like no mere vision: I felt the cooling trade winds on my face, and heard the grackle of mynah birds hopping on the lawns. With the scent of frangipani in the air, butterflies flitted among the red and orange impatiens that stretched out before my feet.

When the time seemed right, I just moved to the Islands, never as a tourist, never with false visions. Hawai`i became a convenient locale, a launching pad physically and ethnically halfway between the United States and Asia. It seemed completely practical.

Tibet took corporeal form for me in the middle of the Pacific Ocean at the very end of the disco era. The XVI Gyalwa Karmapa, the head of the "Black Hat" lineage of the Kagyupa sect of Tibetan Buddhism, arrived in Hawai`i on a world tour. The Karmapa, acknowledged by his followers as a reincarnation of the God of Compassion (and thus in competition with the Dalai Lama who shares that title), had one foot in this world and the other in a state impervious to the karmic laws of cause and effect. As a bodhisattva, he was considered by his followers to be an active element in disseminating the full teachings of the Buddha, a prescription whereby any sentient being could achieve non-reincarnating transcendence.

During the "Black Crown" ceremony, the Karmapa would become the god in an elaborate ceremony that culminated in suspending over his head a black hat allegedly made from the hair of celestial nymphs (*dakini*). At this point the deity would pronounce benedictions to the congregation. The matte black and golden crown was removed, and the high lama resumed the guise of an ordinary Buddhist cleric. The message was clear--with proper meditative training, everyone can be transformed into an emanation of the divine.

The Karmapa's entourage arrived in Honolulu. The ritual began with a sonorous monk-choir, accompanied with cymbals, bells, and discordant Tibetan trumpets. The stage was lined with yellow silk; immeasurable red, green, and salt blue prayer flags fluttered in the bright tropical sunlight. Rapturous Dharma groupies sat lining the aisles, swaying to the ethereal overtones of the monks' chanting.

The appearance of a white-toothed young Tibetan layman as English translator flashed an added dimension to the transformation of the Karmapa. Dressed in a black robe gathered just below the waist with a crimson sash, his long, straight hair perfectly fettered a rare ornament of turquoise and gold. Black velvet boots were trimmed with red piping. A proud Tibetan layman had appeared—the earthly supporter and aide to the imminent epiphany of the Black Crown god. My mind raced: a Tibetan prince, one of those worldly children of the last god-king on earth, the Dalai Lama and his vicars. By such intimate association with the divine, worldly Tibetans must too be possessed with a degree of sacredness, I thought. In comparison to the crass, material grasping of Westerners, any Tibetan seemed a perfected being, cleric or otherwise.

The Karmapa returned to his secular form. In a scene uncomfortably reminiscent of an Oral Roberts revival, the prince then invited interested parties to come forward and take refuge in the Buddha, his teachings, and the community of practitioners—ostensibly to become a Buddhist in the presence of the Karmapa. The initiation was two-fold for me. While the Karmapa's gaze and his tap on my head brought me into Buddhist practice, the prince's escorting to and from the throne seemed symbolic of an introduction to the secular world of Tibet. One could approach the totally transcendent through the relative sacredness of these biological kindred of the sacred bodhisattva. The invasion of my West by lama troops had begun. In the waning glow of the '60s and '70s spiritual experimentation, refugee Tibetan priests were finding a niche. Refugee lamas provided institutional order to many Westerners seeking to perpetuate the inspiration of the preceding decade. The god/king was still on his throne in the Himalayan village of Dharamsala, and all would be well with the flocks of brain-fried psychedelic survivors of that great EuroAmerican experiment. Unlike the Moonie or Hare Krishna cults, the Buddhism professed by emigré lamas seemed an authentic tradition, backed up by millions of adherents in Asia.

I became the student of the equivalent of the high priest of Delphi. Nechung Rinpoche had just then settled in Hawai`i at the dawn of the New Age. A reincarnate lama usually procured his name from the site of his monastery. Nechung (Tib. "a small secret place") had been a tiny hermitage situated in a gully just outside of Lhasa, the capital of Tibet. It was several hundred meters downslope of the largest monastery in the world, Drepung, which at one time held 10,000 monks. A massive rock battlement framed the horizon behind Nechung, in a setting familiar to pilgrims to the rock amphitheater of Mt. Parnassus at Delphi. While Apollo had his laurel trees, Nechung possessed a grove of sacred junipers. And both locations were renowned seats of prophecy. Nechung guarded the State Oracle of Tibet, a shaman-monk who in trace would speak the words of the divine Protector of State. Both Apollo and the Tibetan Protector carried symbols of their art—the bow and arrow. Like Delphi, Nechung Monastery maintained the roles of high priest and oracle in two different individuals. The Pythoness was the mouth-piece of the god, not the mistress of the Ritual. Nechung Rinpoche provided the system and the key whereby the incoherent mutterings of the Oracle could provide meaning to the queries of the Tibetan government and various pilgrims. Perhaps a vague genetic memory of a sacred institution, significant at the very foundation of my own civilization, was activated in the presence of the Nechung Rinpoche. As Delphi was the center of the ancient Western world, Tibet represented the antipodes.

My teacher had a short but powerful lineage. The first Nechung Rinpoche, Ogyen Thinley Choephel, arrived from Mindroling monastery in the 1880s. He was divinely directed by the Great Protector who had taken up residence at Nechung outside of the grand Drepung monastery in Lhasa Valley. Ogyen Thinley was a master of the Treasured Doctrine and was an expert in the practices of the energy channels, the winds, and the bodily *yantras* of the generation and completion stages of tantra (*tsa lung khrul khor*). At Mindroling he had been recognized as the incarnation of Langdro Kunchok Jungne, a disciple of the great Guru Padmasambhava. Langdro reincarnated as the treasure master Ratna Lingpa, a well-known figure in Tibetan Buddhist history.

Ogyen Thinley arrived at Nechung monastery during the tenure of the Eighth Medium, Shakya Yarphel. In 1891, following the prophecies of the Nechung medium, Ogyen Thinley Choephel headed east to Do-Kham to collect the divinely-blessed image of Padmasambhava, an object discovered by Ogyen Larab Lingpa, a disciple of Zongsar Khyentse Rinpoche. The statue was housed at the Tsuglha Khang in Lhasa close to the holy image of Jowo Shakyamuni, brought by

Chapter 2

the Chinese princess Wen Cheng Kung Chu for King Songtsen Gampo. Such images were protected at the Tsuglag Khang for this universe, "so they may not be taken away by the Nagas into their subterrestrial realm." With the image was brought the *Terton Sogyal*, a hidden Guru Yoga text. The first Nechung Rinpoche passed away shortly after Tibetan independence was declared in 1914. The XIII Dalai Lama recognized Thubten Kunchok as the *tulku* of Nechung Rinpoche. Trained in both Gelukpa and Ningmapa traditions, Thubten became a highly realized master in Tibetan astrology and studied Tibetan literature. He was a highly refined scholar in letters. From 1956 to 1959 he taught Tibetan language at the Minorities School in Beijing. Following the flight of the Dalai Lama, Thubten Kunchok was imprisoned by the Chinese.

This second Nechung Rinpoche escaped the marauding bands of the People's Liberation Army in 1962, and settled in Dharamsala, bringing with him some of the sacred ritual paraphernalia of the Nechung institution. He remained there just long enough to re-establish the Oracle close to the Dalai Lama and his exiled government. In 1964 Nechung Rinpoche became a professor at the Ladakh Buddhist Institute in Delhi. Then Rinpoche left for greener pastures. The gravitational movement of the Tibetan Buddhist *dharma* to the West seemed an all-win situation. On one hand it provided a much needed injection of sacrality into a fragmenting civilization. On the other, it provided a reserve of capital which could be utilized to help maintain the lineages of teachers in exile. In 1974, Nechung Rinpoche established Nechung Dorje Ling Buddhist Center in a two-story house in the suburban hills of Honolulu just above the University of Hawai`i.

Befitting its name, the western *vihara*, or temple, of Nechung was a small establishment. It initially needed only a few western students. A dedicated Hawaiian couple, Tanya and Greg, became the managers of Rinpoche's worldly affairs. They operated out of a small, rented split-level on Frank Street.

Nechung Rinpoche was as orthodox a minister as Nels Lundy, the Lutheran prelate of that severe white church back in Montana (also frequented by the Pfaffenburgs, Gronnenbergs, Falkenbergs, and their kith). The Rinpoche offered teaching sessions several times a week to a handful of students—an offering, a teaching, and a dedication. No great shows of religious ecstacy were forthcoming, just the basics: the Four Noble Truths, the Five Skandas, the Eight-Fold Path to Liberation. This was the same sort of universal Buddhism taught in a chapel-waddi along the Mekong, in a massive brick fortress on the steppes of Mongolia, or in the Victorian bric-a-brac salons of San Francisco.

I advanced, though, to the Great Vehicle of northern Buddhism Mahayna, and from that point to the Vajrayana of Tibetan tantric practice. The image of the simple Buddha as physician to the earth multiplied into forms of deities representing the cardinal directions, the primary colors, and particular aspects of the emotive self. There were forms in the early realm, heavenly realm, and transcendent realm. Some had messengers—some had wrathful, protective aspects. One could pick a deity to match one's basic personality, or one that could challenge one's mundane outlook. Some gods and goddesses represented positive ideals of compassion and discernment—others, vicious human emotions of anger and lust left to the Self to conqueror. The point of practice was to understand that the deities were mind-created aspects of self. Good and evil were self-born, and thus manageable.

With the arrival of a priest-sage with the status of Nechung Rinpoche to Hawai`i, a stream of other lamas followed—further teachings, further initiations, each of which came with its package of daily mantras and meditations to perform. As an outward sign of initiation or blessing, each of the lamas would provide a colored string to wear around the neck. In time, my multiple *srungdugs* became a frayed, pale rainbow around my neck—they were never removed.

Rinpoche tutored me in the Tibetan language. The sounds seemed familiar. I would dream of speaking it fluently. Rinpoche was a fatherly soul to me. I was honored to be occasionally invited to sit at his right side.

No one else was aware of Tibet in those disco days of the late 1970s—just this handful of curious students. When not meditating, I entertained the style of a precocious yuppie with a twenty-seventh floor Diamond Head view luxury condo, a periwinkle blue Jensen Healy sports car, and a taste for fine wine and pâté, all this obtained by waiting on tables a mere 20 hours a week at the ultra chic Hyatt-Regency Waikiki. The hotel staffed its public- contact positions with beautiful girls with seductive figures and radiant smiles, and slim, young men with fawn-like elan and sparkling eyes. I was simply decorous to the hotel, that's all—nothing much to build a career upon. The fly-boys came and went.

From Rinpoche, I learned of a small enclave of Tibetan refugees living in Nepal and northern India—exiled supporters of the Dalai Lama who fled Tibet in 1959. Tibetans who were trying to maintain the old ways, it seemed—a very noble cause. They were holding back the floods of modernization released upon them by both the Chinese in their homeland and perhaps unintentionally, by their hosts in developing India. Of all the great civilizations of the ancient world that have come and gone, the Tibetans may be the last living link to an age when ancient oak trees spoke and cloud auguries framed the visions of the day.

Where was this place called Dharamsala, the seat of the Dalai Lama in the Himalayas? It took quite a bit of research to find a reference to the town in the great Asian collection at the University of Hawai`i. A yellowed tourist brochure described the village as a rustic retreat from the dusty Indian summer in the beautiful Kangra valley of Himachal Pradesh. Apparently, Dharamsala had been a watering hole for officials of the British Raj; there was no mention of any Tibetans. Another similarly obscure source suggested that Tibetan refugees had been camping out in the province since the early 1960s. Apparently few outsiders had visited and fewer still had written about their experiences. The Dalai Lama in his first autobiography had written a bit about the site, but only in general reference to the exile experience. Nothing was really known on the outside about these "survivors" from the last ancient civilization on earth.

A scoop for an ambitious anthropology graduate student? Perhaps, but the lifestyle that had to be destroyed indicated the seriousness of my quest. I sold the Jensen sports car; the toy-boy parties were terminated. Abandoned was the idea to purchase the glass condo in the sky. Material objects were sold at garage affairs and flea markets. I liquidated my Western life and departed for India as soon as possible.

The journey to Asia was circuitous. Eastward across the Pacific to Seattle; a train trip across the continent in the dead of the winter; a flight encompassing London, Paris, Frankfurt, Kuwait City, Bombay, with a airplane

Chapter 2

meal rammed down my gullet at each stop. The journey was two-thirds the circumference of the earth (ticketing was cheaper that way). Ultimately, at 3 a.m. on some unknowable date, the harshly lit Delhi airport customs holding area disgorged its human livestock out into the sooty night air and upon the dung-splattered streets.

I spent the next week sleeping off fabulous jet lag at some tiny pension in the suburbs of New Delhi, impassive to the houseboy's interest in my suitcase's t-shirts and his furtive glances at me and my cargo. I recall the lobby contained a framed photo of some holy woman simply called "The Mother." I would lie in bed listening to the banana-walla's cries in the street, and watched commuters piling on buses like an army of ants attacking some hapless dung beetle. It seemed like I spent a month in my room, lying on my bed and looking out on the wild scene of rickshaws hurtling down the street.

I took to the attack myself and headed for Connaught Place in search of a Tibetan face. Nothing—I bought a bus ticket for Dharamsala in Himachal Pradesh, a stop the perplexed clerk had to look up. At 4 a.m. I threw a t-shirt at the lash-batting houseboy and found myself at the Inter-State bus terminal near the red sandstone Kashmiri gate of the old walled city. Dark pillars, figures appeared in the gloom. I stumbled around and coughed harshly from the thick gasoline fumes that enveloped the station like a death pall.

At last, a Tibetan or two. Like a lost dog, I followed them to their bus. Back then, I could not read Devanagri script, nor would I ask the attendant the destination of the bus. I simply followed the Tibetans. I didn't realize at the time that they were scores of Tibetan settlements scattered around India, and we could have been off for any one of them. By some miracle, however, the bus headed north and eventually rattled its circuitous way out of the Beas River valley, a sister of the Indus watershed that drained all of western Tibet. On to Dharamsala.

A dark afternoon—it was 6 p.m., on the waxing side of the winter's solstice. The dewy moistness of a chill rain barely slicked the grey slate tiles of farm houses. They looked like Tibetan houses, yet their image grew distorted by grimy bus windows. It was stoking my imagination, filling in the landscape where hydraulic-fluid, dust, and vomit stains fouled the glass. My heart beat quickly. Tortuously, the bus hoisted itself up through the hill country, past Shaivite temples, Mughal summer palaces, and the cow-dung adobe huts of the Kangravati.

We halted suddenly in a smoky pine forest harshly illuminated by fluorescent tubes. This was lower Dharamsala. Taxi horns blaring, raucous motorcycles encircling, the bus was seized upon by hundreds of uniformly unshaven, barefoot Kashmiri porters. The bus exploded into a stampede of flying cabin luggage, elbows, knees, saris, ankle bangles, and glowing cigarettes. An Englishman grabbed my arm and fought for the clearing to the trail that rose 1,500 ft to the Tibetan village. We found two village boys, somewhat afraid of the night, to carry our luggage. We had no flashlight—animated forms silently appeared and receded.

Out onto the ridge that hung over the city, we ascended to McLeod Ganj, the Tibetan village. It was a moonless, crystalline black night. Lights profusely dotted the mountains and merged with the stars. Sleeping dogs lined the trail, as sentries guarding the mystical riches of what lay ahead.

Although my anticipation of the unknown grew razor sharp, waves of nostalgia inexplicably swept through my body. It was a type of round sentimentality which had no clear mnemonic association. It was not a rational *deja vu* famil-

Dharamsala didn't resemble India at all. Indeed, it seemed more like Bulgaria with its pitched slate roofs and octagonal buildings. It was so frigid in the winter that few ventured on to the roads that steeply ascended up the hills covered with rhododendron trees.

Chapter 2

iarity where new experiences suggest past ones. It was an unfathomable return to a time and place yet experienced.

My entry into the Tibetan world was neither utopian nor anti-utopian.[19] It was not the classical arrival scene typical of the first-contact episodes of anthropologists Firth and Malinowski, who followed the travel genre of explorers like Bougainville and Burton. I had not arrived at a Shangri-La as had Rowell, David-Neel, Mattisson, and Gold. Describing his initial arrival in Dharamsala, the latter sugars his readers:

> In the pre-dawn light the eyes must strain to discern the contours of houses, prayer flags and wooded hills. In the effort, the realness of the place and its people becomes elusive, and the question of its very existence unfolds as the subject of a dialogue before the mind...Here the ancient ways are preserved. They swirl about in a dramatic pas de deux with those of the mish-mash world below, like oil in water. The culture of Tibet—last of a brood of untouched ancient civilizations—hangs on delicately, but with great momentum and determination[20]

What was he talking about? The question of Gold's very existence unfolded as a subject of my own internal dialogue. This village in front of me was not utopia — but here the ancient Western expectations of Tibetan behavior were preserved. My bones ached, my palate was raw, I just wanted to sleep.

My arrival did not suggest the genre of the "repressed colonial" as expressed by Evans-Prichard or Mayberry-Lewis either — no sullen natives, no obvious exploitation of a curious White outsider. It seemed a neutral non-event, with the mild pleasantness of returning to a well-ordered home after the battle with rush-hour traffic. My pretensions were simple — I belonged here, and thus experienced neither the excitement of discovery nor disappointment.

We arrived in the village of McLeod Ganj at 10 p.m. I ditched the Englishman and kept walking the long, deserted street alone until I encountered a prospective lodging perched on a cliff. The stratospheric cement stairway to the aerie of the Kokonor Hotel was harshly illuminated at the doorway by a single naked bulb. A young woman with a cleft palate was vigorously sweeping the steps. I approached.

"Of yourself one single room have not have?" I surprised myself in unrehearsed Tibetan.

"Not have. There dormitory have. Silver not much. Ten rupees day one is," the woman spoke, head down, her sweeping uninterrupted.

"There men many are?"

"No, men many are not."

"Goodness it is. Thank you," I responded.

"Your coals bring."

Not one blink, nor raised eyebrow of curiosity at this foreigner speaking Tibetan. Not fair! I ballooned, proud of my first live-context utterance in Tibetan. I received lodging and a charcoal brazier instead of accolades. It was the first major step in my deconstruction of Shangri-La fantasies.

I had one roommate that night, Lars Ostenborg — from Denmark of course. I introduced myself as a kindred Scandanavian, blown off course by a generation or two. I shared my genealogy: Eric von Falkenberg, with a Prussian father descended from the Teutonic knights of Königsberg; son of Charlotte Ødegaard of Lund, daughter of Elizabeth Fjeld, daughter of the mythical Pauline von Waldeck.

Miniatures

It was no mystery who Pauline was, but where exactly did Elizabeth come from? Grandma always claimed she was related to the queen of the Netherlands. Aunt Alma always seconded that. It seems that Pauline was kicked out of the family:

> The house of Waldeck was honoured by good marriages into most of the princely families of Germany, while two or three of its members had contracted morganatic unions...[21]

Morganatic? It sounded awful. Indeed, Pauline seems to have had a love child. She had been sister to Emma von Waldeck und Pyrmont, the second wife of King Willem III. Emma, known as "the sweetest old lady in Europe," was great grandmother of the present queen of the Netherlands, and thus my great great aunt. The Royal Archives in the Hague traced the von Waldeck und Pyrmont lineage all the way back to A.D. 923. That genealogy showed that I was also related to the Pfaffenburgs and thus to Mother's coffeeclatch mates back home. But I really didn't know much, having never been to Waldeck or had any idea of any relatives living there in Central Germany. I was just a Montana boy, who thought Rev. Lundy's church pancake breakfasts were the height of Scandinavian culture. German culture in exile consisted of singing hymns in whitewashed churches, with the ubiquitous framed prints of Dürer's praying hands of Christ in every other home.

I had finally satisfied my own sense of place that evening, yet convinced Lars neither of my sincerity in understanding Tibetan culture nor its claimed relationship to my own Lowengrin journey.

It was all a catharsis, this first night in the Himalayas, some fifty miles due west of Tibet itself. The unraveling of the mother and father lineages that I told to Lars was a purge of all the Eric-body genetic and cultural miasma of the West. It was tossed at the feet of an unknown Western tourist.

I moved my bed and my nostrils to the open window to prevent asphyxiation from the glowing charcoal brazier placed on the floor by Rinzin, the grumpy hotel attendant. Ghoulish cries emanated from the forest, somewhat between the howl of coyotes and the laugh of hyenas. I imagined the wrathful deities announcing my arrival to Tibet. Throughout the night I was serenaded by the beast-gods, and a strange bird who spent the moonless night calling forlornly to its invisible mate. Drifting in and out of consciousness, I finally stabilized on an image forming gradually as dawn rose: the blue of mountain ice against a dusky pink sky over Tibet in the east. Golden rocks, blue-black pines appeared. It had infinite range:

> We may term such a displacement from an outward to an inward space 'the crisis of the object', using an expression coined by the surrealist artist Salvador Dali in the 1920s, when a bold generation of twentieth-century painters was recovering for Western man the understanding of art as a discipline of the interface between waking consciousness and night, as is shamanic song.[22]

Peering out of the glass, I watched the sun rise over Mt. Dhauladhar, warming rays seemingly sanctified by their passage through the Tibetan air.

From the village a hundred feet below, the crystalline bells of the temple prayer wheel cut through the rising smoke of scores of wood fires warming morning tea. Although quite content to remain in the fastness of my bed and recording the fantasies of my mind, I arose and with Lars walked down to the village.

Chapter 2

Naively expecting to find Tibetans with their yaks doing things Tibetan, I noted only rows of chai stalls, with blond heads and too-long legs popping out of windows and doors. It became evident that the main activity for Westerners here in the Dalai Lama's village was to spend their days in sugary bohemian indulgence, hopping from one tea shop to another, and swapping tales of their righteous indignation towards Third-World inconveniences. Each tea room had its own specialty, it seemed. Some did eggs well. Others had good *roti* bread or cheese. Some had chewy cookies, while all had the standard chow mein and vegetable noodle soup. There was rarely any meat, except during festival times when goat was abundant. On rare occasions, when a cow had been hit by a bus or died of old age, Tibetans would secretly butcher and roast the holy beast under the noses of the grieving Hindus.

At the first chai shop there was Angelica, a vivacious Italian woman who was proud of her affectation of speaking English without the slightest comprehension of the language's grammar or vocabulary. Broken English, I was to learn, was the lingua franca of the various French, German, Yugoslavian, Dutch, and Italian expatriates unwilling to assume their hosts' essential mode of expression.

Pictures at an Exhibition...there was Marcello, a stringy Roman who forced me to attend his lecture on the homosexual leanings of a late pope. Introductions followed rapidly in the acrid, Mother Earth café of *apres mode* flower children.

Here was Ronald, a punk Cockney who hated the queen—and Joyce, an IRA sympathizer who hated both the queen and all Cockneys. June was a chubby Philadelphian eager to force herself as apprentice upon a Tibetan mid-wife while she searched for a magic elixir to cure her father's baldness (he had bought the plane ticket). June recommended that I meet Kip, a long-term expatriate, and now king of the Dharamsala Westerners. He represented the Old Guard, along with Kenji the Japanese *thangka* painter, and a mysterious female anthropologist that no one had ever met. A few other EuroAmerican and Japanese faces entered and passed.

I left roommate Lars here, walked to the next tea house, and found André, an affable Frenchman with terminal rhinitis. Tubercular Marjorie from Scotland was half Buddhist nun and half Western astrologer who had fled to India escaping a failed romance. Marie, another American, was from Vassar. She wore a sapphire velvet dress, tailored to resemble a Tibetan *chupa*. Marie was "doing psychological analyses" on Sherpas. I had a vision of poor Sherpas reclining on tufted leather couches in some overheated Boston office.

This rammage of emigres was well attended by a wizened old child, the peripatetic Amala, the same individual later made famous in Peter Gold's story of Dharamsala. She had few teeth by which to radiate an ever-present smile, but she managed to proclaim a continence of amused indifference within the absurd atmosphere of her little tea house. She made wonderful bread—plain, crusty white loaves. And somehow her chickens laid the best eggs.

The third chai shop on the Baghsunath strip was similar to the others. A few boards for walls, a tin can roof, and the oily roar of a kerosene stove. Tibetans came in, one by one, to observe us for a few moments. I was not one wishing to be confused with my adjacent cohort of local comic relief. The disheveled, fractured, hairy Westerners were the clowns of the Tibetan refugee community.

I wanted to be something else, but it was not clear to me exactly what. Without much of a plan, I began revolting against both the Tibetans' and

It took at least seven layers of clothing to attempt to keep warm during the wet winter at Cow Barn. A neighbor from Germany built a cozy cabin with glass windows and a wood burning stove.

Chapter 2

Westerners' attempts to place me somewhere in a moribund classification system. How great it would be to float above the herd, like some enlightened deity.

In the next few days, all remained the same. Endless rounds of chai shops, followed by an equal amount of cold "comfort calls" in the icy wilderness. I talked at length with the American girl, June, who wanted to study midwifery under Tibet's only woman doctor. She had found the hair restorer for her bald father. All dreams were possible in Shangri-La.

"You have to meet Kip," she repeated. "He doesn't come to town often. Lives in a cow barn up the hill."

On one frigid afternoon. His Reclusive Highness Kip did in fact happen upon Amala's Last Chance Café. Looking up from my sweet milk coffee and roti with Amul cheese, I knew him right away: a thin, high-strung young man wearing an orange shirt, pyjama bottoms, plastic slippers, and a woolen maroon shawl, similar to a monk's palladium. Doleful blue eyes were contained within a curious personality of nervous anxiety and calm bearing. Kipling Beauregard Laperoux, III, I had already learned, was a hopelessly guilt-ridden Catholic man from New Orleans who had abandoned his upper class social status to find himself in the trendy grubbiness of the Third World. Westerners with less tenure in McLeod Ganj deferred to Kip, and on this instant cleared a path through the crowded shop and offered him chairs. Kip nonchalantly greeted his subordinates, sat down, and stoked his small Indian pipe with tobacco.

"Where are you from?" Kip quipped between *chilim* puffs, acting like the caterpillar in *Alice in Wonderland*.

"Hawai`i," I retorted.

"Hawai`i? How could you ever leave? I mean, it must be sooo nice on the beach in all that isolation," he said in a smooth voice. "At Christmas here in India most of us go south to Goa and live on the beaches. You can live on about Rs 20 a week. There are giant pigs there that keep the beaches clean. Not too many hassles from the Indians, but be sure to go to Nepal first to get your three-month visa extension. Goa is pretty far away from the border."

"What do the Tibetans do in the winter?" I asked.

"Guess they stay—some sort of month long holiday happens." Just then June entered the café and joined us.

"What sort of holiday? Haven't you guys ever thought of staying to find out? Aren't you curious about this entirety of experience around here?" I argued.

"No, Eric," June laughed, "what you don't realize is that it's cool in the mountains in the summer. And at least the Tibetans are an easy and uninhibited people to be around for awhile. Sort of what the British used to do in the summer. India is an inferno in the summer. Least they've got less people up here."

Realizing that Kip and June's arguments made sense, I slowly began to confirm that Dharamsala was an exceptionally special place. I dealt with the de facto mayor's wife, the ancient Mrs. Nowrojee, to obtain more permanent housing—Kip had recommended her. All the Tibetans rented from her, an elderly Parsee woman with Anglo pretensions born in the glory days of the British Raj. Yet she bore subdermal resentment to the West that had abandoned her empire and destroyed her privileged social standing. But she had subdivided an old cow barn to provide rooms for Western tourists. What she called "Balcony House" was at least isolated—located perhaps half a mile straight above the village, in the thick rhododendron forest frequented by serene langur monkeys and bitchy rhesus macaques. It had neither water not heat. But it did create a private space, away from the cacophonous clusters of houses in McCleod. My room that I labled "Monkey View," was a tiny alcove of staked slate, with soot covered adobe walls.

My first night in the manger I lay on the wooden *charpoi* bed trying so hard to maintain a reasonable body temperature. I looked out upon the starry night through an iron screen covered with a decomposing plastic sheet. The temperature was dropping. It seemed 20 degress F by now. It also snowed heavily — a wet, sticky snow that incised eerie forms of trees and rock on the dripping Himalayan night.

A bed? I conceived of it in a rather ingenious buying-trip to the Dharamsala bazaar. A wooden platform, laced together by leather straps, formed the foundation of many layers of insulation. First came a yellow 3 x 6 ft. thickly piled Tibetan rug with two snarling dragons and a flaming pearl. This was covered by a Yugoslavian army-issue sleeping bag (bought from a ballast-dropping, green-eyed youth), followed by three woolen army blankets left in the region by Indian troops returning from border conflicts with the Chinese. To add to this puff pastry, I enshrouded myself in successive layers of Norwegian mesh underwear, a flannel shirt, and a natural color wool Norwegian button-down sweater supposedly knitted by great-grandmother Inger Eskehaug in the nineteenth century.

I felt like a freshly chilled halibut on a bed of crushed ice. My mind took off wandering, trying to divert the reality of the petrifying, cold habitat. As I attempted to sleep, the candle fell off the shelf and began to burn the palm matting on the floor. While stamping out the woven mat, a giant centipede appeared and darted angrily towards me. I dispatched it at once with the burning candle. The instant blackness gave forth a smell of frying shrimp, but fortunately revealed no further lower orders that night. I soon returned to fitful sleep and dreams of the Manchu *saman*:

> Shamans are significantly different from non-shamans in three aspects of cognitive style...First, shamans avoid bafflement more than non-shamans. They are imposters of form on diffuse sense data. Second, shamans are more productive in their responses; they are more generative of different responses. Third, shamans seem to have available to themselves their own constructive categories and remain relatively insensitive to the alternative categories provided by the experimenter.[23]

Alternative categories... I was roused by a knock on the door. I flung off my blankets and opened the door. Here stood Kip, who paused for a second and invited me to his room at the other end of the building for Bournvita and biscuits.

Kip's place appeared much larger than Monkey View. He had covered his walls with the *Times of India* to prevent fallout from the cow-dung adobe. And he had furnished it as well as expatriate ingenuity could manage; bits of string, wood, foil, and duct tape concocted strange appliances of unknown function. The room glowed warmly, though, being softly lit by numerous candles.

Kip propped himself up with several cushions and began reading me the litany of his life, the usual story of severe Catholic nun-teachers and the unreasonable moral expectations of his parents. Kip was in India, as usual, to "find himself." Apparently this activity took about four years, and he claims to have discovered it not among the Tibetans (he spoke not one word of the language). Rather, his enlightenment came upon him while sitting on a balcony at deserted Swaraj Ashram, the first Dalai Lama palace in Dharamsala, when a "self-wave" or

Chapter 2

something akin jolted him to his senses. He existed now in the "radiant afterglow" of this experience. Once it passed, I presumed, he would return to America.

I quickly established a routine living on Nowrojee's property. I spent the days talking with Westerners in the chai shops. At around 5 p.m., Kip would come into town, buy a *Times* at Nowrojee's General Store, have dinner, and return with me up the hill.

If lucky, industrious foreigners graduated from cement barracks in McLeod Ganj to Cow Barn, and from chai shop to their own homely kerosene kitchen—all before their visas expired. We lived on the margins of yet another group on the edge. Ironically, the former Tibetan nomads had settled into stable village life, while the scions of European and American bourgeoisie assumed the role of nomads at the margins of a great civilization.

The Westerners formed an enclave within Tibetan refugee society, itself at the mercy of the benefices of India. Tibetans generally kept away from the local Paharis, except for the occasional aggressive Indian boy, overwhelmed by curiosity. (These were usually youths from other villages, and relatively unfettered by adult concerns). What is this? Is it not true that Tibetans are open, gregarious, and expansive at all times?

Sonam Gyatsho hailed from the little village of Kamrao, about 16 kilometers down the valley. He was a rather scrawny boy, about 19 years old and as awkward as any unsure teen. He found me sitting on the steps of one of the general stores, waiting for the bus to lower Dharamsala. He just started to talk with me. Sonam's hair rocekted wildly from his head; on this cold winter's morning, he wore an oversized Indian army jacket, a thin brown sweater, and heavy boots. He and his family were supported by a rug-weaving co-operative established by the Tibetan government-in-exile and India. Sonam tried everything to ingratiate me to him. Tibetan lessons? Certainly. *Thangka* painting? No problem. Errands to the post or telephone exchange? Happy to do that. Like some ancient Persian potentate, I now had someone to do things for me. It took me off the streets, and having Sonam running around for me seemed to better mesh with the expectations that many Tibetans in McLeod had about lotus-eating Westerners. But there was not too much for him to do with me, except to just hang around. I had other priorities on my mind.

In the cold and icy heights of the southern slopes of the Himalayas, I quickly caught a deadly cold, accompanied by a grand fever. Kip detested being placed in the role of nursemaid, but I was too ill for him to protest. I lay in my thin Yugoslavian sleeping bag, space heater on one side, kerosene heater on the other. In a steaming fog, I stared at the newspapers covering the walls. I read old stories about Indira Gandhi and the Minister of Defense, the Syrian president's trip, and the state lottery. I couldn't sleep, and didn't want to move. Endless cups of Bournvita and tea with lemon flowed through my body. All of this stressed poor Kip, no longer snug in his manger away from the fray.

Slowly I began to regain full use of my body, my lungs and head started to clear. One early evening, before Kip had walked up the hill from Nowrojee's, a polite knock brought me to the door. There were two looming male figures; it was very dark, but I could still see the shadows from the crescent moon upon the crisp snow. The man in front seemed thin, the one in back looked more solidly built. I felt a blast of frigid air, and saw the silhouetted, standing figure in the back snort clouds of frosty vapor. Moonlight flashed from his glistening eyes.

"Is Mr. Kip at home?" said the smaller one in the front.

"No, sorry. I think he's still down in McLeod," I uttered, fighting strong resistance in my sore throat. I kept staring at the taller man, who slowly approached the doorway.

"We have a package for him. Oh, please... this is Dorje Dhondup." The bulky dark figure moved to the doorway on a gust of sandal-scented warm air. A clear blue light dripped from the icicles that had formed on the lintel.

"I am called Jimmy," he said in a friendly, resonant voice. He extended a great brown hand, glowing warm and firm; its subtle padding held my fingers earnestly, and hesitated in its release. I stood back to gather in the light.

"My name is Eric. How are you?" I said in Tibetan as I gazed across the broad expanse of his sparkling face. I was used to meeting short and slender Tibetan men, mostly scruffy undernourished, street-wise kids. But Jimmy grew nothing short of magnificent! My cloudy head cleared instantly; my red eyes dried. It must have been at least 6 feet 2 inches from the crown of his wild stock of long jet hair, to the soles of his large, steel-toed black boots. He wore a thick, deep green serge coat over his wide shoulders. A blue flannel shirt fit snugly across his chest. I could see the top of a bright white T-shirt next to his dark skin, with a thin red cotton *srung-dud* around his sturdy neck. A leather thong held a nugget of bright blue turquoise and fell on his chest. A small image of the Dalai Lama was affixed over his heart. I examined the symmetry of his wide face, and noted how well-framed it was by his full mouth and closely cropped ears. Jimmy was wearing new Levi's, heavy tough indigo cloth, size 32-34.

Jimmy's companion could be heard in the background, yammering at length about some parcel. Jimmy's head turned, nostril flared, ears perked. We saw Kip trundling up the hill.

"You look better, Eric!" Kip called out as he climbed the last few steps on the path to the Cow Barn. "How are you feeling?"

"Yeah, the fog just lifted" I jibed.

"What's happening, guys?" Kip asked.

I made introductions all around. Jimmy and his friend brought out the parcel for Kip to give to the English woman who lived next door. Something about a dictionary.

"I can keep it for her," Kip responded. "She's gone south for the week. To Delhi, I think. Why don't you guys come in for tea."

I hadn't realized that all this time we had been standing in the doorway. But the cold outdoors blew out the humid miasma of the overheated sick room. Jimmy sat down on the foot of the bed. He filled the room with his powerful presence, overwhelming us in swirls of warm mocha in the thinning air. He spoke English beautifully in a soft, quiet manner, with precisely chosen words separated by long pauses. He seemed a good listener. But now he talked.

Jimmy Dorje Dhondup was a student at the Tibetan Institute of Performing Arts (T.I.P.A.), born in Ngari region of western Tibet. Born a nomad, from the holy Mt. Kailash, Jimmy's parents raised him out on the open grasslands. At the age of four his family left Tibet. Now he danced and sung, and acted in the classical Tibetan opera. Among the chosen, the finest of them all, he represented the genius of the tribe abroad. I immersed myself in his deep radiance, his glowing prismatic countenance. I sat there transfixed in the glowing room as Kip chatted about the above ground graves in New Orleans, Moraji Desi's urine drinking, and the wiles of everyone's landlady, Mrs. Nowrojee. The wolves were romping, sniffing the wind.

In a quick moment, all stood up. Our noble visitors made an abrupt departure, gliding swiftly off to the south and over the shallow ridge to the performing arts school.

As soon as Jimmy and Jigme were out of sight, Kip turned to me and uttered, "He's a breeder, that one."

Kip's words stabbed me like an icicle. Somehow I couldn't see that tall Tibetan man in shorts barbequing outside a suburban split-level, or loading the twins into the wagon for swimming lessons at the YMCA or softball at Little League. I turned my head towards Kip's partitionless apartment in Cow Barn. I saw my crumpled nest of flat pillows and blankets braided and rolled in a corner. Teacups were strewn throughout, smouldering clay ashtrays sat here and there. Trash cans overflowed with Kleenex. In the sweltering humidity, newsprint peeled off the walls. The electricity went off, leaving one feeble candle light burning on the shelf, casting a shadow of a huge Kip head on the opposite wall.

In a day or two I felt well enough to go with Kip down to McLeod Ganj to see the Tibetan doctor. Amche Chenpo, people gossiped, did very thorough examinations on young men, especially blond foreign ones. Indeed, I felt a bit uneasy while waiting in the long queue. Finally my time came, and a young male nurse ushered me to a room. He asked me to unbutton my shirt and remove my bottom clothes. Strip down for a chest examination? Well, the experience seemed interesting enough for me, so I complied. A few moments later the doctor came in and gave me a big smile. First he examined the urine sample I had provided, noting its color, sediment, etc. Then he examined the pulse of my wrist very carefully, and felt behind my jaw and along my neck. And I smiled when he gently examined my genitals. "Very good," he said, motioning to me to pull up my clothes. The amche wrote a prescription for those hard brown pills that I could be obtained at the Tibetan Medical Center. Enough--I was cured. Upon returning to Cow Barn, I gathered up my clothes, grabbed my toothbrush, and went off to sleep in Monkey View on the other side of the building.

It seemed to have been a month since I saw my own room in Cow Barn, the tiniest chamber in the Nowrojee palace. It was dusty and the black, sooty walls smelled of mildew. Unlike Kip's apartment, it seemed freezing cold inside. Yet my place stood immensely inviting. I smelled the bright camphor of the eucalyptus leaves left under the woven mat that a South African had shown me to ward off vermin. I still had two large white candles, and several smaller ones, and three layers of pea green Indian army blankets on the little *charpoi*. In no time I fell fast asleep, dreaming of the wildwood and galloping stallions with flaring nostrils and flowing tails.

From my window, over the next few weeks, I saw the fury of the Himalayan winter broke across the field and set the dark pines into motion with blasts of freezing ice. Ever so often the monkeys came up from the village and ate the sweet red blossoms of the rhododendron trees, made crunchy by the frost. Nearly every day Sonam would call on my way to breakfast down in McLeod. Would I like a Tibetan lesson? Was there something to carry? Sadly, I never had anything for him, but I often treated him to breakfast at either the Kokonor or the strange, nameless "shotgun" hut built on the literal edge of town. The latter was a delicately balanced wooden cabin, situated between the main road of McLeod village and the 60-degree slope that fell 1,000 meters down to the valley floor.

What it had was a wonderful view of the vast expanse of the western mountains and the plains of the Punjab. Sonam seemed more like a lamprey than a young friend; the more I shook the harder he clung.

I spent most days refueling in one way or another. Breakfast, followed by more tea, a stop at the petrol shop for kerosene. Candles, biscuits, maybe a magazine. Lunch of thukpa noodles or an onion pancake. More tea. Buy vegetables and cheese. Get a Mr. Pik soda at Nowrojee's, then off to the Kokonor for fried noodles.

In the evening I walked up the steep trail to Cow Barn. Just after dark Jimmy would come over, mostly by himself. We would always talk. He was so busy, though, too busy for Tibetan lessons for me. But we would talk. Then he would quietly leave for upstairs, to visit the English woman. She had finally "returned from the south."

Her name was Eleanore, a gentle 30-something woman with short blond hair, a bit like a young Julie Andrews. The walls of her apartment in Cow Barn were stark white from the thick application of plaster. The chalky material appeared to be covered in deep fissures and thin cracks, which showed the black soot lurking underneath. The effect was much like a fine, artistic loaf of charred, floured bread. And Eleanore fit right in the Indian desert aesthetic that she created in her room at Cow Barn. She formed an image of a very proper lace doily — much like an exaggerated Lady Mountbatten. A perfect tea hostess at 4:00 p.m., she became a wanton vixen by moonlight. I did not visit often, she being Jimmy's girlfriend. It was difficult to keep my mind off the resonances of inflamed passions engulfing that room.

The Tibetan New Year, Lo Sar, arrived in the darkness of my great ignorance. I could hear *pujas* down the hill and *dung chen* booming across the valleys. The Tibetans seemed to have disappeared, indoors perhaps. This left the streets of McLeod Ganj and the other villages suddenly alive with Parharis and Punjabis, people from Kulu in their off-white woolens with red and green trim. I imagined this is what the hill station had been before 1959 and the immigration of thousands of Tibetan refugees. I found it amusing when Indian tourists came to take pictures of the colorful Tibetans. Then they took photographs of me, laughing and gesturing me to pose in front of local landmarks. I had become a commodity.

One day during the week-long festival the villagers gathered in the bus square. All the elders, all the old nobility. There stood Amala Lobsang Dolma, the great woman doctor of Tibetan medicine. There were former duchesses, now restaurant owners. Officials in black *chupa* from Gangchen Kyishong had driven up the road to McLeod Ganj. I saw crazy Peter Brown festively dressed as a Khampa. Kip stood far in front of me, wrapped in a maroon shawl. It was time for the great social dance of the season. All the former nobility danced, in large circles swaying this way, then the other. We watched.

We starved. All the Westerners discovered that the Tibetan restaurants closed for Lo Sar, and all the other shops had run low on provisions. It forced the dozen or so *injis* out of McLeod Ganj to the decidedly non-tourist Indian restaurants in Dharamsala. We were, on the whole, delighted by the different fare: curries and complex vegetable flavors, nuts and ghee, in sweet, seductive courses served by youths with long black lashes.

Chapter 2

In time, Lo Sar died down, and the lay Tibetans got back to their routines, but only for a short rest. As the first breath of spring danced through the air, the time arrived for the commemoration of the Lhasa Uprising of 1959 that had sent the Dalai Lama and 100,000 Tibetans into voluntary exile. Every March 10 since that year, the Tibetan exiles have celebrated the Uprising of the People.

The entire Tibetan community and twenty or thirty *injis* gathered in the broad amphitheater at the Tibetan Institute of Performing Arts. After an introduction by the Chief Minister of the Council of Ministers, His Holiness the Dalai Lama, Bodhisattva of Compassion and King of Tibet, approached the podium to a fanfare of *dung chen*. The crowd rose; the Tibetan national flag was hoisted. All begin singing the National Anthem:

> Let the radiant light shine form Buddha's wish fulfilling gem...
> Above our heads may divinely appointed rule abide...
> May the auspicious sunshine of the teachings, the beings of Tibet, and the brilliance of a myriad of radiant prosperities be ever triumphant.

Standing squarely in front of the Dalai Lama on the raised platform, the color guard appeared. Two men, one wearing an Amdo hat, the other a Khampa fox hat and a leopard skin mantle, carried red flags with emblazoned white snow lions, twin symbols of Church and State. A third carried a mace. In front of them stood a muscular man holding the national flag of a yellow sun, snow mountain, and alternating red and blue rays. On his head sat the brocade and black fur *shamo tshering* hat of the central province of Ü-tsang. The Tibetan Institute of Performing Arts marching band stood behind the guard. The assembled masses remained standing to enthusiastically sing the "Song of the People's Uprising":

> Rise up! For ten years now,
> The people have been tortured.
> We've had it down to our flesh and bone.
> In the year 1959,
> The patriots could no longer endure.
> The single choice: rise up for truth and liberty.
> Rise up! Rise up, all Tibetan peoples!
> All peoples of the world.

And the thunder at the very back of the band heralded a truly magnificent sight. Standing above the crowd was Jimmy, his broad shoulders supporting the great bass drum beating the call to the people. His clear brown eyes looked straight upwards, unflinchingly, at His Holiness. My hair bristled. The voices of the people became insistent. Jimmy burned, the drum the heartbeat and the blood of the nation.

Beating the drum. For the shaman, sounding the drum is an extremely self-focused experience, one which the general society experiences only through external ritual:

> the mythological image of the shaman, created in the popular mind by mystifications, theatrical scenes, and sleight-of-hand illusionism, the effects of which, however, turn back upon the mind of the shaman himself and become the aids and generators of his own translation to ecstasy.[24]

I thought of the role of T.I.P.A in the March 10th anniversary. And I thought of the strong spine of the percussant. Jimmy was as Alexander beholding the sun:

> Support and rise up behind us.
> Be witnesses for the truth.
> Tibet follows its true leader,
> The Great Protector, His Holiness the Dalai Lama,
> Undoubted by Tibetans inside and out.
> The red-handed butcher-enemy,
> The imperial Red Chinese,
> Will surely be kicked out of Tibet.
> Rise up! Rise up!

The tribe was renewed. No sooner was the blood up and surging in every soul that the monks and laity began to queue up for the march down through the city of Dharamsala. The line stretched at least a kilometer, from the performing arts institute to McLeod Ganj itself. The red-robed monks were in the front half of the line, the black robed laity in the back. As I watched the parade forming, an elderly monk, with great dignity, summoned me over. He looked around, and saw I was the only Westerner in the crowd. Then he looked at me and asked me with his eyes to stand between the two groups, and to hold one corner of the Tibetan flag. Other monks nodded.

I was dumbfounded. Would this make me a part of the inner community of Tibetan refugees, or would it symbolically demonstrate some sort of "unbounded support" of the West for the Tibetan cause? Was this an international event, or was I chosen as a sop to mollify Indian charges of strident nationalism emanating from Dharamsala? The experience might tell.

And the line started moving, slowly through the main street of McLeod Ganj, past cheering Tibetans and curious Indian tourists standing in shop doorways. *"Inji! Inji!"* squealed a tiny girl, excited by my strangeness. But she looked confused, turning her head quickly to the left and the right for clues from adults whether to cry or laugh. It made me feel like a baboon.

We made the sharp left turn at the western edge of town, and began the steep descent past the exile government headquarters at Gangchen Kyishong to the city of Dharamsala proper. The path clung to the side of the hill as it passed the Ganden Nunnery and the little concrete chai shop built out on a precipice. I passed Kip standing in a vegetable garden. The hundreds of red-robed monks moved through the yellow gate of the Dalai Lama's Central Secretariat, crowned with the great blue and white snow lion seal. "China out of Tibet," "Tibet is Free," "Long Live the Dalai Lama" — the homemade signs were carried aloft by the hundred of lay people immediately behind me.

The queue snaked past the Indian restaurants carved into the hillsides. Matronly ladies looked up from their tea, while swarthy *sadarjis* beamed with a chuckle. Past the Post Office and the Telephone Exchange swarming with callers, down to the open area at the end of town. Here, the Indian press had gathered. Officials of Dharamsala and Himachal Pradesh read speeches of greeting and support, all falling just short of official recognition of the government-in-exile. Photos all around. In a flash the thousands of patriotic Tibetans vanished.

The ripple in the tea cup had passed. In the evening, I learned that my experiences represented the first time a Westerner had marched with the patriots on March 10.

Chapter 2

The Tibetan people marched down the hill through the streets of Dharamsala.

In the ritual calendar of Dharamsala, the Great Prayer, Monlam, followed the new tradition of secular nationalism. In old Lhasa, the Monlam saw the Grand Abbots from the three royal monasteries in the valley, Drepung, Ganden, and Sera, assume direct rule of the capital, aided by the gigantic *dab-dob*, the billy-boy monk police. A type of ecclesiastic martial law would be declared as lamas usurped the authority of the civil magistrates. The traditional Monlam festival served as a mnemonic to the urbane populace of Lhasa and showed that the monastic community was ultimately in charge of matters and superior to the secular administration.

This year the Monlam in Dharamsala became a homecoming of sorts. High lamas from various reestablished monastic outposts around the world arrived, Western monks and nuns, the entire government-in-exile, the former nobility, lay people from throughout India and beyond gathered for a month of *puja*, teachings, and renewal.

At the high point of the celebration, the Dalai Lama himself and his retinue were trumpeted down from the cottage palace to the Central Cathedral, the Tsulag Khang. Here he entered the great hall and ascended the Snow Lion throne. The Monlam provided absolute precedence to the clergy—no laymen or women were allowed inside the temple, and protocol chiefs were assigned, making sure that the seating arrangements of all reflected the internal stratification of both the clerical and secular worlds.

Miniatures

The Dalai Lama sat enthroned upon seven silken cushions in the center of the Cathedral. At his side were the Senior and Junior tutors, accompanied by the abbots of the reestablished Gelukpa monasteries. Lesser prelates and "regular" incarnate *tulku* sat on respectively smaller seats and at a greater distance from the center. The ranking continued through lesser circles of ritual sanctity until the inner walls of the temple were reached. It was an all male holy space: nuns, like lay men and women, were relegated to the outside precincts. Lay officials and remnants of the old lay aristocracy were assigned to positions along the broad windows of the Cathedral, again, according to precedence established centuries ago. The commoners had to find spaces beyond the Central Cathedral, on lawns, and on the road wherever they could find them.

I knew nothing of the rules. I thought myself exceedingly clever by arriving just after dawn and finding nearly the whole space mine. I settled into a nice spot just outside a large, open window which afforded a good view of the interior. No one else was around, and I did not notice that parties had marked their ascribed territories by placing mats and carpets at certain locations along the perimeter. Then the fun began.

The Cathedral began to fill with monks, and well-dressed lay Tibetans began to sit on their assigned mats and carpets next to the windows looking in. Just as the Dalai Lama's procession started, one red-faced Tibetan man reproached me, barking an imperious command for me to leave. I moved over to the next carpet, and was chased away from there as well. I was shooed away like the dog under the table, with nowhere to turn. But then my friend, Karma Lekshe Tsomo, a kindly Western nun, silently motioned me to join her sisters on the mat assigned for them. Eric had symbolically become a nun in the eyes of the assembled Tibetan society! Unlike the international outreach of the March 10 commemoration, Monlam was a time of intense bonding between the clergy and the Tibetan laity—outsiders were distinctly not welcomed. By failing to enter into the formal social order, I was banished to the frontier and effectively neutered.

So began a long series of teachings and *cham*, "lama" dances, the conclusion of which marked the end of Monlam, and ultimately the closing of my sojourn to Dharamsala. The great holidays were over now and it became a time for a break to the city, Delhi. It was now springtime and the apricots in the Kangra Valley were in full bloom.

Kip and I took the slow train to Delhi, seemingly just to find decent chocolate, a real bed, and a nice hot bath. After about a week of gorging on tandoori chicken, naan, and chocolate of various qualities, we returned to McLeod Ganj. The warmer weather brought with it a few more expats from Goa, and we often joined them playing frisbee on the fields outside of T.I.P.A. In a few more weeks, it was time for me to leave and drift off to another realm. It also seemed a fine time to renew my Indian visa. That meant crossing the border.

In May, Kip and I took the overland bus to Kathmandu. The journey, a grueling affair, included overnight stops in Lucknow and a mud hole on the Terai known as Muzaffapur. Here clouds of mosquitoes made sleeping and even eating impossible. At a chai stop in the foothills of Nepal, a lukewarm cup of tea made me quite ill for the last few hours before we finally arrived in the fabled city of Kathmandu.

Chapter 2

The Nepalese capital resembled a little dusty jewel lost in the Middle Ages of Central Asia. It seemed a part of an ancient, pre-Islamic Persia, or perhaps of T'ang Dynasty China. Studded with the artifacts of the Pathans, Rajputs, and the Gorkhali, Kathmandu was an isolated place, even as the Disco Era waned and the second wave of the New Age dawned. Despite its charm, however, an unsettling vapor lurked in the tiny city.

I walked with Kip through the darkest of streets and alleyways filled with innumerable bobbing heads. A strong scent of sandalwood drifted through the humid air of the valley. Even on the roof-top gardens in the dead of the purple night, deep, oppressive attar of roses and heavy droplets of musk and violet filled the atmosphere.

Kip set up his rather impressive telescope up on the roof of the hotel, five flights above the streets. The Valley of the Gorkhali was experiencing an eclipse of the moon. "Don't go out," said the shaman priest we had met earlier that day. "Don't go out." From our vantage point, the landscape of the dusky city turned russet and maroon as the earth's shadow slowly crossed the face of the moon.

"Don't go out." The words echoed as we focused the telescope on the great Swayambhu Temple perched on a hill at the edge of town. Nicknamed the "Monkey Temple," it was sacred to Manjusri, the God of Wisdom. Looking through the lens, we saw hundreds of bobbing lights, firebrands perhaps, flickering through the choking haze of the city. It reminded me of the natives' sacrifice scene at the altar of King Kong. "Don't go out," he said.

After about two weeks Kip and I flew back to Delhi. I returned to Dharamsala just long enough to collect the rugs that had been custom woven for me. I brought a little gift of chocolates for the Nowrojees, and sold my sleeping bad and hiking boots. I gave Jimmy a pair of size 28 jeans and my U.S. Air Force parka. June and Kip and other *inji* friends threw me a going away dinner. There was a fresh tomato soup, and ginger cookies sprinkled with sugar to go with tea. I was loaded down with letters to post and personal messages to deliver throughout the outside world. In my luggage I had stuffed Tibetan medicines for various people back in America, two dozen sandalwood prayer *mala* for the Nechung Dharma center, *thangka*, a real skull cup, silk clothing, and other old Tibetan artifacts, books, and hair medicine for June's father.

In an instant, the heavy door of the Air India 747 slammed shut at Delhi Airport, and I was home.

I had returned to Hawai`i, and spent the next few years in deep graduate studies, attempting to understand more of what I had witnessed in India. I rarely saw my mother in Montana, or sister and brother. Karl came to visit me once on the Islands, and we lounged through idyllic days on Queen's Surf beach and hiked remote trails in the Ka`u Desert.

I was busy wearing Tibetan shirts, importing Tibetan carpets, studying Sanskrit, Asian religions... but it all passed in another blink of the eye. When the sun rose, it was time to return.

Kip leaned up against a lattice of cinnamon wood within the towering pagoda of Hanuman Dhoka Palace. Silver bells glimered under the eves while the ancient city of Kathmandu stretched below

3. The Apotheosis of Captain Hook

> With innocent revels to welcome the day.
> —Henry Purcell[25]

A grey winter's pall settled over Kathmandu, and tourists had fled in direct proportion to the drop in temperature. A freezing rain began, liquefying the filth of the streets. In the late afternoon, broad puddles crystalized in the narrow roadways and paths of the teeming village capital—colorful little Jell-O molds of cow dung, urine, butcher's offal, orange peelings, and election pamphlets.

The previous day I arrived on the flight from Bangkok, carrying a certified ABD (all-but-dissertation, but really all-but-dead) certificate, just in case I wanted to teach, and a stack of letters for hand delivery at Tribhuvan University. I planned to ensconce myself out at Bodhanath, a Tibetan pilgrimage center, and examine the interaction of Western tourists and traditional Buddhist pilgrims. But for now I was getting settled in to the Blue Diamond Hotel, between Thamel and Ratna Park.

It was nearly Christmas. A few disoriented merchants had set off their shops with a few odd garlands of pink, green, and gold Mylar tinsel, imitating the clueless Christmas decorations found throughout the tourist traps of Southeast Asia. Not a Santa, manger, or snowflake in sight, just icy downpours luridly reflecting scattered dull green, purple, and orange lightbulbs. The illuminations to attract nonexistent tourists to empty restaurants, hotels, and shops, seemed as gapingly hopeless as the mating call of the last passenger pigeon.

I was roiling with a bad chest cold this Christmas eve. Having exhausted myself chasing the Mad Hatters of the Kingdom's civil service, visiting the affable but powerless tea party known as the American Embassy, and calling on the under-the-table world of the unofficial Tibetan government, I drew myself out of my warm room at the Blue Diamond to seek brighter inspiration. The streets of Kathmandu were enshrouded in the miasma of an angry Himalaya. Desolation stalked the normally packed tourist ghetto of Thamel.

I had difficulty finding an operational restaurant in these lull times. Tibet's Kitchen, Tso Ngon Café, and Ü-tse Restaurant had easily converted their dining rooms to family rooms. With drooling rug scamps at one's feet, owners as put-upon martyrs, proprietresses anxiously watching the clock, suspicious Lhasa apsos growling, and ancient momo-las snoring, it was impossible to enjoy the happy prospects of a quiet, self-absorbed evening.

I chanced on the Rum Doodle bar, with a promising European face or two in the window, hoping to find some place where the Holiday could be shared. Underneath the portraits of an uneasy looking King Birendra and Queen Ashwarya, I found a drunken Zurich couple arguing in wildly expectorant Schwytzer Dutsch. Heaping plates of pasta with grated buffalo cheese were placed

Chapter 3

before chubby red faces, the delicacies quickly bolted down between volleys. I sat alone, ordering tomato noodles and a Coke with a quarter liter of local arak rum. Good cheer and great tidings to all, eh? Rather than warming my congested chest, however, the liquor bestowed only raw irritation followed shortly by vertigo.

I stumbled back through empty streets to my small hotel and lurched around sleeping bellboys and clerks languorously draped on lobby furniture. Kathmandu indeed! I thought—a city of a hundred anthropologists, where research opportunities abounded 'round every street corner. The ancient city ballooned into a circus of opportune ethnic color and swelled into a bubbling cauldron of successful graduate theses. Spinning, I arrived at my dark room, vomited, and hit the bed like a meteorite. I slept fitfully at first, the pathos of a lonely Christmas and an empty stomach soon clouded my dreams with absurd forms: with an oversized fork and can opener clutched in the other hand, I chased a giant can of Chef Boyardee's Beefaroni through a moon-gladed wood deep in the Black Forest. Eventually I stumbled up a stairway to a pillared galley of an empty Lowengrin palace. In the darkness, the huge can of pasta and I galloped through long passages, dodging sheet covered couches and overstuffed chairs. As I ran, portraits of the great chefs Escoffier, Brillant-Saravin, Point, and finally the grand Hector Boiardi himself passed along the walls. In a clever flash, the animated dinner escaped through a breech in the shadows. Undaunted, I spent several minutes ravenously opening a myriad of doors, all passageways plunged in coal black darkness. Breathless.

I noticed light streaming from under a door on the far side of the hall. I leapt over a harpsichord and arrived at the portal. Turning the doorknob, I stood as an adult Tiny Tim at some upscale Cratchet Christmas party. Of course, I was instantly dressed in white tie, shining as a Habsburg Apollo, with the red and white sash and neck chain of the ancient Burgundian Order of the Golden Fleece.

A long dinner table had been set, accommodating 15 to 20 splendidly attired guests gliding into a gala banquet. A silver coiffured woman approached me, arrayed in a flowing gold and white evening gown, with large diamond earrings and mantilla. She was my aunt—the Baroness Minnie of Milwaukee! The elegant lady eagerly grabbed my hand and led me to the table, asking with relieved concern why I was late. Looking back, the darkened hall had become brilliantly illuminated. Portraits of history's notables stared benignly from the walls, replacing the Great Chefs of the World.

Sparkling light from massive chandeliers glinted off Meisen china and Irish crystal. At the damask covered table sat my father's family: my only uncle, a wealthy physician and his elegant wife with an Arizona tan; several cousins, known only in legend, exchanged animated conversation. Oddly, at the center of the table sat an expertly stuffed white rabbit, cuddled on a bed of julienne radishes and carrots. Delicate courses of pâté en croute and Dover sole béchamel succumbed to a cacophony of rarer aromas and tastes. Harmonious wines flowed with scintillating conversation, while candles burned brightly. Liveried servants wore Tibetan faces. My family hung on to every word of my story of Asian adventure, the return of the prodigal son.

I awoke gradually, fully sated, with a cozy afterglow of a Nutcracker dream suffusing my outlook the entire day. It was Christmas. I decided that day to forego my pursuit of Tibetans through official channels. In Nepal, there was little room for the broad play of Tibetan *rang-bstan* (nationalism), and little chance for me to short circuit the Nepalese bureaucracy for their benefit. I followed my intuition and decided to return to the little hill station in Himachal Pradesh, the center of the Tibetan diaspora.

Suspiciously I handed over 450 Nepalese rupees (about $10 at the time) to a scruffy youth in a side alley travel office, and grabbed my overland ticket to Dharamsala. I would be traveling over the New Year's weekend, on a 36-hour "Super Deluxe Luxury" bus down through the tortuous river valleys of the Himalayan watershed, across the broad plain of the sacred Ganges, to Delhi.

Following to the letter of my committee-approved research design, I diligently kept the week's appointments, meeting with vice-chancellors, university deans and high poo-bahs in a perfunctory attempt to win a formal research permit. In Nepal, Tibetan nationals did not officially exist. Even His Holiness the Dalai Lama was not welcome. In a country that had become entirely dependent on the touting of Tibetan culture to tourists, it seemed absurd that the flesh and bone reality of Tibetans would not be acknowledged.

Teasingly I made my farewell to the lanky boys of the Blue Diamond Hotel, and was promptly overcharged for the taxi ride to the other side of town to catch the mysterious bus to India. The cab deposited me at a strange little hotel parking lot. In a few minutes a long pink and green bus careened up the driveway. As it pulled into the yard, panicked Indians and Tibetans shot their luggage upwards to acrobatic rooftop porters. The more sedate hesitated a noble minute, then stuffed their life's possessions into the hold at the rear. As I attempted to jam my heavy suitcases into the back compartment, a polite voice called out from behind a large suitcase: "Please take your time, sir. Will get your bags on."

To my astonishment, there was a tiny man working in the trunk of the bus. Amid the backpacks and trunks filled with smuggled Chinese goods, I saw brown eyes and a rapid glint of smile.

To my further surprise, my seat reservation, the choice #3 by the window and door, was actually honored. No middle aged men feigning decrepitude, no sacred old ladies pulling Brahminic rank—the seat was mine, with plenty of leg room. This must have been the "Super-deluxe" aspect of the otherwise battered trundle cart.

I looked around at my traveling companions for the next two nights—a group of ancient rough and tumble Tibetan women with seemingly hundreds of Chinese down jackets filling their bags. One dusty foreign girl bound a scarf tightly around her head and fled to the rear. The middle seats were occupied by local commuters. Nepalese men were destined, in Super-deluxe style, for their home villages at the periphery of Kathmandu Valley. The front section and the glass enclosed cab was studded with thin, teenaged Tamang boys.

The Tamang youths were the drivers, conductors, and porters for the adventure. They were accompanied by their buddies, all sharing the surname Lama. The wiry Tamangs are Buddhist and Tibeto-Burman speakers from the recesses of the southern Himalayan range. Like the Sherpas, Monpas, and Mishmi hill people, the Tamangs were porters by caste for centuries—bus transport service was a predictable concession to modern times.

Inexplicably, the seat adjacent to me up front remained unoccupied until the very last moment. Suddenly, the five foot tall man that I had found in the trunk bolted aboard, proclaiming to his Tamang cousins that the seat next to mine would be his. He was profoundly tendon-bound, built like a wolverine, and as strong as a man twice his weight. So Sangay Lama sat down and asked if I was traveling alone. Scarcely could I utter a response when he flew up, squawking orders for the relaxed, socializing Tibetans to take their seats. Then he ran to the back of the bus like an angry ferret, scattering heaps of bed rolls, contraband parcels of Chinese goods, box lunches, and metal thermoses littering the aisle. In just a few momemnts he was climbing through the luggage racks, screaming at passengers to stow their flotsam, Super-deluxe style.

The bus finally wound its way out of Kathmandu city and was out on the open road, the conductor contentedly punching tickets. Sangay Lama eventually returned to his seat, dusting off his hands like the mouse in "Tom and Jerry." His age was impossible to discern—anywhere from 20 to 55. His strident personality seemed an immense compensation for his small stature, making him a formidable but amusing character.

The Tamang boys adjacent to me started an animated conversation: "If you're traveling alone, stick with us. . .we'll take care of you," piped Lopsang, the bespectacled spokesman of the cohort, "these are all my cousins, and we take care of the bus. Just follow us, not to worry."

Here sat Migmar, a handsome pup making his first trip away from his Kathmandu home. He spoke cautiously in convent English, and seemed apprehensive of his cousins' unabashed spontaneity.

Little sleep that first night on the bus. The twisting mountain roads through the Terai, the animated Tibetans in the back, and the perpetual stops and starts, boardings, and honkings made rest impossible. Sangay kept bolting up to hassle passengers. Returning he would proclaim, "No sleep tonight, I think. Tomorrow I sleep."

The Indian border along the Terai was reached at eight in the morning, in the wild savanna known for its rare rhinoceroses, Bengal tigers, and as the home of the Buddha. For some inexplicable reason, the two foreigners on the bus had to visit the security office located in a concrete bunker at the side of the road. The dusty girl in the swaddling cloth from the back of the vehicle and I entered the building and turned over our passports. Officers studied each page carefully, made scribbles, checked rosters. Two men then engaged me in light conversation, one finally asking if I had any American coins for his collection. Am I going to travel 6,000 miles and spend two nights on a bone rattling bus with my pockets full of useless dimes and quarters?

We returned to the bus, where real police had descended and were in the process of scolding the old Tibetan women. While they threw a large bag off the roof and into the gutter, one of the momo-las slipped me a down jacket, motioning me to put it on. I looked up at her, smiled, and made her a deal. I would wear this 1960s chartreuse green polyester parka through the border, despite the 80 degree heat, if I could wear it the following night. "Agreed! You smart boy!" she cackled. Meanwhile, Sangay Lama scampered about, shouting euphemisms and exhorting the Tibetans not to smuggle. He adjusted his *topi* hat, picked up pieces of police-rifled luggage, and stowed them indiscriminately throughout the coach.

We crossed a litany of sacred rivers between Bihar and Uttar Pradesh, each one necessitating a rising cadence of *mantra* from the Hindu passengers. The Gangetic plain, endless stretches of great flatlands splattered with torpid villages, finally gave way to a smoky night.

Migmar was bright-eyed but wary, like some sea otter baby taken out to deep water for the first time. Everything he now experienced seemed new and unanticipated. Around ten that night, the glassy eyed driver finally pulled off the road for a hour's nap and a passenger stretch. Sangay caught Migmar in the aisle and gave him a bear hug for no apparent reason. Migmar squirmed. From sitting 28 hours, more or less consecutively, I felt by now completely numb from the waist down. But I managed to stagger off the bus into the hazy countryside, my legs like oaken logs before me.

In the murky landscape, we had parked next to the tracks of the Indian State Railways. I became envious of that more sedate means of traveling across the subcontinent. Two of the Tamang boys ran off to a cane field and returned, munching juicy stalks, the fibrous pith no match for hard, white teeth.

Migmar stood with me. As in some backlit Gill Reid painting, the amber moon of a steam locomotive headlight slowly filled the dark atmosphere. Reddish coals, deep earth rumblings, and acrid smoke was followed by the blurred faces of unknown people being transported to unknown places. In cadenced state, it appeared as Migmar's first train. "It's so big," he said softly. I battled the urge to explain the structure and function of railroading to this young man, Lionel style. I resisted giving him the moral story of American enterprise and the thrill of immense power and speed.

Back on the bus, the Tibetans were either imperiously sawing logs or mirthfully taking snuff. I had Momo-la's chartreuse jacket for that cool night on the Gangetic plain. The teenaged crew were apparently exhausted, settling in quickly. Even the wiry terrier Sangay gave up his aisle patrol. He collapsed in his seat on my right. But he fought on even while sleeping, continually adjusting himself, searching for elusive comfort. My right arm seemed to be the culprit, as he punched and banged it throughout the night. Finally, like at a border crossing, I raised my arm. In a split second the little Tamang man was curled up with his head on my lap.

So the night was well spent. The red sun finally brought with it the slums of Delhi, with vultures slowly spiraling upwards. The bus looped along broad avenues and halted at an urban campground filled with hirsute Iranian teamsters and blonde backpacking English girls. I handed the down jacket back to the monodont Momo-la with a wink, and gave my adieu to Sangay as he ran off to prepare for the return trip to Nepal.

The camp that the bus had been delivered to lay in a large, walled park, like an old American drive-in, with a cluster of wooden huts in the center that served as office, boiler room, and showers. Banks of windowless cells encircled the center, each the length of an unfurled sleeping bag and barely wider than a bus seat. It wouldn't do for a body that had been lashed to a creaking metal rack for the jarring 36-hours transit of the subcontinent. I thought of ten years earlier, when my powerful American student loan dollars could afford the finest old hotel in Delhi.

But little had changed. On Janpath Street at Connaught Circus in New Delhi, the Tibetan merchants were gone, but their memory lived on in a perverse way. From what had been an open bazaar of refugees selling antique *thangka* and heirloom jewelry, Indian merchants hawked cheap souvenirs of vague Tibetan art from neatly numbered stalls. I wondered if the Tibetans of Dharamsala had disappeared too.

Still unrested, I headed immediately for Kashmiri Gate terminal. At the same spot a decade past, I again boarded the shiny night bus for Himachal Pradesh.

I remember little of that night—burly Sikhs muscling themselves on and off the vehicle, women vomiting. Images were just that—detached fragments,

Chapter 3

scraps of brightly colored sari, bits of curried *pakora*, discorporate utterances of unintelligible languages. They floated past my raw body, unrelentlessly aching, like sounds in a distant corridor of some feverish patient's wardroom. These were the signs of life happening elsewhere, not my own.

The seemingly endless night broke into an over-brilliant morning. As the sun rose over the hills, the jerking metal box of humanity began to heat precipitously. Limbs of the living dead of India nodded as gracefully as those trundled out on fourteenth century plague lorries.

Death and its power of transformation became more vivid with closeness to Dharamsala. It reached its climax at the bus stand of lower Dharamsala, as scores of panicked souls fought for precious space on the next bus for the Tibetan village of McLeod Ganj. I found myself impaled on my own weighty luggage and wedged firmly by arms and legs of 80 or 90 struggling Tibetan and Parhari commuters in an oversized aluminum beer can driven by a suspiciously skeletal man. From my standpoint, a successful 2,000-foot climb to the Tibetan village in this version of Charon's raft seemed highly doubtful. Indeed, about halfway into our tortured progress up through the bare cliffs and switchbacks, the bus belched black soot and shuddered to a halt. At that instant, all bolted out of the coughing bus and scattered like cats from an overturned dumpster. Vultures swirled in the ominous skies. Moving about 200 feet away, I glumly sat down on a rock.

Soda trucks seemed to arrive at the central bus stop in McLeod Ganj every hour of every day.

A sudden breeze of mountain air instantly enlivened my flickering spirit. I picked up my luggage and began to climb the hill. Soon I found myself at Forsythe Ganj, a little cantonment of Indian Army officers sent there to help fortify the nearby Kashmiri border. Some men stood out on patios barefoot, in khaki uniforms and scarlet turbans — young attendants polishing their boots, beads of sweat glistening on their chin straps. McLeod Ganj and the hazy palace of the Dalai Lama lay in the great beyond, across terraced farmers' fields of yellow mustard; a tiny mountain stream extended up through the dense forest. I adjusted the straps on my baggage, tied to my back, on my waist, over my shoulders, and drifted off and up through the deodar and rhododendron trees.

I floated over gardens of pastel red and blue sweet peas and odiferous geraniums, and glimpsed the circling raptors high overhead. Little rivulets of meticulous cultivation flowed into narrow fields of flowering yellow. Here was a glen as pristine as Darjeeling before the British tea plantations were established, or Pokara Lake before the Gurkha invasion.

As I climbed the last 100 yards up the valley, I thought of the great changes that must have befallen the Tibetan community in exile. No longer destitute, the new refugees' prosperity had grown in proportion to the rise of the fame of the Dalai Lama on the international stage. McLeod Ganj had metamorphosed from camp to capital. I arrived to order, calm, the trickling of springs, and the faint smell of musk and sandalwood. Looking back, I saw the silvery blue bus far below, now enshrouded in an asphyxiating cloud of black smoke.

Lightheaded from dehydration, I glided into the first chai shop off the main square. "Kalimpong Café" — this was new too. A tidy, bright corridor with photographs of mountains hung on light blue walls, the restaurant was wedged between Rinzin's Donut House and the soggy front of what used to be a homey Indian eatery. Leaving my dusty bags by the door, I wearily sat down on a stiff wooden chair at an awkwardly high table. In an instant a thin figure appeared over me. I had been covetously examining the display of soda bottles along the shelf. My gaze fixed on the inviting bottles. I ordered a "Mr. Pik," an over carbonated spring water that I remembered from years back.

"Oh no! Mr. Pik's been bad today. He's too hot," an overgrown Tibetan boy proclaimed incredulously. I turned to the side and caught the radiant countenance of a happy young man about twenty years of age. "I've got something else for you." By now the room had turned a pulsating electric blue. My heart pounded wildly as the boy disappeared.

In a second the handsome youth returned with some sort of effervescent froth that barely contained itself in its bottle. It opened explosively. Fascinated, I focused all my attention on the bottle, its smiling moon face label mockingly leering at this reckless foreigner. While the sharpness of the chilled tonic helped counter my alarming dehydration, its frigid rush gave me an immediate headache. I called the boy over to request a large pot of black tea.

"No food this time, yeah? Just things to drink, right? Okay, no problem. Relax." He laughed as he ran off to the curtained kitchen in the back to ask his mother to set up the hot water.

He returned promptly. Slowly the blood returned to my head as I sipped the tea. With it vibrant images half-composed of the present space and half of a pleasantly strange fantasy flooded my head. I saw tables covered with vases of flowers — vermilion red and black-streaked poppies and crocus painted butter yellow. The front window box, trimmed in pink geraniums, looked out upon neat

Chapter 3

Germanic cottages with homey mottos painted in Gothic script over doorways and shutters. Jersey cows with large bells placidly moved through the village, indifferent to the passing of buxom blonde girls on mopeds and the blur of an occasional BMW. In front of me, condiment jars suddenly had faces and names to them, a Mr. Salt, a Miss Soya.

I looked at the mountain landscapes painted on the walls with bright enamels. I examined the Hindi cinema calendar that stood next to a hand colored portrait of the Dalai Lama. A pyramid of Cadbury chocolate bars stood on a little shelf in front as an offering.

As I slowly sipped my hot Darjeeling tea, it struck me that perhaps this chai shop was really a play restaurant. Nothing here seemed real. The hammy young man, if he existed at all, greatly overacted his part, being a sycophantastic host to embarrassed visitors from the outer world. He provided a campy show to please a jaded, world-weary patron, no doubt — a charming operetta complete with a supporting cast of attractive brothers, sisters, mother, and father happily dancing through their duties in a state of frivolous gaiety. They were sort of a Sherpa version of the von Trapp family with the fawning eldest son as Maria. What a wonderful attempt at Shangri-La!

I drank my leafy tea, becoming more hyper-sensitive to the nuances of my self-conjured illusion. It seemed no longer Dharamsala, but a place ripped out of the fabric of time and space that surely no one else had experienced. Objects were familiar, but ever so slightly knocked out of phase. All was bathed in a sense of the uncanny, and spread heavily with a frothy kitsch. While the dogs of rationality suggested a simple matter of exhaustion, I felt an extraordinary feeling of auspiciousness and excitement, a being on the verge of a transformation. There existed an undercurrent of strong color, a vibration of an impeding apotheosis. It became too much to behold; I had to leave the surreal café.

"You come back! You come back!" the grinning image of the Cheshire waiter panted.

Sure...sure, I really need to rest, I thought as I walked out his door and onto the now muddy streets of McLeod Ganj, past decrepit beggars, shoving Indian tourists, raucous motorcycles, and fuming buses. I turned the corner to find familiar Baghsunath Road, and headed like a dog to my old home at the Kokonor Hotel.

Up the stairs, still dimly lit by a bare bulb, I found my cement block room at the Kokonor Hotel. Ten years after, Rinzin was not here to greet me, nor to my splendid relief, were the ghosts of the Old Guard. I had the former dormitory room to myself. I stowed my roll of rupee notes under one of the mattresses. McLeod Ganj had electricity now, but no running water. Thus, the excreta of humanity and the offal of the burgeoning tourist industry was now brilliantly illuminated.

I set off down the road to purchase two large plastic pails: one to wash off the accumulated catacomb grime of my transit ordeal, the other to soak my heavy clothes. After a trip to the stall at the Kokonor at the end of the long hall, I returned to my stark room three shades lighter, placed a papier mache mask of the blue god Mahakala on the wall above my bed, and entered a long, dreamless sleep.

January in Dharamsala developed into a bright affair with few Tibetans and even fewer tourists. I paid a call at Nowrojee & Sons to see if the old dowager was still alive. Mrs. Nowrojee (Mani was her first name) had survived, but hadn't an inkling who I was until I told her. Now practically bald, a few wisps of

The road from Baghsunath to McLeod Ganj was nearly empty that winter. There was no snow. The dry mustard terraces, the deodar cedars, and the tall pines shown brightly in the stark Himalayan sunlight.

Chapter 3

henna jutted from the sari draped over her head. Yet she still owned nearly the entire village, and ruled it as the stern mother Indira had ruled the country. The Tibetans, according to her, were her wayward children, and many of them had run away.

"All the Tibeti have gone! Gone South, big jobs in Delhi, off selling their sweaters!" she scoffed. "Now, good sir, do you have a nice place to live? We received your letter and you must know now that we have remodeled Balcony House. It is really very pleasant and you must let my *chokidar* show it to you. Very nice, indeed."

Cow Barn! My mind recoiled. Balcony House would be filled with the zeitgeist of the Old Guard, memories of Kip, and the resonances of Jimmy. I bid Mrs. Nowrojee my sincere regrets and walked away.

My thoughts turned on the golden half light of the Byzantine stable of years past, when the meadows and woods were resonant with the chatter of monkeys and redolent with the fragrant smoke of Tibetan hearths. It marked time on the very edge of old Tibet, the last camp of an ancient nomadic people.

Although I had barely returned to the village, I could sense that it was all gone. The *nono* princes and the old duchesses were disappearing. The young Turks had come of age, and were impatiently anticipating their country's liberation. It seemed interminable to wait for the miracle. The God of Time also challenged the nerve of the new generation born in exile. Not content to entertain the phantoms of the increasingly mythical past, the young exiles of Dharamsala had begun an uninhibited plunge into a new fantasy based on the consumerism of the West and its exotic blue-eyed blonds. Paradoxically, this stampede away from the homeland had begun by those who had first revisited the land of their ancestors.

As if to slander the successes of the administration of the Dalai Lama, the Chinese government had recently swung the forbidden door wide open, permitting Tibetan refugees to visit the occupied country for the first time since the exodus in 1959. Beijing went a step further, blatantly encouraging Tibetan repatriation by offering jobs and cash to restless Tibetan refugee youth. Seduced, many young boys and girls of Dharamsala and other camps visited the Chinese Embassy in Delhi to apply for the special "Overseas Chinese" visa. There they would be seated in comfortable chairs, served tea and cigarettes, and would otherwise be treated with every respect and nicety—provided they did not use the Tibetan word *Gya-mi* when referring to the Han Chinese. Such a term implies that the Tibetans are something other than Chinese, and its use would send most consular officials into a state of red-faced apoplexy.

While it still was the center of refugee life, McLeod Ganj had become a hybrid, unlike either its Tibetan or Western parents (was it ever Indian?). Perhaps a mosaic of both, it was a totally new presentation of Tibetan culture: subtle, seductive, and proud, where once the dramatic, honest, and self-deprecating prevailed. The West had found a readily accessible Shangri-La, despite the wild irony that such a phrase evokes. It bore absolutely no resemblance to the homeland Tibetan capital that the local tourist bureau appropriated to refer to McLeod Ganj as "Little Lhasa." In the last ten years, Tibetan exiles had become so used to the wide-eyed infatuations of Westerners, friendship had now become a matter of qualification. Only the wealthiest, most politically powerful and celebrated foreigners were worth one's time, to all but the unworldly old and the very young.

The day after my arrival, at about ten in the morning, I walked down the muddy street to find my breakfast in one of the many chai shops. I took a seat in an empty restaurant, next to a window, and began to write in my journal. The window overlooked the street, and many Tibetans walked past, doing their prayer wheels, running off to school, or heading for work in the rug cooperatives. I looked up to see two young women, perhaps in their early 20s, standing across the street, pointing at me and giggling. How rude, I thought, and returned to my writing.

Later that morning I saw the two women again on the street, talking with a third. Oh no! They saw me! But instead of pointing, they cautiously approached, twittering all the way. I didn't know what to expect.

"Excuse, please. Excuse, please!" one girl said to me, eyes downcast.

"I think, no...eh...my friend, here, my friend Dolma says you are a big movie star," she continued, red-faced. "Please tell us."

"Is that true?" I countered.

"Yes! Yes, we have seen you in the video cinema," the women stated. "I'm sorry I cannot remember your name, but you are very important."

"Oh, no!" I laughed. "You must mean someone else. I'm not a movie star, never in movies."

"But, please. You are. Please, no need to be modest," flustered the second young woman. "I have seen you, too, in many videos." The third girl nodded her head.

My eyes were popping out of my head with disbelief. I could not deny anything, nor establish my real self with these women, or with anyone in this village. This is Dharamsala, isolated, but well-known to the outside world, I thought. How is this possible? As I walked away, the girls turned to each other with hands across their mouths, and jumped up and down in a fit of excitement.

A star without portfolio. I fancied myself as Brad Pitt, shining dangerous, crystalline sky blue eyes in all directions. Perhaps I was Richard Gere—that would be logical. He was a good friend of the Dalai Lama and had visited Dharamsala many times before. The worn trail of thousands of Western visitors to Dharamsala had not eliminated the power of imagination and the fascination with all things Western.

Despite the propaganda of the Tibetan Ministry of Information and the Pollyanna visions of empathetic scholars, Tibetan culture had **not** maintained itself in exile. To survive in India and Nepal, it had become a parody of itself, selling an image that neatly conformed not to tradition but to tourist expectations, and much of that built upon generations of Western Shangri-La musings. It would be a curious experience to discover how deeply layered the novelty had become.

These appraisals flashed before me in an instant, blankly standing before the Anglophile Mrs. Nowrojee while she rattled on about the advantages of the Roman alphabet. In that brief moment, the formal hypotheses of my research that had eluded me and my committee of six profoundly august Asian scholars had fallen into my hands.

I left Nowrojee & Sons and headed out onto the village streets and down the paved trail to the Central Tibetan Secretariat, descending the hill to Gangchen Kyishong. Following a curious Western tradition from Marco Polo through Walt Disney, I presented myself to the Tibetan government as the first order of business. To be absolutely true to form, it was the Dalai Lama himself I should call upon. But the hierarch was in Bodh Gaya in Bihar, enthroned at the center of the Buddhist world—the spot where the Buddha himself experienced nirvana.

I shared this presumption with nearly every foreign visitor that had ever visited old Tibet or its successor state in Dharamsala. When presented with an

Chapter 3

acclaimed pinnacle of the exotic, it was a universal Western urge to take oneself to their leader. As Cook demanded of Kamehameha and Cortes of Montezuma, every Western warrior in Tibetland had to see the Dalai Lama.

Casually visiting the Dalai Lama was hardly a Tibetan tradition. Self-ascribed importance becomes a convenient psychological defense for coping with the anxiety of immersion in the radically novel. The homey farm girl Dorothy, when presented with the obstacle of Miss Gulch, conjures up a tornado to do her bidding. When confronted with the bafflement of Technicolor in Oz, she seeks out the awesome Wizard to help her make sense of the exotic. She journeys to him in the company of extraordinary locals with crippling low self-esteem. And she travels through the strange land not as a simple school girl but as a deity, a "Good Witch" who has inherited the ruby slippers and the powers they possess. Dharamsala was indeed crawling with herds of Dorothys and tribes of Scarecrows!

Down the winding road, through the forest I trekked, to the government community of Gangchen Kyishong. This village of civil servants of the Dalai Lama had grown from a ragtag collection of rented tin huts in the 1970s to an imposing labyrinth of ministries and monasteries. It now reflected the immensely enlarged status of the Dalai Lama to the outside world.

I left my card for the Director of the Library of Tibetan Works and Archives, my official sponsor, with a bored receptionist. And I visited the office of the Minister of Information. What had once been a tiny office in a cement walk-up would soon be replaced by a sprawling complex of glass and marble. At the adjacent construction site, its name was already spelled out in golden letters on the pediment, highly appropriate: Office of Information and International Affairs. Spreading the official line about Tibet and the diaspora was essentially the exiled government's only foreign business. Having recently published articles in the Library's *Tibet Journal*, and the Office of Information's *Tibetan Bulletin*, my name was vaguely known. But my persona was scarcely distinguishable from the perpetual stream of yellowed-headed tourists who jostled their way to Dharamsala for an audience or for the latest information on the possibility of visiting Tibet.

In my ten-year absence, the monastery of the State Oracle had been splendidly rebuilt by Western funds. There had been radical changes since those carefree days when as a kid I had enjoyed the morning sunshine with the Nechung Oracle on the balcony of the tiny reestablished monastery. He had since died, as had the abbot Nechung Rinpoche, my guru. The grand monastery and its halls of Elysian mystery were now strictly forbidden to foreign tourists, an action that only inflamed Western curiosity. I expected the managers of the Nechung Dharma center in Hawai`i to arrive in Dharamsala any day.

My old Hawaiian friends, Tanya Retro and her husband Greg, had "brought me to the lama" and hence into a practical relationship with Buddhist teachings and the Tibetan language. And through my broken Tibetan I learned from the monk sentries at Nechung Gompa that Tanya and Greg had not yet arrived. One monk guard seemed only to recognize my words, "Tanya," "Rinpoche," and "Hawai`i" before falling back into sullenness and subsequently booting me off the property. I couldn't help but think about that portion of his bed and *tsampa* that I had paid for over the years.

Fortunately, the event conjured up my last attempt at polite formality, as I had thought befitted an agreeable Western graduate student. May my professors spin in their endowed chairs! No illusions, no more illusions, I thought.

The Apotheosis of Captain Hook

All eyes on His Holiness, a wonderful scene unfolded when the Dalai Lama's tan colored Mercedes careened around the curve on its final approach to Thekchen Choling in McLeod Ganj. Just in time for Lo Sar, he was returning from a long pilgrimage in eastern India.

While the Tibetan nobles once rode in palanquins and on horseback, their modern civil service equivalents commandeered government jeeps, motorcycles, and Marutis. This left the commoners, as ever, to shuffle up the steep hills on foot. During my own 1,000-foot climb back up to McLeod Ganj, one careening jeep nearly hit me—I leapt into the nettles instead. The vehicle was occupied by three or four Tibetans and one apparently privileged Western woman—all looking very serious. The blue car blazed with an enameled snow lion crest, the seal of the government of the Dalai Lama. As I walked further up the slope, a dusty, rose red jeep dashed by. I caught a glimpse of a blonde Englishwoman and a middle aged Tibetan man with a pigtail. I continued past the open gutters of the nunnery. I saw the site of a new hotel under construction, the works of the Yong Ling orphanage newly opened in a former mustard field, and the soon-to-be opened Chocolate Log tea house next to the most fetid drainage in all the village.

Returning to the Kokonor, I salved my scratches with Bacitracin, took two Tylenol, and headed for the dark hotel dining room. An oil cloth curtain covered the entry to the large gathering place. Typical of McLeod Ganj establishments catering to Western tourists, the room contained half again as many tables as could seat guests comfortably. The same rock hard, Carmelite convent chairs, which despite their designed restraints, did little to contain the grubby margins of the half dozen freaks who were draped across them.

I ordered a fried green tomato chow mein, with a side of mutton stuffed pancakes, and prayed for the best (it cost me about 80¢). The old, predictable, and

Chapter 3

absolutely adequate cook had left several years back, perhaps when Rinzin moved to Delhi. A new family ran the establishment. The kids operated the front of the house, or rather giggled and gossiped, while their sweating parents, hard pressed at the stoves, shouldered most of the burden.

I had table partners. No great coincidence in a town as small as McLeod, but seated adjacent to me were the pigtailed man and the blonde Western woman from the red jeep. The young woman was an American, a graduate student in Indian philosophy at some small private college in Massachusetts. The stocky man was none other than a leading scholar at the Tibetan Archives—an *acharya pandit*, in fact. I was familiar with Paljor Taring's work, and he even knew of mine. I could sense he was not impressed with this information, nor perhaps with that of any other foreigner with the pretension of understanding Tibetan culture from the outside. But he liked blonde women. This particular couple, Angela and Paljor Pandit, appeared to be on a date yet I felt myself drawn into the interaction. Perhaps it was Angela's expedient to displace Paljor's amorous ambitions.

Paljor had recently returned from a broken marriage in America. Like Queen Hope of Sikkim, his Yankee wife had kept the kids, and he returned to his community with tail curled 'round. Angela was soft-spoken, subtly expressive, and irritatingly brilliant. She waxed deftly in entertaining her curious instincts while avoiding the "rebound transference" of the broken-hearted Tibetan across from her. She was also plainly honest: she liked Tibetan men and that is frankly why she was here.

Momentarily I glanced up at a portrait of the last Prime Minister of pre-1959 Tibet. I slowly realized that Paljor affected the mannerisms and obsolete dress of those same, long-passed dignitaries. Having failed to be an American, he now seemed determined to be more Tibetan than anyone else in Dharamsala.

Since the dog had eaten my research proposal, I approached my tenure in Dharamsala viscerally. I would improvise, and not restrain myself. After all, except for the feline Kenji, still painting *thangka* in Dharamsala and banking a fortune selling them in Tokyo, I was the sole representative of the Old Guard. That gave me a right to set myself apart from the normal refugee expectations of Western tourist behavior. Khampa Peter didn't count, of course, for he " went bush" years ago. The point of ethnography is to plunge deeply and jump back out of the abyss. I would go where I wished, *en suite* if I liked, and examine whatever caught my fancy. I would present myself as a cross between a soot-caked Alexandra David-Neel and a hyper stereotypical Nordic Nanson.

Young, engaging, and six-foot four, Oliver the Canadian received overflowing attention. The Grand Dowager Nowrojee, in particular, took a special interest in Ollie, making sure he had the freshest copy of the *Times of India* waiting for his daily visit to the general store. He was a Coldstream guardsman in her lost world of cricket on the green, and strawberries and cream garden parties at the vice-regal lodge at Simla.

Ollie rented an A-frame hut from the Western Dharma people of Tushita, Lama Zopa Rinpoche's embassy at the Tibetan diaspora capital. It was just west of Cow Barn. Like many a tourist, Ollie wasn't sure why he had come to McLeod Ganj. He knew nothing about Tibetan culture and religion. But he thrived in the bright mountain air, and enjoyed the modest decorum that Tibetans were prone to display. It was with Oliver that I first began to examine the new and preposterous.

Ollie and I would spend days lying about in the sunshine of the cabin, eating lotuses and free-associating. A family of rhesus macaques had moved into the adjacent A-frame, taking over the lodgings of a rather prissy Western nun who was on holiday somewhere in the south. One afternoon we watched in glee as the balcony door flew open. Clouds of flour billowed out of the shack, followed by flying saucers, plates, and half-eaten boxes of biscuits. One elderly female monkey bolted out clutching a Buddhist rosary; a juvenile immediately followed, covered with honey and newspaper scraps. Too bad Walt Disney was still frozen.

Hanging with Ollie was great fun and without many responsibilities; we were like children. One morning after breakfast we visited the monastery of the Ngapo Lama, the abode of the ancient Tibetan shaman who was the official weather maker for the community. Zilnon Gompa was new to me. The orthodox "red hat" order of the Nyingmapa had actually established a beach head within the Holy See of the Dalai Lama's yellow hat Gelugpa church.

One morning Ollie told me there was someone at Zilnon he had to visit. An elderly monk had taken a liking to the strapping Canadian, and Ollie was returning his kindness. Ollie asked me to go along to help translate. We stopped off at Nowrojee's to buy the standard monk-visit food, cookies and biscuits. Luckily Mrs. Nowrojee was in lower Dharamsala, meeting with her attorneys over the matter of converting the McLeod Ganj motor garage to rooms for tourists. Walking toward Zilnon on Baghsunath road, I glimpsed the kids of the Kalimpong Café running in and out of their shops like monkeys. The waiter from my first encounter there had inexplicitly dressed in a spotlessly white Tibetan shirt as he siphoned kerosene from the barrel into storage jugs. I counted two sisters and a younger brother, all with an indelible Tibetan apple cheeked complexion. The young man was by far the most animated, darting here and there, laughing and tossing things out of the door. He teased his siblings while Lhasa apsos scurried around his legs. As I continued to stare, the waiter soon recognized me at this distance and waved. I managed a short salute, and Ollie and I continued our walk. I still didn't know his name.

Passing the site of old Amala's "Last Chance Café," the atmosphere once again became quiet. Lucky Amala. She had gained international notoriety after being featured in Peter Gold's slick book *Tibetan Reflections* and moved to Switzerland when her hut was bulldozed to build the monolithic Hotel Tibet. Oily smoke drifted upwards out of wooden shacks along the route, and soft sounds of water taps and Tibetans clearing their throats filled the air. We walked past my own Kokonor and four other hotels built recently, then progressed around the infamous concrete public latrines that had been contributed by some foreign agency many years ago. The outhouses traditionally marked the boundary of the village, yet three or four new chai shops now lay beyond.

Zilnon Gompa had been constructed on a nearly vertical slope within a few feet of the Tibetan Institute of Performing Arts. Ollie's monk friend was found in an adjacent cottage. He struck me as a simple old man, and his old robes attested to the fact that he wasn't the celebrated Ngakpo shaman I had thought. His room was strung with laundry, and a young girl of about 19 was in the back doing chores. Was she his wife, perhaps? Ollie and the monk began a predictable "it's a small world" show-and-tell with Ollie's watch, the golden hair on his arms... The monk displayed his rosary, pointed to the Buddha on the wall, and handed his tall friend a bag of string—little, blue knots of string. These were talismans, *srung-dud*, to be unfurled and worn around the neck for three days as a blessing from the

Chapter 3

Ngakpo Rinpoche. Ollie threw me one as an afterthought. I was not the lama's favorite.

The two went on and on while the girl served us a small lunch of samosas and tea. The old man kept smiling at Ollie the entire visit, while my eyes wandered about the room, fixating upon the upholstery of the chair, the calendar on the wall, the cobwebs in the corner.

Hyped as the eerie citadel of the ancient order of the Nyingmapa, Zilnon had been about as inspiring as a Lutheran pancake breakfast back home in Great Falls. I had hoped to see some of the mysteries of the great Nyingmapa founder, the Guru Padmasambhava, who could turn fire breathing demons into saints. I opened up my string, and tied it around my neck. Ollie and I walked back to town.

Soon we were in the center of McLeod Ganj, where I ran into the Kalimpong Café waiter at the bus stand. I was slightly taken aback with his overt familiarity—slightly and unaccountably shocked as he bounded over to me. I didn't know why I deserved the attention. But what a curious, animated fellow, I thought. His name was Da 'od Gyatso, an unusual but beautiful Tibetan name: Ocean of Moon Light. Oddly, I had never really met him, other than as a one-time patron of the restaurant. On that occasion I had been in a serious state of dehydration. Nor could I now look upon him directly, either. His unbridled energy seemed too much of a contrast to the chalky old monk at Zilnon we had just visited. I was struck, however, by the young man's unaccented, idiomatic English, spoken in a slightly affected but resonant tenor. He was disarmingly engaging, though. I had to venture a question: "Why aren't you working right now?".

"It's my day off. I get to go out once a week. Usually I go and see my lama. That's why I'm wearing this new shirt. I really work all the time, from 6 in the morning to 11 at night."

"It must be very hard," I said, pawing my feet in the dust.

"Sure, I take care of my whole family...all the brothers and sisters. So I have to run the restaurant all the time. I couldn't finish school..."

I felt Ollie impatiently prodding me to move on.

"I want you to come by the restaurant anytime," Moon Light urged as I began to move away with Ollie, "we have much to talk about, Eric-la." I felt a pang of free-floating anxiety. Panic—a lithe Burmese cat had just jumped into my lap, rubbing and kneading. This seduction could be a scandal. What about my fieldwork? What would my dissertation committee say?

A blubbering Sally Struthers slowly walks through a pig pen somewhere in the Third World. She picks up a tiny child playing in the mud, and implores the bloated couch potatoes back home that life is unbearable "out there." Timed to appear right after dinner throughout the U.S., the ad is designed to maximize the feelings of social guilt by linking it with gluttony. The sobbing, plump American celebrity suggests that for the price of a cup of coffee, these scruffy children can be fed, housed, and educated for a month or so. A simple reach for the checkbook is all that's needed to alleviate the unbearable guilt generated by viewing this squalor. If the patron wishes, he or she may send a card to their adopted child. In return, the child (i.e. the agency staff), will provide a photograph of the remarkable changes that the child has undergone due to the donations. Suddenly, the waif is transformed into a smiling child wearing a crisp school uniform, is speaking English, eating with knife and fork, and hoping one day to have a bright red Jeep Grand Cherokee snugly parked in front of a split-level ranch house in the suburbs.

For the cost of a Chicklet, anyone could vicariously raise a child, anywhere from India to Peru, to be a flag waving, burger eating cheerleader from Des Moines. What more could a generous, compassionate Westerner want? For starters, one could throw a Lady Edwina Mountbatten pique and go out and save the world first hand. It could be an all-win situation: the host society would love the free attention, the audience back home would applaud, and the guilt of excessive riches would be reduced by a degree unattainable through passive measures. Combine these motivations with the spell of a handsome people from a fabled land living on the brink of extinction, and you have hordes of would-be Lawrences of Tibet streaming into the Dalai Lama's mountain retreat. By 1987, Save Tibet had become fashionable. Never mind that the Western powers turned their backs on the struggling state after World War II. Never mind that in 1977, the Dalai Lama himself had difficulty even securing a visa for a private visit to the United States. And never mind that for a generation of Western academics, the mere mention of Tibetan studies to those who controlled the portals of academia would bring on polite nods while one was being escorted to the door.

I thought I had little in common with these modern Crusaders who piled off the buses clutching the Peter Gold Sutra and the Tantra of Lonely Planet. After all, I had been quietly fighting for Tibetan freedom for ten years now, I was Old Guard. Having saved the piebald snail darter and the Malawi wood tit, well heeled environmentalists imbued with neo-Enlightenment tenets kept pouring into this village in the Himalayas. It was important to retain my standing in Shangri-La, however, being the direct heir of the Heinrick Harrer generation of "authentic" Tibet explorers. I had carved out a nice fiefdom, and planned on decorating it with images appropriate to my fantasy. The new zealots would bear scrutiny.

I would always have a Xeroxed copy or two of my latest article to pawn off on any literate tourist, interested or not. And I found an interesting space in which to write. The Toepa Hotel dining room had become the favorite watering hole for the chic tourist intelligentsia. It was run by Samden, a great friend, a solid citizen of Free Tibet. Here I could usually find the latest news on the opening of the Tibetan border to overland travel. They had the information, more accurate than the CIA.

To conservative Tibetan refugees, the thought of dealing with China, at any level, was anathema. Until the homeland was liberated, travel to Tibet did not exist as a possible course of action. Through their well intentioned but insatiable curiosity, Western tourists would destroy what was left of Tibetan culture back home. What China could not accomplish, a mass of wealthy, unknowing foreigners could. Only the Dalai Lama and his top advisors saw the benefits that might be gained by the crack in Tibet's otherwise complete isolation. The older exiles of McLeod Ganj were aghast—the Western tourists were even taking their kids on the jaunt to Tibet!

The youthful Western Action Heros were well prepared. At the Toepa Hotel, burly Australians and studious Japanese communally plunked down their new guidebooks and poured over the details. The Toepa was a war room bunker, shielded from the very real Chinese spies and most Old Guard skeptics. The plans were Rube Goldberg, but canonized by the instant veterans who had just returned.

During the winter of 1987, a foreign visitor to Tibet had first to travel to Delhi, or preferably Kathmandu. Then one visited the Indo-Arab Bank and telexed a request to China International Travel Service in Beijing for permission to travel to China overland (do not mention Tibet!). The telex had to be accompanied with a wire draft of U.S. $30.00. Then you waited exactly three days and returned to the bank. The officer would read all the incoming telexes before you. Like the modulated prattle of a dining room hostess, the officer inevitably cantored, "Wilson party of six...Van Patten party of four..." A few days later, when the Chinese Embassy consular section opened, one would take a cryptic dot-matrix slip from the bank telex and fill out a visa application. Do not mention Tibet. Those that did received a one-month visa. Those that wrote "China" on the form got three months or more. After another week, the great red seal of the People's Republic would be placed on your passport, and the race against the immediately valid visa would begin.

Discussions of how to arrange surface transport, how to exchange money, and other practical matters filled the dark hours of many a night at the Toepa. Led by gender stretching New Zealand women, who rolled their own cigarettes, tactical and strategic courses of assault against the plateau were discussed, voted upon, and memorized.

I thought of the old '49ers off to California. I thought of a vintage photograph: White American pioneers lined up with their wagons at the border of Oklahoma Territory the first day of the Homestead Act. Since Tibet had been open to low budget tourism for a year or so, tourists could rarely boast of being the first Westerner to visit any particular site since any awe-inspiring length of time. The game was now modified, in sporting measure, to encompass qualified firsts: Who would be the first EuroAmerican woman since Madame David-Neel to walk across Tibet with no money? The duration of stay in the Forbidden Realm itself became an exercise in summiteering. Seven years in Tibet was exponentially better than six years in Tibet. Who could design the best disguise in order to most closely blend in with the indigenous people? Who could have the most fun deceiving the Chinese without getting shot? Gamesmanship would run close to brinkmanship on this lofty board.

At the Toepa, the plump, acerbic Ritz was accompanied by another young woman from New Zealand. Julie had closely cropped hair surrounding a bony frame, a perpetual trekker. The older Tibetans mistook her for a boy. She tended to hang out with the young Tibetan men. They were all perplexed, however, with her ritual breakfast of Marmite on toast and bee pollen on boiled oats.

Anne hailed from England, as sweet and temperate as Lewis Carroll's Alice. She seemed a reincarnation of Eleanor of the Cow Barn of years past, bookish, self reliant, and stuck on Tibetans like gum on asphalt. But Anne stood as a model of the new Tibetophile — her infatuation was broadly defined. Instead of merely plotting to bed one fine hunk, she wanted to cuddle all Tibetans to her bosom. Whereas Angela savored the fragrance of one superb rose, the voluptuary Anne delighted in the bower and boudoir, garlands of gardenia, and Tibetans by the armful.

The Apotheosis of Captain Hook

Anne, Ritz, and Julie were soon joined by Lulu and Pierre from Quebec, aid workers sent by their government. The Canadians were accompanied by a very unusual young man. Swiss Tibetan Werner Dorje had just arrived from Europe and had been plunged into a severe identity crisis. Westerners took turns to show him what they expected from a real Tibetan man. More German than Tibetan, Werner Dorje wallowed in the type of self-pity and feeling of inadequacy that often is expressed as arrogance. German angst. Over 1,000 Tibetan refugees had been settled in the Alps in the early 1960s, and as the *National Geographic* had attested, the colony had thrived, adapting to the best of Swiss culture while maintaining a strong Tibetan identity. For Werner, at least, it hadn't worked. He spoke fewer words of his ancestral tongue than most of the foreign tourists in Dharamsala. His deficiency was ill concealed by this mask. Further serving to alienate him from his Dharamsala cousins, Werner displayed expensive cargo—a Puma Gore-tex™ jacket, Nike shoes, even a Nikon camera around his neck. As a result, he was completely shunned by the local Tibetan community. He had become an attachment to Lulu and Pierre and the rest of his closer kindred, the Western tourists.

My buddy Samden, the sturdily built Khampa woman who expertly managed the Toepa Hotel, had a keen eye for making money as well as great desserts. Samden learned how to bake excellent banana, chocolate, and carrot cakes for Western munchies. In a munificent gesture of gratitude to India, she "adopted" six or seven children from the dirt poor State of Bihar to the east. They became her kitchen and dining room staff. Ranging in age from five to ten, the kids seemed genuinely happy playing restaurant from six in the morning to ten at night. It was perhaps an additional gauge on how bad conditions were back home in Bihar—the children would wail pitifully when sent back to visit their parents.

While the patrons of the Toepa were obsessed with everything relating to Tibet, the local Tibetans had practically nothing to do with the Toepa guests. Young Tibetan ladies stopped in to visit with Samden, sipping tea and gossiping in Tibetan about the foreigners. Monks in groups of two or three often took a light, silent lunch of noodles between long prayer sessions, eyes peering out from behind their bowls. But oddly, no Tibetan refugee was ever seen joining the group of tourists and their plans for liberating their country with land rovers and walking sticks from REI. The kingdom of the carrot cake stodd proud as a preserve for those practical folks in-the-know and those waiting to be. The Toepa glowed with spotlights and maps, green visors, and cryptic codes passed between strategists— one expected to see field phones with generator cranks. The preconceived fantasy of Tibet seemed to be sieved through arduous adventure.

Next door presented a radically different scene. I began to realize that my hallucinations here were based in disturbing reality. The Kalimpong Café could be more appropriately named "Westward Ho." Here, Ocean of Moon Light's dream of the golden West burst through a thin veneer of denatured Tibetan decor. Kalimpong represented not the hardtack Tibet of the Toepa, but its cloying opposite—rendered pith, all sweetness and fluff. Cherubic nomads danced with their cuddly yaks on bright frescoes. No place in all the Tibetan world was more blatantly covetous of the West nor more fantastic in its display of Shangri-La.

Ironically, in the process of presenting a spurious image of Tibet, Moon Light played the consummate Westerner. He became confident through the attentions that foreign tourists amply provided. A properly modulated stereo filled the narrow room with Chameleon and other Europop, providing a bright background

Chapter 3

to the Moon Light show. He seemed well turned out in his Swatch watches and snugly fitting turtleneck sweaters over Levi's 501 jeans and suede loafers. His world marked the place in Dharamsala where Tibetans and foreigners exchanged their fantasies, where effete orientalists and occidentalists found kinship. Did Eric still have any further illusions?

A popular place for bookish Japanese, the Kalimpong Café created a clean, tidy sanctuary from which to taste the hospitality proffered by a happy Tibetan family. Governmental officials, great lamas, and renegade Tibetan essayists mingled with the more innocent of foreign tourists. Soft, peach skinned Western patrons of the Kalimpong Café were padded, coaxed, and tickled into gentle participation.

Phala, the head of the family (he had no other name?), had been the cook at the Gang Kyi Restaurant in McLeod Ganj. He was thoroughly trained in the art of the Chinese wok. A Khampa, he had married a beautiful Sherpa girl in Kalimpong, and set about raising a very large family. They arrived in Dharamsala some time in 1982. While Phala became the most valued cook in McLeod Ganj, Amala sold noodles on the sidewalk at the bus stand. Soon, they accumulated enough money to lease a long, narrow shop stall from Mrs. Nowrojee. Hardworking, the McLeod Ganj neophytes had managed to collect much of the dinner trade in the village, a fact hardly appreciated by the pioneer establishments and their vanguard guests, the Old Guard. Newcomers they were, and newcomers they remained.

Despite my intuitive misgivings, I was drawn to the place again. Two weeks into my formal apprenticeship as an anthropologist, I stopped into the Kalimpong Café for a light lunch. I had just walked the three miles up Jogi Bhara Road from the Library, and was typically lightheaded. Heart pounding, I entered softly and found the long, painted hall practically empty.

"Always working?" I greeted Moon Light, who jumped over a chair and presented me with a menu.

"Yes, sure. It's awful, really. I'm always here. My brothers and sisters get to go to school during the day, so I have to be here with Amala who cooks."

"What about your Phala?"

"He has to be out all day to go to the bazaar to buy supplies—petrol, and other things for the restaurant. Since I'm the eldest, I never got to finish school. I am needed here and I cannot leave. I'm here by myself with Amala. I am 100% pure Tibetan."

That last line demanded my attention. I took my eyes off the menu and finally looked up, intently, at Moon Light. I saw a pure, golden being about 20 years of age, delicate features framed by strong eyes and firm jaw, with a complexion flawless even by Tibetan standards. I was afraid of that.

We spent a few moments simply looking at each other, an exercise not all that unfamiliar between me and some of my new Tibetan acquaintances. But now I had the same uneasy feeling one might have in a primate house, a gentle but anxious probing, a bright glimmer of a recognition between cousin apes, an instinct to communicate. It did not put me off my lunch.

I needed a friend in town, more formally called a primary informant in anthropology lingo. Had Moon Light sensed this from the start?

"Eric, it's a past life connection," Moon Light offered, "I think maybe brothers. Yes, I'm sure of it."

At that bombshell, he left the table and ran to the back. He talked to his mom. In an instant or two, Moon Light returned with coffee and told me he had ordered food for both of us—a boastful prerogative of being the manager.

"Your money is no good here!" he proclaimed. I want you to take all your meals here. From now on, you are part of the family."

Moon Light then left me to fuss over the waves of fresh-faced tourists suddenly flooding through the door—wide-eyed Japanese wearing neatly pressed *chupa* and sporting new rosary beads, hands politely folded, smelling of camphor and sweetly laundered, soft cotton.

I sat alone in my thoughts, intrigued by the audacity of this skinny boy's proclamations. It seemed ironic that this prancing gazelle was a direct descendent of Chinggis Khan and his hoary swarms. He also brought forth images of the decadent Manchu court in its last gasps. Moon Light resembled a decadent Pu Yi amid the lotus ponds and eunuchs, with powdered, grasping dowagers ornamenting their coal black, dyed hair with golden brooches. The fierce horsemen of the steppes and the reindeer hunters of the taiga along the Amur River had become peach-blushed actors in the Beijing opera. Lines from a Chin dynasty poet floated past:

> The Actor Zhou elegant wanders,
> The youthful boy is young and delicate...
> Fragrant skin, vermillion cosmetics,
> Simple disposition mixes with notoriety.[26]

The Chinese agents down the street in McLeod Ganj must be splitting their sides in self-righteousness. The unconquerable barbarians of the Western frontier have succumbed to the decadent effetisms of the Occident. Is this why China opened Tibet to tourism, I wondered, to soften up the incorrigibles?

"I am pure Tibetan..." Moon Light Gyatso's words stabbed me resoundingly. From my anthropological training, pride of racial heritage was always stretched over an abyss of shame. It went against everything I had learned about Tibetan cultural identity, and inclusive, Buddhist universalism. However, like the pride of pedigree among the European ruling class, the *mana* of the ancient Hawaiian practice of royal incest, close genetic associations function as a visible sign of divine prerogative among the masses.

As applied to the Mongols and their affiliated tribes such as the Manchu and Tibetans, the concept of the power of "bone lineage" (T. *rus*) was professed by the ruling elite. To be a Moghul ruler of India, or a khan of Bukhara or Samarkand, it was necessary to trace descent from the illustrious Chinggis Khan. And for Western colonial romantics, if one's own heritage was opaque, one could transform it through the Exotic Other. The illegitimate T.E. Lawrence loved the Bedouins, for among the Arabs, they were the only ones with blood lines as pure as their horses. Such notions, while considered fascist when applied to the Western self, linger as they apply to the inhabitants of the last strongholds of the Asiatic Other. The Tibetans, suffused in the aetherial light of profound geographic and chronological isolation, attract many Westerners as the last representatives of a powerful and pure stock. And of course, Westerners themselves haven't been pure since Eve did her thing in Eden. Moon Light was a Tibetan of such concentrated heritage that his eyes nearly crossed. What were the Ash Boy's intentions when he called himself "pure?"

Chapter 3

Life settled down a bit. Now I was an anthropologist, so I thought, examining how Tibetans in exile constructed notions of national identity and solidarity. I set out to map the village, using the tried-and-true old fashioned Tibetan explorer way. Not bothering to use a compass, I climbed to the top of every building in McLeod Ganj and drew sight lines to various landmarks — the central *stupa*, the hill of the Dalai Lama's palace, the bus stand. Then I walked through the village counting my paces between buildings — *every* building, every chai shack, latrine, and hut. Intersecting sight lines, more pacing, tying in, weaving a map from all perspectives. In a matter of time, I had a rough draft. Slowly a clear and hopefully accurate map emerged.

During the last week in February, the shops began closing as Tibetans sequestered themselves in preparation for the New Year's celebration. In fact, my own hotel technically closed. I was awakened very late one night with a hesitant knock at the door, and asked to go into the dining room. In the dim light of a 20 watt bulb, the hotel staff stood, bags at their feet. Are they going to shoot me, I wondered. After an embarrassed silence, they told me that all were going on extended visits to relatives in Delhi and other scattered refugee communities. If I could would I please pay two months advance rent? An odd and untimely request. But I just so happened to have 600 rupees under my pillow (about $60). Could I get a receipt? Paid off, the family bounded out of the hotel in a flash, the girls struggling after their parents, dragging heavy luggage down the long stairs. Phala raced the engine of the rented sedan. They left! They left me alone, I had the entire Kokonor Hotel to myself. I could rent out rooms if I wished to the hordes of desperate tourists presently descending on Dharamsala during this most colorful and intense festival of Tibetan refugee life.

But the closing of the hotel also meant no water, not that there ever had been any anyway. And the dining room remained a black hole. I was quite alone in the four story mausoleum, the bare lightbulb at the end of the long corridor mocking my continued tenancy. Why did I stay? Perhaps it was the warmth of ghosts clustered in the dank corners of each room.

Obtaining food during the week long festival presented anxious moments. Even the lusty Toepa was to close for the holiday. I really didn't want to accept the hospitality of Moon Light's family at the Kalimpong Café. So like refugees among refugees, tourists scrounged and scrapped like monkeys, buying up the last of the cookies and tins of biscuits from the Indian shops in the bazaar.

At the Lo Sar festival of purification, Tibetans lock themselves into their houses, and engage in the fiercest, most frenetic cleaning rituals on the planet. Scrubbing, painting, disinfecting, changing drapes and screens, washing rugs and bedding, new shirts for everyone. Purge the old, regale in the new, whitewash the walls, end useless relationships — gather together all accumulated rubbish of the past year and toss it into the fire. New Year's was a catharsis of mind, body, and soul.

New Year's Eve slipped in as silent as a tomb in McLeod Ganj. Exhausted Tibetans took to rest or prayer. Bored tourists roamed the empty, unusually tidy streets, looking for a Times Square, any gathering. At about 8:00 pm I met up with Angela, the American, and shared a dinner of biscuits and sardines on the steps of the bus stand as night fell. As if on cue, villagers began to stream from their houses. Soon, the streets were packed with excited Tibetans. The first volley of Chinese fireworks exploded somewhere over the Toepa Hotel. Then another. In no time fireworks were ignited everywhere, without regard for nearby hay bales, autos, or kerosene drum. Angela and I climbed to the roof of the Green Hotel. It was an all-out war, with bottle rockets zooming past our noses, exploding a few inches away. No one minded if a rubbish pile or two caught fire. The entire sky leapt ablaze with light, noise, fragmenting red paper, and choking smoke.

Angela and I adroitly dodged the incendiaries, and found refuge in the Friends Corner Café near the bus stand. It stood brightly illuminated on the outside, with silver foil letters on the glass proclaiming a party. We cautiously looked about — a dozen young Tibetan men were occupying the seats in the center of the room, while 20-something Tibetan girls stood in groups along the wall, giggling. All eyes expectant, the patrons fixed on Angela and me. Ta da! Real *inji* to lead *inji* dances. With no Twila Tharps in the audience, the young librarian and professor felt no shame as we began to flail our limbs in absurd asymmetry.

I found Moon Light with several empty beer bottles in front of him and sat down next to the youth. The other boys were passing around a small bottle of

The roof of the Green Hotel was perhaps the best vantage point to see the original beehive settlement of Tibetans. It was also an ideal place at Lo Sar to view the barrage of bottlerockets and silver fountains.

Chapter 3

horrible Indian rakshi rum. The bar's stereo was fully cranked with the latest tunes pirated from Singapore. Oddly, while Angela and I were the sole foreigners in the club, only English could be heard.

"Eric! This is great. You found me in this silly state," Moon Light chirped, "glad you found me!" I looked askance at Angela, standing along the wall. Moon Light was smoking cigarettes and carrying on conversations with three or four different men. One was Racoon, a schoolmate of his who got his nickname from deeply set eyes. Suddenly Moon Light, pride of a generation, slumped over, head in my lap.

"He'll be okay. His just needs a little nap," said Racoon who grimaced and gulped down a swallow of rakshi.

A few minutes later, Moon Light was up and gadding about. I walked over to Angela, who busied herself trying to play the serious anthropologist. Together we watched as girls danced with girls, boys with boys. Again, everyone tried to get Angela and me to dance together, as if to bestow upon the crowd our "vast" knowledge of the latest steps from the West. In reality, I could barely keep to the beat. Moon Light joined us briefly, but soon passed out again. This time he fully stretched out on the bench, with half his body in my lap, ready for a long snooze. I sat down, and laid one protective arm across his chest; the other cradled his head, all black disheveled silk. Moon Light fell soundly asleep. It was clear this 20-year old needed something, someone major in his life. He had apparently chosen me.

"Wonder what the tourists are doing tonight?" Angela quipped, one eyebrow raised. I looked about: the girls were still standing in their groups, discretely pointing and gossiping about their friends. The boys struck to their own cohort, too, quietly speaking to one another.

"Angela, when are you planning your trip to Tibet?" I asked, intensely aware of my legs numbing from the pressure of this young Tibetan man snug in repose across my lap.

"Are you going, too? I thought your work was here?" she questioned.

"I'm going to do whatever these people do. Looks like everyone is talking about heading north to Tibet this spring. If I stay here, there'll be no one around."

Angela and I decided to dance again, despite the stares of the crowd. No sooner had we started, however, that I found myself dancing with a revived Moon Light. Angela wandered to the back wall to save her chair. I felt rather uneasy, all eyes still watching the wallflower Eric teach the Tibetan EuroAmerophile the secrets of contemporary Western dance.

Hours later, it seemed, I returned to Angela, who had been quietly stowing away the beers. She now seemed immobile in her chair, but with eyes engaged in self-satisfied comprehension of the totality of the odd world about her. She was an Empress Victoria, a grand she-elephant, indomitable, whom no mere Tibetan boy would dare ask to dance.

Throughout the night, the young men ran out of the café to smoke or piss on the side of Nowrojee's house. In the cold winter air, the occasional tourist scurried past the milling gang of benevolent local toughs. Soft intimacies spoke of spring trips to Tibet, the chance of adventure, and escape from the forlorn constraints of a life of serving oatmeal to foreigners. Racoon reached out and softly kissed his male companion on his cheek.

The fresh air brought a certain lucidity, which had escaped me since I had arrived in the village a few weeks ago. Dharamsala no longer represented the center of the Tibetan nation, with its mental topography of exile, distance, and glorified maintenance of a receding past. A more mobile generation had made it somewhat marginal. The Tibetan diaspora was becoming a transnational movement. By this time in the late 1980s, with the real Chinese frontier only 50 miles away, one could finally go beyond into the new Tibet. Even the Dalai Lama himself spent more time touring the world than in his little village in India. For young Tibetans and many foreign tourists alike, Dharamsala was no longer the "Little Lhasa" destination, but a place to bone up on Tibetan culture before the real thing.

New criteria for the establishment of Tibetan identity had rapidly developed and were expressed in cultural hybridization, selective borrowing, inventions of tradition, and linguistic "code-switching" between languages—all anthropological jargon that may explain some of the phenomena of refugee reality. It had been my colonial imperative as an anthropologist to confirm that pristine Tibetan culture still thrived in exile after all these years, whole and neatly bounded. The *inji* expatriate Old Guard once stood as sentinels against cultural pollution of what had been deemed by the Dalai Lama's government-in-exile as traditional. The process had been one of acutely conscious and artificial selection of essential traits to carry into the diaspora. Oddly, it was the role expected of me by myself, the Western activists, tourists, and the aging administration of the Tibetan government-in-exile.

The She-elephant dozed off in the bar while my new classificatory brother and I danced and drank until dizzy. It was 4:00 am when Moon Light and I eventually left the fuzzy party and walked slowly past the bus stand. It was very late and very silent out on the streets. Monkeys could be heard snoring in the giant rhododendrons above.

Down the hill and deep within the recesses of Nechung Gompa, home of the State Oracle, monks were chanting sonorously to welcome the spirits of the Year of the Wood Rabbit. We could hear the great *dugchen* horns reverberating across the valley. The Dalai Lama and his retinue would soon arrive in grand state to formally question the Oracle and obtain his augury for the New Year. At sunrise, the Tibetan pontiff would bless the people. But now, a cold drizzle fell from the black sky, and all the mortals of McLeod Ganj walked slowly to their beds.

Moon Light escorted me back to the Kokonor Hotel. It seemed like a giant concrete hanger at some deserted Cold War airfield, empty to all but us. I got to my room and switched on the light. He had never been to my room before; no one else had either.

"Are you sleeping by yourself tonight?"

Moon Light's clear words struck me with terror. What should I do? What does he mean? I thought of the three beds in my room. I felt my head spin, my stomach upset from too much Tibetan *chang*. Was I about to make an embarrassing spectacle of myself? Oh, what did he mean?

The pause grew unbearable. My words blurted out: "Yeah, I am very tired. It's late. I'll meet you in the morning at the palace gates." With that, I reluctantly sent Moon Light vectoring slowly in the direction of Kalimpong Café. Did I see a hint of disappointment on his face, or was it just my projection? Was I protecting myself or his own naivete?

I now was alone in my empty room with the three beds, smug and self satisfied that I had behaved like a disaffected scientist. Ice ran through my veins,

Chapter 3

my feet were blue. The bare light bulb on the ceiling painted deep shadows on the beds, which were by then making a slow orbit around my head. Suddenly I became violently ill. I pulled the wash bucket to the foot of the bed, and made good use of it that night. An excess of New Year's gluttony, but a relief that I did not share the spectacle with another. The room spun and gyrated for hours, yet I continued to debate Moon Light's nocturnal fate; the tigers had been at the door. Eventually sleep won the battle with my convulsing body. Finally it was quiet.

4. Frontiers of Experience

> ... to regard ourselves as beleaguered innocents and those we meet as shameless predators... is to ignore the great asymmetry that governs every meeting between tourist and local... and that we, often courted by the government, enjoy a kind of unofficial diplomatic immunity with all the perks of authority and none of the perils of responsibility...
> Pico Iyer[27]

I awoke a few hours later with great anxiety. Grabbing my silk presentation *khatag*, I rushed out the door. Tibetans in bright new clothes were scurrying everywhere, ladies trying to run in new and unfamiliar heels. It was a steady flow through town, through the tight alleys, over newly sprouted mud puddles, around the hundreds of beggars lining the road. Purified vessels moving in unison, steadily forward for the touch of the god.

As old as the order Primata, the laying on of hands from a dominant individual to a subordinate conveys the ordination of protection. This benediction is a sacred rite, an invocation to the deity that is followed by a transmittal of divine *mana* to the supplicant. Usually it is done through a ritualistic intermediary, a priest. As in many other traditional cultures around the world, the Tibetan New Year drove the universe into a state of chaos, only to be reordered again by the oracular knowledge and its effective execution by priests. This chaos allows the accumulated novelty of the novel to be channeled into familiar lines, a restructuring nevertheless redolent with refreshed meaning.

It was the touch that brought it all back into order — from the Protector of Tibet to the people, the sacred was brought to the profane. The metaphor is expanded throughout Tibetan society. It flows from the strong to the weak, reestablishing and reordering familial relationships according to accumulated circumstance.

Near Tsuglha Khang, the Central Buddhist Cathedral of McLeod Ganj, I spotted a flash of white in the crowd. I had expected Moon Light to be with his family, but there he was all alone. Remembering a common Asian thought, the state and condition of an individual during the first moments of the New Year established the pattern that will continue throughout the year, I realized this was an auspicious moment, a "point of conjuncture," as structuralists would say. There he stood, radiant like a freshly scrubbed Apollo. Was my new adventure to be a *Death in Venice* or an ordination into holy mysteries? That which I could not understand would be reborn in a different world. I leapt over to Moon Light.

As the crowd began to funnel single file through the security gate next to Namgyal Monastery, I instinctively placed both hands on Moon Light's shoulders. Despite the sacred nature of the solemn epiphany of the Dalai Lama, families were being ripped apart by the sheer crush of humanity. An old woman suddenly vanished from the top of an embankment, and was caught by the crowds below.

Chapter 4

Humble folk close to the fence were swept onto its sharp points, snagging hair and clothing and scraping knuckles. The crowds pressed Moon Light up against me. He and I would experience the blessing together—the urgent, shoving masses would not break him from me.

Inside the palace compound, all padded quiet and orderly. The earliest spring flowers were beginning to bloom, and the walkway to the Thekchen Chöling Palace was shaded in evergreens and flowering rhododendron. In the presence of the Dalai Lama, the shoving masses were transformed into a disciplined assembly of smiling, relaxed anticipation. Everyone quietly unfurled their silk *khatags* and placed them around their necks. The chamberlain and his aides paced the procession, moving people forward or holding them back. Another official received the *khatags,* his arms piled high in flawless white silk.

Directly in front of Moon Light in the queue was an ancient, grizzled man being held up by his sons and nephews. Trembling, he was brought before the Dalai Lama. "Who are you?" the pontiff inquired, "What is your name? How is your health?" At that, the old man burst into tears, and was led away sobbing.

Moon Light then stepped forward, his head bowing up and down, his black hair streaking across the snow white scarf around his neck. The Dalai Lama smiled, and placed his hand on Moon Light's forehead. And then my turn. Remembering all too well the last time I received his blessing, too scared to look up, I now gazed squarely at the face of the Dalai Lama. The huge Phil Silvers moon face smiled and shook my hand. I even managed to exchange a few mortal words with the God of Compassion. Farther down the line, an official wearing a brown *chupa* placed a red *srung-dud* cord around my neck, symbolic of the return and transformation of the white silk *khatag* offering.

With a grand headache, I returned to my room at about 8 a.m. and fell dead asleep. While oblivious to the world, a pontifical messenger appeared that morning at the Kokonor Hotel bearing a luncheon invitation for me to Nechung Monastery.

As the short man presented his envelope, Lewis Carroll's words crossed my mind: "The Fish-Footman began by producing from under his arm a great letter, nearly as large as himself, and this he handed over to the other, saying in a solemn tone, 'For the Duchess'." The lamas of the State Oracle of Nechung were hosting the Dalai Lama's ministers, a tradition retained from old Court practice. Tanya and Greg had apparently thought I would enjoy observing the solemn formality of a government banquet. Each *kalon* would be seated according to seniority, rigidly toasting each other according to ancient protocol. Of serious countenance in black *chupa*, they would taste the ascribed victuals, having first refused three times according to the stilted mannerisms in the style of the Ch'ing dynasty. Yet I could hardly stand up on that auspicious day. My head still reeled from the *chang* and its bacterial side effects.

When the spinning subsided, I hauled myself out of bed at 4 p.m., relieved at having spared the sacred Moon Light a spectacle of my mortality that night. Yet the New Year's revelry continued out the window, down into the streets. I felt the excitement of a new age coursing through my fibre—I was crossing the line this first day of a new world.

Cleverly disguised as an anthropologist, with camera, cassette recorder, notebook, and pencil, I slipped out of the Kokonor and found myself in the ribald afternoon streets.

The town was packed with dirty, noisy, superficial, arrogant, drug-crazed, neophyte, circus freak-show *injis,* embarrassingly treating the native New Year's celebrants as inmates in some cute petting zoo. It had become the duty of every patron-seeking Tibetan refugee to convince the prospective sponsor that he or she was certainly not one of that burly lot. A Tibetan succeeded by isolating the patron through flattery.

The bus stand, having stood well to disgorge its last festival tourist, had become a dance stage. The older generation, festooned in traditional costume, practiced almost-forgotten folk dances and sang sonorous ballads—close, and impervious to the gawking crowd. Large circles of heavy-footed men, followed by the same of women, ponderously orbited the bus stand while tourists, Peterbuilt young Tibetans in nylon windbreakers and Nike shoes, and the absolutely befuddled Nowrojees, looked on. I saw Peter Brown himself in the same circle, nine years later, yelling and stomping like the Khampa he had become.

That day was spent drifting from one gathering to the next, eating strange, sugarless cookies and a Tibetan party mix known as *kaptse.* Butter tea and *chang* flowed from every thermos. Every pleasant sensory wave overwhelmed my body, which rallied and steadied and bobbed up for more. I was fed until bursting at Thupden Dawa Sangha's house, his chopsticks placing select pieces of goat's liver directly in my mouth. It tasted like soap—but a great honor to be thus fed, my face wreathed in smiles. Mounds of roasted fava beans and dried white grapes were set on tables; little hills of rock sugar were placed in front of softly burning altars.

The next day, the last of *Lo Sar,* was the traditional time to form new relationships, ones that would last throughout the year if not a lifetime. For that reason, everyone satisfied with the status quo of their lives had to maintain a guard. Moon Light had asked me for a meeting that morning at Friends Corner, away from the Kalimpong Café. This would be a formal petition, I suspected, to be his sponsor.

This concept of Tibetan patron, *sbyin-bdag* (pronounced "jin-da") had broad connotations. It could refer to the special relationship between the Manchu emperors of China and the Dalai Lamas, whereby the Ch'ing monarch vowed earthly protection to his priest and the high lama granted a benediction upon the imperium. In modern Dharamsala, a "patron" could be simply asked for bus fare to Delhi and back.

Away from the seductive sweetness and polite manners of the Kalimpong Café, I found myself again alone with Moon Light, in what became our own turf. It was at Friends Corner, a real space, with smoke and strong coffee, where I prepared to record his soliloquy. As his long, tan fingers picked up a cigarette, and as he proclaimed the goals of his life he seemed to acquire a sudden maturity.

I had heard about his self-sacrifice as eldest of his family, how his father would be abusive, taking away his camera. His siblings were all in private schools, Moon Light had to drop out of upper school to work at the restaurant. His tack made me feel a bit like Jack Bailey on the 1950s American t.v. program, "Queen for a Day." Could I really help, should I facilitate his western fantasy? All the problems of an innovative young refugee in a land of constrained opportunities—I suggested that he project into the future:

Chapter 4

"I think it's best to be free and single. Don't you think so? I think that's best. Yeah? What do you think, Eric."

I nearly spat out my coffee. This boy was proclaiming the life of a secular monk, and I recognized the similarity with myself. His would be a world of light and flight following the Apollonian dream. By this statement, he was refusing the chthonian morass—the questionable delight requiring the sacrifice of the self in the endless chain of the Great Becoming.

"Freedom is what you need," I blurted, feeling a little like a jingoistic Statue of Liberty, "You should get away from this place for awhile. It seems as if too much is expected of you here. You probably need to become familiar with yourself." I reddened as I said those words, thinking of the epitaph of the western psyche, carved upon the lintel of the Temple of Apollo at Delphi, "Know thyself." So abused it seemed trite, it was the motto of the self-sufficient god, and his pilgrims who traveled to the center of the earth to receive his wisdom.

"I want to travel. Here I am, Tibetan, and I have not been to Tibet. How do I know I'm Tibetan? We are just "different" here, from what the Indians think. I can't just wait until my country is free!" Moon Light said with frustration.

I thought of Manjusri, the Tibetan Apollo. God of light and wisdom, *swayambhu*, self-created, brandishing a sword with which to sever the fetters of earthly attachment and ignorance. I thought of my first dark, ominous night in Kathmandu, the blood red lunar eclipse backlighting the stupa and temple of Manjusri, Swayambhunath.

"Do you know what I'm doing here? I said. "I'm not a tourist, you know. I need someone to work with me, someone who could help me in language. You see, I'm writing this book on the Tibetan people for my degree, and I need someone clever to help in my work."

"I know all that—*I* want to be your assistant. We can go to Tibet together. I would feel really safe with you around. I really feel safe."

That put me over the line. Moon Light was gnawing at some long dormant protective instincts in me. He knew exactly the effect it was having. "You need to experience your own *rang-bstan*," I reiterated with the Tibetan term for self-empowerment. Finally, I summoned the conviction to look into his eyes: "Maybe that's why I am to help," I said cautiously.

"You understand all this?" Moon Light asked.

"Yes."

Was my own path superior to that which my friend would be compelled to live without my interference, in anonymity, perpetually ignorant of the arts? Without my influence, his life would be shortly compromised with a family-arranged simple-hearted sweater girl, and the life of dirty diapers and an endless oppression of fly-blown mundanity would be his in poor India. The gods were giving me a living human being to take care of, to educate. His eyes told me that he was not of this place. It would take super-human strength to overcome 2,000 years of the societal demands of Central Asia and India. Overriding cultural predestination would require single-minded determination. I felt a sword placed in my hands. Ocean of Moon Light would be my protégée, my very own. Batman and Robin against the Chinese foes! It was a heady prospect. My mind went wild with projected images.

"When is your birthday?" I blurted out, embarrassed by an uncharacteristic lack of reserve.

Frontiers of Experience

"I'm 20 years old," Moon Light said proudly. "Around late July, the 27th I think, 20 years ago in Kalimpong I was born. My Phala and his family had just escaped from Tibet."

The 27th of July, 1967—I shuddered involuntarily, my mind vainly grasping for a point of reference other than the remarkable coincidence of my own birthday on that date eons before. My intuition sensed that his remark was somehow of apocalyptic importance in my own infinitesimal corner of the Universe. In an instant all action stopped; hazy figures of life froze, smoke arose and slowly disappeared. In the eternity of the moment, the planets themselves seemed to have reeled past, one by one, eclipsing, orbiting, some waxing into beach ball blue, others into vermillion red crescents. Electric blue vapor veiled my eyes, chased by the acrid smell of ozone and the deep tones of warm earth. I saw images of great green and yellow gourds, knobby and smooth. I was covered with a great numbness. Mindfulness flickered in the background. With great effort, I finally broke through the mental paralysis, and pawed through the ragged shroud covering a flashing sky.

I slowly returned through a crackling haze of static, and became acutely conscious of sitting squarely on a hard chair, my feet coldly fixed upon the cement floor. A door led right into a large kitchen, which was full of smoke from one end to the other. Kelsang sat on a three-legged stool in the middle, nursing a sneezing baby. She was the proprietress of the restaurant/disco, by neighborly regards a strong businesswoman, steeled to the vicissitudes of life in exile. Her husband had run off with the cook. A personal tragedy, but not totally unanticipated. It told of a baneful pattern in Tibetan culture—Tibetan men seem almost superfluous in the maintenance of a traditional household, especially among the nomadic herders and trading families. They were more like flying drones in a hive of female workers.

Kelsang began to banter with Moon Light, occasionally shaking her baby to make a point. Standing behind the bar, she had been glued to every word of Moon Light's oath of fealty. Doubting, accepting, warning, convincing. She was the Achela—the Big Sister, the older woman—Kelsang showed off her knowledge, chatting at a great clip. I thought of the droopy-jowled Duchess in *Alice*:

> Speak roughly to your little boy,
> And beat him when he sneezes;
> He only does it to annoy,
> Because he knows it teases.

The experienced world of Kelsang was not yet for Moon Light. He would not be taunted into the world of responsibility. He remained untouched, unfettered. Moon Light stood as a tidy Ohio farmer's midnight field on the first day of spring, covered with a smooth sheath of white, crystalline snowflakes.

"Wait awhile. I still have my travel plans to make, and work to finish in Dharamsala." I interrupted Kelsang's entree. I looked intently at Moon Light. "When can you be ready?"

"April! When my brothers and sisters get out of school." Moon Light said with a sudden surge of newly found confidence.

"Keep very quiet about this, *Cho-la*." For the first time with me, he used the term of address for brother.

Chapter 4

Moon Light's family had invited Angela and me for their evening feast that night, the final evening of Lo Sar. The Kalimpong Café had reverted to a private dining room. An altar had been set up with ancient symbols of renewal—green barley shoots burst forth from a soil-filled coffee can; a ram's head of colored butter sat in a plate of candies. Above all was placed a softly illuminated portrait of the Dalai Lama. The main table was set with vast plates of wheat and rice noodles, candies, fruit, green beans, red chilies, chocolate bars, *kaptse* cookies, *momo* of all kinds, and that most forbidden of the foods of India, beef. Whose cow is missing? No one discussed the matter, but instead gazed, drooled, and fell upon the yak-like contraband like a quiet pride of lions.

Then pancakes. Pancakes of every imaginable description. Someone once told Last Chance Amala that *injis* lived on such things in the West. Phala even brought out cigarettes. And *chang*—no cup could ever remain the slightest bit less than full. The metaphor of over-brimming riches, to the point of exploding, soon made my slightest movement painful.

Taking leave of my new family, Phala, Amala, and the little sisters and brothers, I walked Moon Light back to his dormitory-like room below the restaurant, and by my design, did not see him again for over a week. I felt overwhelmed by his naive trust, one that had developed strongly in his twenty short years of life. Such a crisp, white page existed nowhere else. A fleecy cloud to inscribe one's dreams upon. The good words or evil deeds to be subsequently written would be my responsibility.

The day had just begun, and I lay enveloped in the invincibly clear mountain air that seemed pure oxygen. Farther down the hill, I wandered to dappled spots in the woods no tourist had ever found. Amid offerings of Amul cookies and marigolds, small shrines to Shiva nestled in the deodars and rhododendrons. This god of the snow peaks, sitting in lucid self-realization, erect at the elation of his own existence, was a machine of limitless potentiality. Shiva, the god of creativity, who by forgoing the object of his lust, became perpetually engaging, indefatigable.

I returned to Friends Corner that evening. The bartender took an immediate interest at my arrival. I caught Kelsang smiling at me, sitting at a booth holding her child. It was on the verge of turning into a pig, like the story of the Abbess Dorje Phagmo up on the plateau.

"I saw you in here the other day," the bartender uttered. "You were with some pretty silly Tibetans. These boys at Lo Sar! Would you like to drink beer?"

My eye cocked at this mild slight to Moon Light, but I agreed to listen to the bartender's story. This man seemed about 22 years of age, dark complected, with a largely unkempt appearance and threadbare Hong Kong clothes. Tall and skinny, yet somehow handsome, his left temple had a large, reddish keloid scar. Da Duk ("Powerful Tiger") left a general impression of a not-too-successful street fighter, a personality formed largely by video game heros. He would become an ambivalent companion for Eric, neither here nor there, engaging and repugnant at the same time.

"Angela is my friend, too," the bartender offered, probing for my reaction. "I'm helping her learn Tibetan. I know that you are helping Tibetan patriots, so that's why I have to talk with you seriously. You are important, right? I think that you may be a film star...maybe Mr. Chuck Norris."

Frontiers of Experience

Ah, I supposed it fit—certainly the flattery did. I was too fair and small to be a Rambo, and I had the requisite blond hair, moustache, and hairy arms for the *inji* master of the Asian arts of self-defense. But no desire to flip ogres on their back, and cash in on the wisdom of the East. Bruce Lee had been one of the handsomest man of the twentieth century, that's it.

"You have to be careful with silly Tibetans. Lots of these young boys and girls are just trying to find patrons for their own benefit. They don't give a shit about Tibetan freedom," Da Duk cautioned. "They're just idiots. And so, Mr. Chuck Norris, have you had your dinner?"

The bartender ordered Kelsang to prepare a large plate of momos, grabbed another liter of White Pelican beer, and found a table. Da Duk's place at the bar was immediately and quietly taken by an older man.

"I don't think you are the bartender here," I suggested.

"Hah! They don't know how to treat guests right, so I help them out," Da Duk boasted. "I have had formal training in five-star hotels in Delhi—the Ashoka hotel. I know all about how to treat *injis* in the correct way."

He ate dinner like a famished Woody Woodpecker, yet managed to hold a conversation on several topics at once. Da Duk blathered endlessly on the psychological aspects of fine table service, and provided a thesis on the categories of tourist personalities. As he finally began to point the conversation in his own direction, he halted.

"I can't tell you all my story at Friends Corner, Mr. Chuck Norris—too many spies, silly Tibetans that like to gossip." I looked over at Kelsang filing her nails, nonchalant in studied indifference. We walked over to the concrete fortress of the Koko Nor. So began the last testimonial and petition of the New Year.

Da Duk, unlike many other refugees of his generation, was born in Tibet—in Amdo near Kumbum, a famous monastic estate associated with the present Dalai Lama. His father and uncle were soldiers in the Tibetan army during the 1940s and 1950s—his uncle was somehow attached to the court of the Panchen Lama in Second City, Shigatse.

The tiny baby Duk was smuggled out of Tibet by his desperate parents in 1962. The family tricked the Chinese for a permit to visit the border region for a holiday—they never came back. Like most Tibetan refugees, Da Duk's father and mother left their house and shop, all their possessions behind. Crossing the border on what became a well-trodden path, the family eventually arrived at Kalimpong and Darjeeling. From these old Tibetan immigrant cities they went to Delhi for the child's education—a convent school followed by refugee settlement schooling. Baby Duk and his family finally moved to Dharamsala, enrolling their son at the drama school. It provided a perfect education for a refugee patriot—the Indian nuns for the English, the settlement school for rough-hewn Tibetan cultural indoctrination, and the Institute of Performing Arts for traditional manners, grace, and polish.

Powerful Tiger then joined the Indian army, to be with a regiment that patrolled the northern frontier, to chance fighting the expansionistic Chinese. He spent a few years wearing the scratchy khaki woolens of the 12th regiment of the Pathan rifles. Eventually discharged, Da Duk found a job waiting tables at the grand Ashoka Hotel in the diplomatic section of Delhi, and from that platform stepped into some sort of position at the American Embassy.

Chapter 4

The story rattled on, food vanished from plates. Powerful Tiger had married a Tibetan girl, who died giving birth to their son. Despondent in mourning, Da Duk was hit by a truck while aimlessly bicycling through the crowded streets of Delhi. His face was badly scarred; his work at the hotel terminated. And just a few months ago he had returned to Dharamsala, where his mother now took care of his son.

Da Duk finished his beer. He presented me with a photograph of an infant dressed in ill-fitting yellow and maroon swaddling clothes.

"He's a monk!" I gasped.

"No. He's too young for that," Da Duk stated. "He's a *tulku*."

"A *tulku*? Have you confirmed this with the Dalai Lama? I asked, naively.

"Dalai Lama is impossible for us poor people to reach. He's surrounded by ministers who don't care for the needs of us," Da Duk cried. "Every time they tell me to go away."

"Who do you think he is?" I recalled the great lamas that had passed away in the last few years—the Karmapa, Kalu Rinpoche, and my own teacher, Nechung Rinpoche.

"I think...maybe he's Ling Rinpoche."

That lama served as the Dalai Lama's smiling senior tutor, a very high position in the Gelugpa sect. The predecessor's holy body was currently being dried in a gigantic box of salt prior to his installation in a fiberglass stupa. The orphanage at the edge of McLeod Ganj had been dedicated to Ling's illustrious memory. I had never heard of such a claim by a Tibetan; was there any reason to doubt Da Duk? Maybe I never had been in such a position of trust before. After all, just this morning another Tibetan had spilled his guts out before me. Was the symbol *Om* printed on my forehead? I felt flattered by his confidence.

"What do you need for confirmation?" I asked.

Without access to the Dalai Lama, Da Duk's only possible choice would be the semi-mythical Panchen Lama himself, then residing in Beijing. As an incarnation of the heavenly Buddha Amitabha, the Panchen Rinpoche could be reckoned the spiritual father of the Dalai Lama. The Dalai Lama was an avatar of Avalokitesvara, the active emanation of the Great Red Buddha of the Sukhavati heavens, Amitabha. If the Dalai Lama could not be contacted, it seemed a reasonable course to seek out the advice of his spiritual colleague, if not historical rival.

"Of course, I will go to Tibet," Da Duk puffed.

The late Panchen Lama never went into exile. Many said that he had Chinese sympathies. After all, he had been the Chinese candidate to the throne of Tashilhumpo, that parallel Gelugpa government in Shigatse. The Panchen Lama eventually expressed nationalistic sentiment by denouncing conditions in Tibet and wound up in prison for many years. As part of his "reformation," the Chinese put Rinpoche in charge of the Office of Buddhist Affairs, and could even visit his former estates in Shigatse. The thought of meeting the Panchen Lama reminded me of the clever but highly illogical Steve Allen and Jane Meadows t.v. program, where historical figures from different times entertained each other at dinner.

Da Duk told me of an elaborate scheme to visit his uncle in Shigatse, who having been a retainer in the court of Tashilhumpo, would refer him to the lama's men in Beijing. Da Duk would travel overland to Beijing and secure an audience with the Panchen Lama. He would then present evidence of the divinity of his son, who would then be recognized. Da Duk would also use the opportunity to present his uncle's claims for remuneration for his past services.

A journey, an audience, a way to travel down the circuits of the history that should have been. Second chance, second city, second lama. I thought carelessly, without commitment: a visit to the Panchen Lama would still be a choice experience to add to my collection of world prelates.

"You don't care much for women?" Da Duk abruptly asked.

"No..." I choked, with caution veiling astonishment.

"Then, Mr. Chuck Norris, you should become a Big *Geshe*!"

"But I'm not a monk!"

"No problem. You're fighting for Tibet like I am, but doing it in a studious way, writing books and all. That's the same as a *geshe*!" Da Duk chirped.

"Er, I don't think so. Anyway, I suppose you want to accompany me to Tibet, with Moon Light?" I could not believe I said those words, but it was too late.

"Moon Light's parents will never let him go, so it is no use waiting. He's just into clothes and showing himself about anyway. I am a patriot, and have that business to do in the homeland. I am serious. We can take Angela. Two *injis*—for protection."

"Da Duk, why Angela?"

"She'll make marriage certificate!"

I was gone. Left Dharamsala in the late afternoon several months later with the couple from the Canadian relief agency, Lulu and Pierre. Gunther Dorje, their odd Tibetan friend from Switzerland, sat by himself several seats ahead. It felt nice to have left the mayhem of McLeod, the land of the 1,000 outstretched arms. We snuggled, relaxed fully, in the seats on out late afternoon bus ride to the railhead at Pathankot. Lulu was a slightly corpulent young woman, Pierre tall and balding. Both presented themselves as charming conversationalists, mixing an easily unflappability born of several years relief work with the perquisite youthful energy. Gunther Dorje, tall and slim with thick glasses, presented a mixed sort— focused, edgy, petulant, thoroughly Germanic. He spoke Tibetan poorly and carefully guarded his Nikon.

After about an hour and a half of twisting down the road through pink seamless orchards of flowering apricots and fields of mustard, we arrived abruptly at the Pakistani border town of Pathankot. Thunk! Here we were in the dust under a broiling sun in front of the British built railroad station.

Remarkably, we had reservations for a compartment on the Siligiri Express bound for Delhi. When the train finally arrived, it did so on a track different from the one posted. As this realization stampeded through the crowd, we were hard pressed to jump the tracks with all our luggage and make it into the vestibule before the bulk of the herd. Typically, the roomette was filled with freeloaders without cot assignments, each of whom required a polite, personal inquiry of health before being shown the door. Eventually we worked our way to the back of the compartment, towards the open grated window. Arms, legs, bags, porters carrying trays of food, conductors, army personnel. Gunther Dorje managed to throw most of the backpacks over the luggage rank, and was busily creating a nest for the late night trip to Delhi. Lulu got herself in a difficult position, backed up against the window grate by the crush of men in the front. Like a snake slowly navigating through the tall grass, an arm wound its way through the grate, grab-

Chapter 4

bing an inch or so of Lulu's ample buttocks. Laughter from the platform, followed by another blind arm, searching. Lulu simply lifted the arm away, rolled 45 degrees, and gave us a slight smile.

Soon the train lurched and was off down the silent rails. With the sweltering temperatures of the plains dropping with every minute, I caught flashes of green from the track signal lights glinting off the metal window frame of the coach. Night passed through the broad valley of the Jamuna, through ancient Moghul towns, Chandigarh, Ambala, Wazirabad.

The red sunrise brought the four of us to Delhi and out the door onto the platform far off in the haze, not at the convenient arcades of New Delhi station near our hotel, but the Old Delhi terminal in the immensely crowded, gritty Pahar Ganj. All I could see were people swarming, saris darting in front and to the side. Turbans and sweaty beards, leather sandals, drooling kids. I saw the taxi queue far off in the dreary atmosphere. It would take hours to pass through the human horde. Somehow in situations of desperation, group consciousness springs up out of nowhere. Suddenly, and without a word to one another, the four of us arranged ourselves in a football wedge—backpacks in front as battering rams. And we began moving. People began moving aside. Then more quickly they jumped away from the swiftly oncoming juggernaut. Finally, the crowd parted down the middle like the Red Sea. And a golden yellow taxi stood ready at the end of a shaft of sunlight.

Lulu and Pierre decided that we all could save money on a room with the four of us sharing We did, in one of the Government of India's experimental tourist high rise hotels. Two beds. I slept with Gunther Dorje.

We parted in the morning. The Canadians and Swiss Tibetan were busing it across India to Kathmandu. I had managed to get a seat on Royal Nepal's 2:00 p.m. flight to the Nepalese capital. But first, I dashed over to the Parliament buildings to catch the Tibetan women's protest, held annually on March 12. Two and a half hours later I found myself back in Thamel, back at the comfortable Blue Diamond Hotel with the boys still dozing in the lobby.

The first order of duty in the capital, I thought, was to present myself to the government. Never mind that this had actually been done out at Tribhuvan airport, and that the government was actually that of His Majesty the King of Nepal's. I was operating under the system that had prevailed since the travels of Abbé Huc: when Westerners came a-calling to Tibet, audiences first had to be made with the ruler before any other business. It would be a serious breech of etiquette not to give one's salutations. Although I had actually presented a research proposal to the head of research out at Tribhuvan University, the government I was concerned with was the Ganden Khang Sar, the Office of Tibet. I carried in my bag no less that seven letters of introduction written on official Library of Tibetan Works and Archives letterhead, a division of the Department of Religious and Cultural Affairs, Central Tibetan Administration. Written in the most florid of Tibetan scripts, the papers were embossed with a great red seal—what the Old Guard called "Dalai Lama stationery." These were all signed by the Director, a great favor to me.

The location of the Khang Sar was a well guarded secret, as I had realized when I set out to meet the Representative of the Dalai Lama. No street names in the diplomatic section, a heavily forested part of town. Soon I eyed a row of yellow colored shops with multi-colored Tibetan rugs hanging out in the sun. The smell of noodles frying was heavy in the mid-morning light filtering through the

I found hundreds of Tibetan women demonstrating in New Delhi, commemorating the Women's Uprising in Lhasa of March 12, 1959.

branches of the heavy pines. I saw an alleyway with a rooster or two strutting through the dust. Hens and chickens were making short shrift of pea pods scattered on the ash colored earth. As I walked down the path, the lane became smaller and smaller. Finally a sign appeared that read "Office of Tibet" in red enamel over a yellow background.

The Tibetan mission was a jumble of small buildings, and I could not find a single sign of life. I entered the reception room to find emptiness. I waited; I practiced my rehearsed lines in formal Tibetan. Still nothing. I was trembling. There must be someone here! Finally I mustered enough fortitude to pick myself up and walk gingerly down the long hall. As I stepped along the hall, portraits of past Tibetan minsters looked down. All were wearing black or brocade *chupa*. Some wore *shamo tsering* hats; other wore the "flying saucers" as the McLeod Ganj boys called them.

Quite suddenly I heard voices and the clanking of silverware farther down the hall. My heart raced. I turned the corner into a lunch room and was immediately plunged into the presence of His Holiness' new representatives to Kathmandu and to New York City. A woman in a blue silk blouse, looking all too much like the Dalai Lama's sister Pema Gyalpo, sat with the two men. An older male servant stood trembling at the end of the room. They all looked up at me in frozen silence, expecting me to speak. Panic stuck as I saw an orchestra conductor turn to me and flick his baton. I took a deep breath and let out a cavalcade of mumbles and squeaks, the sound as structureless as a wire terrier running on a keyboard. I forgot to bow, and to hand the Representative my letters of reference wrapped in a white *khata*. I stuttered on, my hands perspiring.

"What is your name?" A sweet voice finally broke the morass.

"Eric, sir," I sighed to the woman, all pretense washed away, "I have come to introduce myself to you. I just came from Dharamsala, and will be working on social research with the refugees here in Kathmandu.

Sonam Dargye, the representative to Nepal, pulled out a chair.

"Sit here, please. Have you eaten?" I noticed that they had all finished. I was obligated to eat, but I had to refuse three times. With that, the elderly servant who had been scraping plates was sent into the kitchen. Quite suddenly a bowl of soup was placed before me. The servant's arms were extended straight in front of him while he faced the floor. Another mad scramble, and a large spoon appeared, glinting in the sun now forcing its way through the half shuttered window. The man took a filthy brown rag and polished the spoon, then placed it ceremoniously before me, again face down and arms extended. He backed away and returned to scouring his pots and pans.

"I think America is very much like Tibet." said Rinchen Dharlo, the new representative to North America. I thought of the Wild West and the Indian Wars. He thought of the Liberty Bell.

I slowly choked down my noodle soup. We talked about the Chinese and the difficulties of the Kathmandu office, working under the graces of a Nepal petrified by the overwhelming Chinese giant to the north. Sonam then took me into the main task room that, following lunchtime, had become a busy nest of over a dozen phone-answering officials. This room was dominated by a large map of Tibet and a smaller one of Nepal, dotted with 30 or 40 refugee settlements.

I finally had the presence of mind to remember my letters of introduction, addressed to three or four members of the Kathmandu office. Smiles went all around.

The ordeal ground to an end. I walked back out on the alleyway, the chickens still strutting, to the idle hours of early afternoon on the street beyond. Night fell quickly that day, without much fanfare. Several weeks to go before Moon Light would arrive, I contemplated, as I settled into my thin cotton sheets at the Blue Diamond. I wondered if Moon Light's parents would let him leave. Several weeks to go. I lay awake at the familiar sound of brass and aluminum pots being washed by the neighbors on the adjacent rooftop apartment.

Kathmandu is best described as a tonic poem, an olfactory realm, a city of the nose. Long ago brilliant sunshine of a green valley gave way to deep clouds of the raw exhaust of the street. With this was mixed the cloying scent of incense, the dark patchouli of Rama, of Krishna's lustful musk. It glowed bright with the Islamic attar of rose, and the bright streaks of Shiva's supersonic sky blue. We all lived in a sort of shimmering, crushing miasma of golden amber, which muffled all sounds. Residents of Kathmandu were like Carl Sagan's hypothetical gas beings of Jupiter, floating around its dense clouds of brown, deep red, and caramel yellow. As I walked down the main street of Thamel, the tourist region of the city, the smells of cinnamon toast and chamomile tea brought me instantly back to my earliest memories of gadfly San Francisco in the early 1970s.

Frontiers of Experience

Under the swirling clouds of the orange-tinted atmosphere, I had the time to sit in cafés all day, eating insubstantial this-and-thats, and stirring buffalo cow cream into endless pots of black Darjeeling tea and Kerala coffee. No pretense to work, except to watch the progression of young Europeans dance through the urban Himalayan fields. At the Bakery Café, Karl and Ross from times past were at the forefront of my consciousness, as if I had internalized their very being and had myself become one with them.

By now, Lulu and Pierre had arrived, sans Gunther Dorje, and had set themselves up with the Canadian relief agency working out of the Nepalese capital. They found a little cement block to live in, unfortunately situated between a marsh and a dump in the center of town. I got a call at the hotel to come and see them.

The taxi could only go so far. The house was in an open area, unusual for the crowded city. A path led past overgrown bushes to a scattered cluster of new houses. Rabid dogs prowled one side of the house, while fat malarial mosquitos lurked in the shadows on the other.

"We got a telegram from our friends back in McLeod Ganj," Lulu related. "They say that Moon Light's parents aren't going to let him leave."

"Gads. It's probably too busy at the restaurant to let him go," I responded. "If I think I know him, though, he will make a break for it. Angela is on her way in a couple of weeks, and the three of us will start the paper trail with the Chinese."

"Do you think he will make it?"

"Make what?" I asked.

"The permission...don't forget he's a refugee" Pierre added.

"I don't know, who knows?" I foreclosed, rubbing Lanocaine on my mosquito-bitten face.

It was late and I spent the night on a mat in their front room, provided with a sheet and a tiny veil that seemed somewhat ludicrous to be utilized as a bug net. In the morning I was off to Thamel. It would be the last I saw of the French Canadian prophets of gloom for many months.

By now the scene of the fuzzy-lipped boys in the Blue Diamond Hotel lobby began to ferment like an overripe peach on the window sill. The luxuries of the cheap cafés, the easy access to smiling Tibetan faces plying the tourist trade, all began to melt into a narcotic pool of indolence. I laid awake at night to the tinkling of brass pots being washed, thinking about the bloated bodies of the German couple who overdosed on heroin in the room just around the corner. But at least the wait would eventually be over, I would re-enter the clear air, and roam above and beyond the valley, with spotless Purity beside me.

Returning from dinner at the Rum Doodle in Thamel, I dodged long haired girls and paramilitary dressed young men from the West. From the cacophony of voices and bicycle bells on the streets, I heard an unmistakably grating, startling voice. "Mr. Chuck Norris! Oh, Chuck Nooorisss..." sailed the catcall from the second floor window of the Yak n' Yeti Café. It was Da Duk! Stupidly I had thought he would have to stay in Dharamsala. Didn't he fail to find a sponsor for his Panchen Lama quest? Aaaargh, there was no escape for me.

Could he give me Tibetan lessons? Do translation? Clean up? Da Duk wanted in. How about a valet? Someone to haggle for me in the bazaar? I wasn't about to budge. He wanted to stay with me in the Blue Diamond until Angela

Chapter 4

arrived from Himachal Pradesh. Then the three of us would go to Tibet. So he thought.

"But what about Moon Light?" I asked.

"He'll never come. His parents will never let him go. You just have to realize that, Eric. You could wait forever here."

In about two weeks, Angela arrived with an American boyfriend in tow, much to Da Duk's displeasure. She scrutinized the situation carefully as we went through the byzantine procedures of arranging travel permits for Tibet. To the bank, to the telex office, to the Chinese embassy, back to the bank—I'd like to buy a vowel, Pat. Finally, when the Great Red Chop of the People's Republic of China had been pressed onto our passports, she informed the Duk and me that she was traveling by herself. Some excuse that she had to wait to pick up a stack of Tibetan freedom literature and Dalai Lama photos, and it might take awhile for them to arrive from India. I knew better. Da Duk's jaw fell to the floor.

That evening, the scrappy Da Duk broke down when I told him I was waiting for Moon Light.

"You can only take care of one! You're going to leave me behind."

Early the next morning I headed for Bodhanath. I needed an ally. Thinley Dhondup was an old friend who had visited Honolulu selling carpets. This time, I met some of his family. There was a younger sister, and an "uncle/father" from his mother's polyandrous marriage. Over millet *chang*, Thinley listened to my story and suggested I abandon Thamel in the center of Kathmandu and find a room at Bodhanath. That night, I moved my things into a large green room that reeked of fried noodles. It faced the outer ring surrounding the great *stupa*. A family of gigantic Khampas ran a store downstairs. They kindly attended their old Momo-la, who lived just down the hall from my room.

I had been in Bodhanath about a week, meeting a baby goat one day and a real witch the next. At night I listened to the sounds of silvery bells from the eleven or twelve monasteries built around the holy site. At 3 a.m., the monks across the street began chanting, and the dark forces that lurk in the Valley began to dissolve. This day shone brilliantly, as pure and stark as clear blue ice in a glacial lake.

When the sun was up, I headed the eight kilometers back to Kathmandu. I needed supplies, coffee, cheese, cold medicine. It was fortunate that I towered above the crowd by a few inches. Thus I could look into the faces of those approaching. I could scan the hundreds of faces instantly. I had done this every day for three weeks now. Many of the thousands of faces were becoming as familiar as those in McLeod Ganj. Suddenly, near the cheese shop, I spotted the smooth face, jet hair, and yellow nylon jacket of Ocean of Moon Light about half a block ahead. I felt great elation! I had to catch up with him; he didn't know where I was living. He was by himself! Get there.

I tackled him from the side in the intersection and held him hard.

"You escaped!" I gasped.

"I left. Hah! I just told them I was going, and they let me. How are you, brother?"

"I have lots of stories to tell you. Angela has left. Da Duk is here."

"Oh. I didn't know any of this, Eric-la. But I made it, yeah?"

His smile beamed. The crowd flowing around us smiled, one by one, as they passed.

Frontiers of Experience

I moved Moon Light in with me in Bodhanath. The Khampa family took to him well. He was after all a Khampa on his father's side. His own Momo-la was a Khampa grandmother just like the matriarch that lived here. He kept himself clean and respectful to this new family. My cold began to abate. Soon Moon Light and I would be heading over the mountains and across the high plateau to Lhasa.

Bodhanath, being a pilgrimage locale, is a convergence point for large numbers of Tibetan pilgrims, vendors, and Western tourists. I felt a deep sense of relief having kept my faith in my friend. Da Duk was nowhere to be found, and Moon Light had settled into a comfortable stay with me in our Khampa room. On one of these beautiful spring evenings, Moon Light and I had been buying provisions for the trip to Lhasa in the bazaar that surrounded the monument. A young Tibetan man approached me, explaining in English that he was collecting contributions for the Tibetan refugee settlement at Solo Khumbu. Despite the fact that I was with a fellow Tibetan, he didn't anticipate my lack of naivete on the matter of refugee aid.

"That's odd...the officials at Gaden Khangshar tell me that the Solo Khumbu settlement is to be discontinued," I said.

"Well," the solicitor defended, "the program is associated with a monastery in Dharamsala, home of the Dalai Lama." Then he opened a large black ledger, and showed me signatures and figures. "You see, these are Western donors to the project."

"Which monastery?" I pressed.

"The S.O.S. one, Save the Children office, a part of the work of His Holiness Dalai Lama.

I knew he was bluffing. "But which monastery?"

"Ah, a Nyingma monastery!"

"Yes, but *which* one?" I grilled.

"You know, the one by the Tibetan Library — the small monastery next to it," he squealed.

"Oh, Nechung Gompa. You must mean Nechung, but they're not really Nyingma. You must mean Zilnon, up the road in McCleod Ganj."

"*Yes!* — that one!" he retorted.

Moon Light was giving me the eye. No matter. I paused for a second, then went in for the kill: "But...the group at Zilnon don't have a program like that. I'm sorry, I'm not really interested."

I turned, with a compelling urge to toss my mane in royal displeasure. Instead put my arm around an embarrassed Moon Light and walked away.

Moon Light's own dealings with the Chinese embassy had been direct and successful. He merely walked into the office, located in an overgrown garden, claimed that he wanted to visit his homeland, and was immediately given a Chinese passport normally issued to Chinese living abroad. I was suspicious of this "Return to the Motherland" document, but any sort of political overtones were irrelevant. It seemed merely an expediency.

We were ready, just the two of us.

Scarcely an hour passed, though, as we relished the victory of having ordered papers, before Jens the Dane entered the mix. I had chatted with him briefly while I waited for Moon Light to finish at the Embassy. When we walked back through Thamel, we found Jens sitting, sipping tea. He stood much taller than myself, with long, stringy yellow hair. His thin nose seemed bit too sharp; his

Chapter 4

knees were boney; and his eyes were unfortunately piggy. Yet he presented himself as one of the most easy-going lads ever, a reservoir of calm. So honest and clear when he asked if he could travel with us—we both said yes immediately.

We discovered that the most convenient means of traveling to the border could be a chartered taxi, one that left from Hotel Metro, deep in the seedier part of Thamel. We talked at length to the driver. How long was the trip? How much for us three? How many times have you done this? What's wrong with the bus? Finally, in Tibetan and English, we guaranteed a price (about $20 each). And a time. Tomorrow at 6:00 a.m.

Moon Light and I hastily returned to Bodhanath and said our goodbyes to Thinley and the Khampas. We came back to the Hotel Metro within the hour. That evening, while squeezing into the crowded room, we heard a knock at the door. Expecting Jens, Moon Light and I were shocked to see Da Duk standing there. The Cheshire Tiger presented a special mess this time. His hair stood out all over his head, and he glistened with sweat. He barely noticed Moon Light and spoke nothing but English as he told of his plight. Apparently he had been "detained" by the police for drinking beer. In fact, he confessed to spending the 600 Rs I had given him a few weeks back on beer and marijuana. He needed to go with us because he had nowhere else to go. This time I believed him. I don't know if I felt compassion or confusion, but I agreed. Moon Light followed the kindness of his heart. No problem with laid-back Jens.

It seemed preposterous. One Dane, one German-American, and two Tibetan refugees hailing a cab for Tibet. It might as well have been a spaceship to Neptune. But here it materialized: out in Kathmandu's Durbar Margh, stood the little Datsun B210—suitcases and backpacks secured in the trunk, with four passengers in jeans and madras shirts, heading for the most fabled and inaccessible land on the planet. The sense of absurdity was profound, akin to taking a dark-paneled, Muzak infused cosmic elevator into space. A Sunday outing, a taxi over the edge, we sailed into the great dark blue void.

We broke the familiar bonds of the valley, passing the adobe multi-storied apartments, the moon face of Bodhanath stupa, and the steeply pitched pagoda roofs of Bagaon. His elbow out the window on a warm spring day, Da Duk sang along with Madonna, the goddess/slut of the Western World. Bouncing along on a superb highway, dark pines zipped past us. Within the hour, the view unfolded to the Solu-Khumbu range, its prize being the great peak of Everest itself. No natural boundary ever seemed so profound. But the path to it was well worn: for two decades, side-trip tourists flocked to the border town of Tatopani just to try to steal a glimpse of Tibet. Those Shangri-La seekers, however, could not see to the other side. The sheer size of these mastiffs blocked all vistas, even of the high-flying clouds. It was just a wall of grey.

One had no sensory foreknowledge in the approach to Tibet. It was pure up—in a state beyond vertigo. Our Western reality piled up against this boundary, plastered in broad strokes with the gravity of centuries of failed expeditions.

After another hour we arrived in a village of three wooden huts. A gigantic, rather intimidating sow wallowed in the ditch adjacent to the the little restaurant we found. Da Duk chatted patronistically with the hosts, like a city slicker at some general store in the Ozarks. A proper boy, Moon Light maintained a studied smile, wiping his hands unconsciously on his cotton handkerchief. Jens, with mouth agape, inhaled the rustic gestalt—the village urchins, the honest, country fare. I watched the pig frolicking in the dung and dreamt of cream puffs.

Eric had figured whenever it was overcast, the bombs would not fall. It was an uneasy time as Christmas blanketed our Third Grade class.

The Milwaukee Road's *Hiawatha* ran around the Mississippi River Valley, all the way to the Himalayas. Here, Eric's aunt and uncle enjoy a picnic while train patrons drink their cocktails, zipping past at 100 mph.

A single ray of the rising sun illuminated the topmost parapet of the fortress of Gyantse, its tiny windows looking blindly out upon long-vanished enemies. A path led to the empty tower at the apex of the peak. It was guarded by a wizen old woman whose toothless grin spoke of wild times in the remote city.

Moon Light took it upon himself to get the passengers laughing, desipte the fact that the bus had no springs. The little boy next to me kept feeding me White Rabbit milk toffees until we finally rounded the last curve of the canyon. We then entered the broad valley of Lhasa and glimpsed the Potala palace upon its little red peak.

At Boudanath on the eastern side of Kathmandu Valley stood a gigantic mound of compassionate white light. It had beautiful blue eyes. How different it seemed from the ruddy glow of Swayambu Temple to the west. "Don't go out!" cautioned the shaman.

Eric sat in his koa chair in the condo in Honolulu, dreaming about his life on the edge of Tibet.

A tea party occured while rocketing through the wilds of Montana

Tatopani ("hot water")—it seemd some sort of failed tourist resort. It had its beginning with the construction of the Chinese-sponsored "Friendship Highway," a road that ironically remained closed at the international border from the 1960s to 1986. Tatopani developed into a minor destination for tourists who were only permitted to gaze across the forbidden border into Tibet. Since the opening of the border in 1986, would-be entrepreneurs had given up the pursuit of dollars, pounds sterling, and yen when they realized that tourists only wanted to rush through the murky frontier zone as quickly as possible.

About a mile beyond Tatopani we were unceremoniously deposited at Kodari, a wooden shack flying the twin-pennants of the Nepalese flag. In a puff of smoke, our driver had picked up a tourist couple and headed back to Kathmandu. The magic chariot had vanished and we were on our own.

This border crossing between Tibet and Nepal extended through a remarkably steep canyon. The Josh Koshi cut through the Himalayas in a series of violent waterfalls that were unrivaled on earth. Gigantic boulders lined the stream floor, forcing white water into wandering, turbulent maelstroms that could swallow highway embankments in a matter of minutes. Far up on the Tibetan side of the canyon perched the parallel border town of Zhangmu. This is the "wall of Shangri-La" that gullible tourists once paid well to merely gaze at. The Chinese established their customs office at Zhangmu, and in theory a bank, hotel, and restaurant. The village was nearly 1 kilometer in elevation above Tatopani, reached only by the switchbacks of an 8-kilometer foot trail.

The Nepalese government hut at the end of the Kathmandu highway at Kodari was swarmed by tiny mountain porters, of indeterminate age but single-minded determination. Sizing me and my luggage up, a persistent little tough began his tout. I felt resentful and immeasurably old—neither Moon Light, Da Duk, or even the Dane were approached by the porters. The slyest wolf had picked out the weakest in the flock, eh?

"Its so far, and all the way up!" the porter began.

"No, its okay." I steeled as I looked at the sheer cliff ahead of us.

"You not regret! I walk with you anyway," he laughed like a hyena as two Gurkha soldiers stamped my passport. I laced up my new, heavy-duty hiking boots and strapped on my overstuffed backpack.

Beyond the hut lay the "Friendship Bridge," built by the Chinese as a thinly veiled intimidation—China could now easily invade Nepal if the latter faltered in doing China's bidding in South Asia. The red and white arched bridge spanned the narrow, roaring chasm.

Spotting the thin red line painted on the roadbed in the center of the bridge, Moon Light started running.

"Wait!" I cautioned. "Lets cross it together. Better to jump across the line!" I motioned to the remora porters to stand away. My two Tibetan buddies, the Dane, and I linked arms, jumped, and alighted upon the sacred land.

Running and hopping, we grabbed each other in self-congratulation. We even shot a beaming smile at the Chinese sentry strolling at the end of the bridge—the first of many smiles that became a survival stratagem in dealing with the People's Liberation Army and the Public Security Police: "So happy to be back in the Great Motherland!" "How very kind." "So nice that everything is efficient...orderly!"

Chapter 4

Much has been written about border territories—parcels of no man's land that are neither here nor there. They are always filled with danger and excitement, a netherworld inhabited by peoples on the edge of existence.

The 8-kilometer trail at the Nepal/Tibet border occupied a strip of space the woodsy equivalent of an airport transit lounge, really a *non-place*. Like in most states of liminality, we had officially left one phase, but had not entirely entered the next. The Tibetan borderlands were inhabited by the porter bands, male Neibelungen whose only law was their own. They were quite literally middle-men, who lived by transporting goods between (or around) Nepalese and Chinese customs. The barefooted troll pirates lived in tiny huts made of wooden lath and shipping crate panels. Their population of tiny people must have been in the hundreds—perhaps their narrow world extended the full length of the Tibeto-Indian border, through Arunachal Pradesh, even to Myanmar and beyond.

Meanwhile, off in the smoky, scattered patches of forest, border encampments were housing scores of PLA inductees. But the Chinese solders were far more content to brood over their lowly, near-exile posting than impose actively the law their duty required. The brigands of same-age, same-size, tribal cohorts provided more than enough security to foil any mass invasion by unruly foreign tourists.

The four of us slowly climbed the steep trail up the side of the canyon, the path covered on either side by the sharp thorns of light green nettles. Stands of giant juniper and dark pine were relieved by frequent open areas filled with landslide talus and rapidly growing, broad-leaf shrubs. Two porters persisted in following me, waiting for my fragile health and new hiking boots to take their toll. They knew their trade—within a few minutes, the unyielding leather cut cruelly into my heels. Warm and sticky blood flowed from flayed skin and blisters. My suddenly disloyal comrades continued on ahead—Moon Light occasionally looked back with anxious concern. Sitting down on a rock, I gave in to the jackals, negotiating a rather surprisingly low fee to carry my pack to the village. Wiping away pride, I changed into tennis shoes and accepted my label of tourist.

We eventually caught up with Moon Light, Da Duk, and Jens. For the last kilometer, Moon Light and Da Duk walked several meters ahead. We would not speak to each other nor show any other familiarity until well beyond the eyes of the guards. None of this had been planned—we just separated in case difficulty arose with the apparent Westerner/Tibetan refugee association. This abrogation of loyalty made me feel sheepish.

Fortunately, there were absolutely no difficulties. The two Tibetan refugees were welcomed with smiles and bureaucratic brevity. Jens and I were greeted by a tall Chinese woman, with an outrageously wide-shouldered uniform evocative of a hostess on an imaginary interplanetary space liner of the 1950s. Next to customs stood a monolithic CITS (China International Tourist Service) hotel with a spectacular view of the churning chasm below. Over-built and under-staffed, the Zhangmu Palace seemed little more than a large, concrete cell block with carpeting.

"No room! No room!" quacked the desk clerk while vacuuming a thick rug. They expected a group tour sometime within the week. For the sake of "efficiency," all those big, stark rooms would sit empty until the buses arrived. It made their work easier, explained the clerk, to process 60 guaranteed people in a half hour than wait around all day for "not know people."

Frontiers of Experience

Relieved of not having to stay at this Alcatraz, we straggled up an additional kilometer to the village proper—a terraced affair, much of which seemed in the process of slumping down the slope. Here we "not know people" found a bank to exchange hard currency for Foreign Exchange Certificates, a monopoly money the government required of tourists in all transactions. Being grossly overvalued, its circulation additionally alerted entrepreneurs in the countryside that gullible tourists were nearby.

For this first day in sub-tropical Tibet, the Chinese segregated Tibetans from Westerners. According to official policy, Tibetans were returning Overseas Chinese, and like all Chinese, officials thought best to keep them separate from further "corrupting influences" of the barbarian West. Moon Light and Da Duk found lodging in a garage-like building which served as a dormitory. Jens and I could find only a large room at a truck stop, ten beds for ten white faces—no regard for any gender differentiation. Old women fulfilling the adventure of their lives were piled in with green teenage boys practically unaware of this rare historical opportunity to enter Tibet. The "hotel" had no lavatory facilities—only several porcellaneous metal bowls to wash in. Water, I was told, would be provided in the morning in thermoses. Ineffectively protesting at being separated from the boys, I begrudgingly claimed a bed in the Westerners' room, and settled into a long night of the sound of tourist discomfiture—sneezes, teeth-grinding, joint-cracking, snoring, incessant coughing, farting. That morning I discovered that the wheels of the Chinese truck parked in front of the hotel had made a sheltered and convenient toilet for my fellow inmates.

While street dogs stretched and scratched at first light, I sprinted across the zigzag town to Moon Light's dormitory. There, several Tibetan men were sitting out on the steps, enjoying the sunrise. Moon Light and Da Duk laughed with new friends. Because of their green uniforms with red trim, Da Duk was having fun referring to the ubiquitous soldiers of the People's Liberation Army as "parrots." One of their new friends, a bus driver from Lhasa, had been stranded in Zhangmu by a landslide just at the edge of town. Crews had been manually hauling rock and debris from the slide for several days now, and they expected a bulldozer that afternoon. The driver had lost his group when the tourists would not wait for the slide to be cleared. They simply walked over the debris to the next village and caught a public bus to Lhasa.

Facing the financially ruinous prospect of deadheading his Japanese minibus back to the capital, the driver suggested that we form a group ourselves. Moon Light, Da Duk, and a new buddy named Tenzin would ride free; being only honorary locals, Jens and I would pay a nominal fee; the tourists would be charged the equivalent of $50.00 each. The agreements set, we chartered the bus for $500.

I returned to the truck stop in my new role as tour escort—now we had to sell the package. Several ragamuffin foreigners were mildly interested in the "luxury coach," but many more believed the landslide would not be cleared soon—precious visa time was ticking away. The latter would walk the 5 kilometers to the local bus stop and pay about $8.00 for the rough, crowded, four-day journey up and across the airless Tibetan plateau.

I regressed to the Tibetan lodge, and joined the group in the sunlight who were smoking cigarettes. The afternoon wore on with no sign of activity at the landslide. Tons of rock and earth not only had taken out 100 meters of roadway, it had pushed three concrete houses off their terraces and into the canyon far below. In the chasm, the glacial torrents fell thousands of feet in seven or eight

Chapter 4

stages, over smooth limestone boulders the size of elephants. We watched, with infinite faith in our scheme, as a dozen or so tie-dyed tourists clambered across the precarious pile, dragging suitcases. Finally, at 4:00 p.m., a red dot appeared on the switchbacks far above us, like a mite crawling down a yellow tendril. It was a bulldozer, slowly leveling a path through the great slump of earth.

When the machine finally arrived, we tied a sturdy rope between the minibus and the dozer, and despite several serious slips, we eventually succeeded in crossing the fall. On the other side, three formerly skeptical tourists ran towards us. I happily took their $150, and we were off. Reaching the local bus stop, we gained an additional passenger—the others in their group quickly turned away in pride. We settled back in our minibus, a roomy new coach with pert mustard yellow gingham striped curtains and a refrigerator loaded with Mr. Pic, Thumbs-up, and Tsingtao beer. Beyond this point, the Chinese highway crews were blasting to widen the road. This hardly deterred the single-minded driver, who simply drove over the buried charges and detonation wires. By nightfall we had traveled a mere 35 kilometers, but had climbed beyond 14,000 feet, not only out of the sub-tropics, but beyond all vegetation entirely. We ascended to the high Tibetan desert in starlight.

The town was Nyalam ("Fish Road"), the home of Milarepa, the famous Tibetan saint who walled himself up in a cave for most of his lifetime. Another cavernous CITS hotel, which seeing a busload of foreigners, allowed us to stay the night. A goose-stepping "hospitality attendant" barked house rules in broken English. Characteristically, the foreigners of both genders were shown a long, bare cement room lined with beds. Da Duk, Moon Light, and Tenzin were given a slightly smaller room on the other side of the lobby. It had an extra bed! From down the corridor, Moon Light waved at me to join them. I silently picked up my bag, slipped past my roommates busy at their toilette, and tip-toed by our now catatonic hostess. It was an immensely comfortable rest, with featherbeds and silk covers, away from the wheezing tourists engaged in gossip long into the night. Fuzzy warm in Tibet with red blooded Tibetans, I drifted into a lyrical sleep.

The next morning we left Fish Road and began a cloudless climb. On the immediate left side of the bus stood Gosainthan, at 8,016 meters the seventh tallest mountain in the world; on the right, the endless plateau of Tibet. At this altitude, the clear thin air rendered distances indecipherable. More than anything else, the unique effect blasted the message to me that this was Tibet. Armed with incorruptible clarity, I looked out upon an ancient past. In the air I could almost feel the reverberations of the sounds of a civilization so recently expired.

It was just after 9 a.m. when the slope leveled out. We had reached the watershed of the Jogi Koshi, which due to the unusual geological history of the region, lay on the north side of the Himalayas. When the island of India collided with the continent of Asia, the ancient streams of the latter cut through the uplift as fast as the mountains rose. Our precipitous road had followed one of these tenacious rivers, and we had reached its headwaters. It began in a flat, boggy tundra, exactly 17,500 feet above sea level. To the north lay the watershed of the Brahmaputra—below us, the Ganges.

A small offering had been placed at the pass, in reality only a broad hummock on the flat plain. Travelers had festooned the rock cairn with multi-colored strips of cloth, remnants of prayer flags tied on to branches set into the pile of stones. Lacking a proper prayer flag, Da Duk yanked a small chunk of hair from his head and tied it to a twig. Then the gods of the wind were summoned with

"*Lha gyal lo!*" — the gods are victorious. The two Tibetans and I cavorted like jackrabbits on the delicate alpine meadow, photographing strange pink flowers growing through bluish ice crystals. Back at the bus, glum tourists huddled for warmth and gasped for oxygen like carp in a stagnant, brown pool.

We continued on the gravel road, never encountering so much as a long-haul army truck. Moon Light had moved to the front of the bus, riding shot-gun with the driver. Da Duk stretched out in the back, fumbling with the collection of cassettes that one tourist brought aboard. Across from me sat a young Italian woman, Flavia, gazing vacantly out the window and singly softly with Sting on her headset. The light buff of the upholstery set off her fine black hair; the sharp folds of the apricot-colored linen curtains accentuated the crisp lines of her Roman profile. In the background, the light blue Himalayan range rose abruptly from the rocky plateau. The entire composition was naturally framed by the bus window — it seemed a remarkable bracketing of one reality against another. With the indigo sky and the ethereal nature of the mountains, I was reminded of a much more familiar scene — the cabin of a 747 flying over the Colorado Rockies or the Alps. I silently lifted my camera and froze the scene.

Silence. A wild black yak dashed away at the approach of the minibus, kicking and jumping furiously into the airless vacuum. Thin dust devils rose as sinuous tendrils against maroon-colored hills. Fine powder began to sift into cracks as the thin wind accelerated with the heat of the day. I tasted manganese.

It seemed we were reaching the end of a global tether. We could see no sign of civilization other than the tiny capsule enveloping us; this brought us a growing apprehension. The little boy Eric remembered the fear of Apollo 13. How much fuel could this bus hold? It was past noon, and a steady diet of stale Chinese

Chapter 4

cookies was becoming inadequate. We rounded a sharp curve and suddenly turned off the road. In front of us were three low, block houses. As the dust cleared, I could see the light green uniforms of the PLA—I instinctively went over to Moon Light.

The driver said nothing, halting the bus in front of the barracks. The women tourists ran straight to the outhouses, while the men lit up cigarettes. Jens found a ball, and began a high altitude game of basketball with Moon Light and Da Duk. I followed the driver into one of the grey buildings. Several skinny Chinese men in baggy polyester uniforms sat behind desks, stamping huge stacks of papers. The driver gave one soldier in a glass booth a five yuan note (about a dollar), and received a slip of paper from another man at a table. The driver then walked into a cavernous hall and sat down at a lonely table with a dozen chairs. Presently, the tourists wandered towards the barracks. No sooner had they entered through the doorway than a sergeant ran forward, screaming at them in Chinese. Flailing his arms, pounding the table, then pointing into the large room, his discomposure was baffling.

"Calm down! We're not in prison," one of the older men from the group suggested to the ranting sergeant. Finally, as a harried cook burst through a door and ran to the driver with a plate of vegetables and rice, it became apparent that this was a meal stop—an army mess. Pay first, then take your chances. The rules were set, despite the fact that we were hardly credit risks—a bit difficult to run out on a check when you're at a Chinese army camp separated from civilization by several hundreds of miles of frozen desert. I forked over the five yuan to a man in a glass booth, who gave me several receipts, each in a different color and all with various chops and signatures. Da Duk asked for one of these. I assumed he would use it to deceive the waiter.

Da Duk went back outside while we joined the driver at the sole table. Two soldiers paced back and forth at the back of the room, trying to restrain themselves from staring drop-jawed at our exotic knot of yellow-haired foreigners.

From the mess window, I saw Moon Light, hidden in the shadows of the bus doorway, munching on cookies and picking through a bag of trail mix we had hurriedly bought in Kathmandu. He seemed uneasy, glancing at his watch frequently.

A commotion at the door—it was Da Duk brushing back bellowing soldiers. As the martinet approached our table, the guards stood away. The grand Duk casually pulled out a chair, and wielding a pair of metallic chop sticks, chuckled, "They owe me at least a bowl of rice! Hah!—the idiots."

I returned to Moon Light like a protective hen, quietly coaxing him to eat. It was far too late for that. He seemed clearly upset, and embarrassed as the tourists began to gather by our vehicle. Across the faces of the foreigners were plastered the toothy smiles of uncommitted politeness. They were visitors in an alien land, possessed of that state of uneasy bemusement born of dangerous novelty. At this repast with the enemy at 15,000 feet, some Westerners experienced the questionable thrill of being probed and herded like cattle to the feedlot. For the two young Tibetan men, one scammed a meal at Chinese expense, the other withdrew in disgust.

We pulled out of the Chinese occupation camp and headed back across the dusty plateau. In a few minutes, the minibus entered the mouth of a broad valley. I spotted a solitary cloud in the distance, unusual for its lone placement in the azure sky. Nor did the cloud become distorted with the passage of time—it neither moved nor changed. With rising excitement I realized that it was no cloud, but a massive Himalayan peak. We were approaching Dingri; the form could be no other than the ultimate itself—Mt. Everest. This is the only angle, at the head of the broad Rongbuk valley, where one can truly appreciate the bulk and loftiness of Everest, a white chunk of rock and ice rising unimpeded another 15,000 feet above the stark plain. For foreigners and Tibetans alike, a glimpse of the North Face of Everest is a great rarity and a heart-stopper.

I nudged Moon Light. "Chomolungma!" he blurted as he turned his head. The native name for the peak spread through the bus like a shotgun blast. In a few moments, we pulled over at the junction with the trail to Rongbuk Monastery. There, sixteen tourists simultaneously removed cameras from rucksacks, and checked "Everest" off their itineraries. "Momo Lung Ta!" one shouted, sounding like "dumpling wind horse" to the Tibetans.

One of the most disconcerting activities of the Western tourist confronting superlative topographic landmarks is the need to "bracket." Galen Rowell and Tom Lehman have the ability to capture the natural mysteries of Tibet through photography; tourists do not necessarily have these skills, nor is it usually necessary to develop them. Bracketing invariably places a familiar face within the frame, poised against the object of the tourist quest. The purpose is to show structure or detail of the object with no greater detail than the minimum needed to simply recognize it. The sole purpose of this ritual is to inspire envy and provide proof to couch-squirmers back home.

John photographed Flavia and Mt. Everest. John and Everest were snapped by Louise, and so on down the ranks. Da Duk in his threadbare American flag tank-top and Moon Light wearing his Puma windbreaker, posed with the bus instead. I returned to the vehicle and dug deeply in my bag for my red fox Khampa hat with the mulberry green silk streamers. I was set to great the massif wearing Tibetan clothes.

Signs of life increased. Convoys of PLA trucks filled the road with gritty blankets of dust appeared the deeper we went into Tibet. I spotted a flat-topped house or two. These adobe structures were washed in a light blue-grey, with red and white stripes painted along the window sills and lintels. Ferocious black dogs, essentially giant Pekinese from hell, lunged at their chains at our approach, red mouths foaming.

In a few hours we arrived at the town of Tingri, waving like Queen Beatrix in her coach, the bus immediately surrounded by villagers. Our driver attempted to go out, but two men blocked him. Eventually an old wizen headman approached. He spoke a few words of welcome to the driver, then looking up at us sitting in our seat, smiled broadly and motioned us to come over and visit him. I stood close to the driver and headman, who cautioned us about the Chinese checkpoint 40 miles ahead. The driver smoked my Marlboros, the headman used snuff. Most of the women of Tingri turned away or covered themselves to avoid being photographed. Children stood their ground, tough and scrappy, and crowded around each strange Western beast.

We sailed through the first Chinese checkpoint, and spent the next five hours bouncing along the gravel road. Finally, we entered into the broad valley of the Tsangpo. Checkerboard squares of mint green and beige from the farthest distance signaled barley cultivation and reflected the richness of increased population. We were now in Tsang, one of the two ancient central provinces of Tibet.

Chapter 4

It was a sooty arrival into Shigatse, the former capital of the province. Ruled by the Panchen Lama, Tsang almost became a serious contender for independence under the influence of the British in the early twentieth century. From above the black pall of dinner fires, the golden roofs of Tashilhumpo slipped past, highlighted by the ebbing sunset. Animated Moon Light and Da Duk ran up and down the aisle in excitement. The day-long vibrations and bump and grind of the gravel road stopped suddenly as we glided on to smooth, black macadam. We halted at a crossroads truck stop near the Panchen Lama's yellow palace. No room at the inn for foreigners: Da Duk and Moon Light jumped off and disappeared into a maze of darkened figures, trucks gunning noxious engines. I was furious—I had expected, hoped, that Da Duk would separate from us this night. I was surprised at Moon Light's carelessness, heading out with his nemesis for a night in the Tibetan city. Despite his garb of silver armor, the knight's squire had vanished. Eric was left in the dust.

We drove on through the inky town, arriving at foreign accommodations near the old bazaar. We were spirited away by a boisterous innkeeper to a second-storey courtyard. Dormitory rooms opened onto a commons filled with chairs and tables. Thin cotton laundry hung like *inji* prayer flags. A gangly blond man sat on a table, weakly playing a flute while pale young tie-dyed women wrote letters, sipped camomile tea, and rewound fading tape cassettes by hand to save the batteries. One of the Tibetan kitchen women brought in an empty basin and a thermos of hot water into our room. It was meant for all six people. But no sooner had I placed my bags under the bed than a male skin-head dove face-first into the basin, turning the precious water a dark grey. I found a tap outside instead.

We beheld a loudspeaker morning—some socialist zealot had erected gigantic bullhorns atop a cliff overlooking the city. The populace was thus awakened each dawn by the "East is Red" and an admonishment, in Chinese, to be good, productive citizens for the Motherland. "Chicken talk! Just chicken talk," a disturbed French woman named Valerie exclaimed.

Tashilhumpo? It was not quite a museum, with velvet cords and carefully lighted displays. The great monastery of the Panchen Lamas, on the other hand, was anything but a genuine center of Tibetan religious culture. It stood intact; perhaps some official had suggested it would make good tourist fodder. The Chinese had pretty much thrown it open by and for the unknowing. An army of monks, actually poorly paid CITS agents, were ensconced at every corner, in every chapel. Voyeuristic tourists and these slightly embarrassed pseudo-monks wandered through dusty halls, each completely ignorant of the historical significance of Tashilhumpo. I felt surprised that a major portion of the monastery stood intact. The divine statuary seemed authentic. One building held an eighty-foot image of Maitrea, the Buddha of the Future, of beaten gold. I circumambulated its base, running my hand along the warm mirror surface of the massive lotus blossom upon which the image sat. It is real, I thought—the Chinese could never restore such a magnificent work, and most certainly would not do so in pure gold just to convince tourists. Reassuring, Tashilhumpo, with its silver tombs of the Panchen Lamas, appeared to have survived without the official red chop of socialist historical "restoration."

Lopsang, our party loving bus driver, was staying on in Shigatse, eager for the next tour headed back to the Nepalese border. From private mini-coach to a battered Chinese public bus, our fall had been rapid. Without my Tibetan friends for the first time, the blunt force of the Chinese transportation bureaucracy confronted me. The population had to make bus bookings at a mud wallow at the southern edge of town. From Tibet at its most sophisticated, I entered a China at its most primitive.

"*Gyantse! Gyantse! Doa xiao chen?*" I muttered through the opaque window. "Tomorrow? Next day? I discovered it was hard to mime the concept of tomorrow. Eventually I heard the dulcimer "*yao, yao.*" Not understanding the fare, I slipped the agent the largest banknote I had, a starchy crisp 100 yuan note, and hoped for the best. Suddenly a chit appeared, accompanied by a blizzard of multicolored *remembei* notes with shiny aluminum coins on top. Jens and the others proceeded to imitate me, and were quicky given tickets.

From the bridled chaos of the ticket office, we wandered back to the hotel through the hyperdeveloped Chinese section of Shigatse. Enter one gigantic Friendship Store, designed to dazzle with spacious chrome and glass, pyramids of Peony Brand and Flying Horse cigarettes. Huge flagons of evil-colored perfume were bedded in vibrant silk pillows next to huge chunks of Manchurian ginseng and royal bee pollen. No real person could be seen buying a thing, however — it was a museum of consumerism, a device to light the slow burning fires of want among the Chinese and Tibetan urbanites. I bought a pencil, and joined Jens, Moon Light, and the French noble woman Valerie out on the main thoroughfare. The young woman reminded me of a mother superior with her closely bobbed hair, ankle socks, and steely determination.

Petty capitalists lined both sides of the wide Shigatse street. Children's clothes spread across a blanket, a dentist with a foot-pedal drill, a Muslim vendor hawking kebabs on a brazier — it was not Taipei, Shanghai, or any other prosperous Chinese coastal city. Instead, Shigatse proclaimed its weathered Silk Route heritage, its essential Central Asian nature.

We came across the Neighborhood of the Photographers, an odd place that turned tourism on its head. Each of the seven shops had painted large backdrops in front of their kiosks, embellished with props — a chair or perhaps a table. I remembered that these dioramas had been common in the Victorian West, and were popular in Imperial China with the advent of photography. Looking about, I was instantly reminded of the pompous poses of old Dowager Empress Tzu-shi (Ci-xi!) with her eunuchs, gliding amid painted clouds and lotus pools mimicking the goddess Kuan-Yin and her attendants. And so the tradition survived here, among the homesick Chinese posted to barren Tibet. These backdrops articulated the subjunctive — the dreams of what could be, or what should be. There were no scenes of Tibet — no Potala, none of the magnificent Himalayas. It constructed a window into the fantasias of every-day Chinese and assimilated Tibetans. We found expertly drawn scenes of comfortable living rooms. The richly colorful depth of shading and subtle plays of light, the round, overstuffed armchairs and sofas, were nothing less than life-sized copies of the backdrops used by Disney Studio animators in the 1940s. One tableau included a painted television set and the radio from "Donald's Day Off." Another set included a cardboard automobile, no doubt the red roadster from "Mickey's New Car."

Valerie smugly shrugged off the photographers' tourist touts, and we walked slowly through the remainder of the bazaar back to the Tibetan district. Main street in the Chinese section was being widened, and everywhere were new plantings of trees. But the slick, paved downtown ended abruptly. The boulevard opened up onto the dusty, old Tibetan market. And above, rising like a broken fossil, the ruins of the huge Shigatse fortress towered in somber shades of ocher.

Chapter 4

Here in Tibet's second city, officials of the rival Tsang state built a *dzong* to match the Potala in Lhasa for the court of the Panchen Lama. Similar to the Dalai Lama's palace itself, the structure's foundation incorporated the hills and crags overlooking the city and river. The fortress was dismantled centuries later, stone by stone, by Tibetans staring into the barrels of Chinese rifles.

"It's no ancient ruin," I told Valerie, "it was blown up by the Chinese — the Cultural Revolution!"

"Here!" The French girl handed me her shopping bags and camera. "Take my picture, will you?" So, dressed in her Tibetan men's jacket of black *sheema* wool trimmed with silver, Valerie, grand-daughter of le comte du Manor de Juaye, chose to be photographed against a backdrop of genocide.

In the corner of the bazaar a terrifying apparition appeared. A great black mastiff hobbled towards us, its body wracked in shudders. Muscular spasms flowed through its body in waves of agony. Foam oozed from drooping lips. Rabies! I had endured the costly dead duck vaccine in Kathmandu to spare me one of my greatest fears. And here I was face-to-face with the horror of hydrophobia. This dog would be dead shortly, no doubt torn apart at first stumble by the packs of wild dogs roaming the abandoned *dzong* above. I backed down the narrow passageway to the brightness of the street. Furtively, I scanned the crowd for the pastels of life.

There was uneasiness. The atmosphere seemed charged with ions, as if building up for a grand thunderstorm. Da Duk had gone out, apparently scurrying for phantom ancestors that would make all things right. Moon Light continued being lost out at the truck stop. Just the Dane and I remained to poke around for something to do, preferably away from the hoary tourist ghetto. Jens and I went to dinner, down the street and to the west. The café was a tiny, two-tabled affair in the Tibetan sector; typically it was run by Chinese. We were joined by Valerie and two others from the hotel. Conversation seemed impossible, as the waitress loved to loudly argue with the cook in the other room (Pepper! Pepper! Pepper!). As with every other Chinese restaurant in high altitude Tibet, the staff pressure-cooked the rice to order, involving an inexplicable and agonizing wait.

We sat at an open window, and gazed out upon empty streets. The sun was setting, and the wind had kicked up. Presently, a sturdy Khampa man in his thirties appeared, wearing dusty, heavy white clothing. He wore his hair in two braids plaited with red silk tassels, coiled around his head like a turban. I spoke to him, making note of his magnificent, deep red coral plug suspended on a leather cord around his neck that he was showing for sale. I asked the price of the marble-sized gem. He smiled. Jens then encouraged the pilgrim to join our table.

We ordered tea. The Khampa gave his price — 50 yuan. Khampas, as most Tibetans, do not bargain. He honestly expected the first price. Still, 50 yuan seemed a fortune even to myself in this economy (even though it was only about $6.00). I hesitated — I changed the subject, fumbled, smiled. Silence. Even the waitress had stopped her bellyaching. I heard a dog barking down the street. A Chinese man, looking somewhat official in his dark grey suit, and somewhat drunk, then glanced through the window and entered the small café. He spoke in a quiet, but obviously agitated manner to the waitress, now cowering in a corner. His eyes focused on the Khampa sharing our table, and became irate, shouting abusively at the nomad. The 6-foot Khampa stood up, and backed himself out the

Dong Lin

The old and the very young in Tibet had time to engage in pilgrimage, an ancient method of merit-making in cultures throughout the world. Anthropological fieldwork could be considered a type of secular pilgrimage.

Chapter 4

front door. Instantly the middle aged Chinese businessman was on him. In the presence of five Western tourists, he kicked the Khampa repeatedly. We were shocked—frozen. Silently, the Khampa managed to run away, as the Chinese man brushed himself off and continued his progress down the boulevard. Then the rice arrived.

Assuming the restaurant's complicity in this merciless attack, we protested in a subtle way. We sat—we dawdled over our food for hours. Our group occupied their valuable chairs all evening. Would-be patrons looked in, noted that the restaurant was full, and moved on. The piqued waitress could do nothing.

Eventually Jens and I left this scene of foreign occupation, and walked down the empty street back to the tourist ghetto. I felt a sudden over-pressure, a blast of air between the Dane and myself. A dance of sparks ignited on the sidewalk before us—a spinning, clattering sound, and a thunk of wood and metal. "Gut gøtt! En åxe!" screamed Jens. I immediately turned around to encounter a crinkled old woman bent over in toothless laughter. A Khampa Momo-la had showed her two grandsons that she still had it! She was an excellent axe-thrower. Still dazed, I managed a weak smile at the ancient Tibetan Annie Oakley, all in good humor having survived this demonstrative brush with death. With my adrenaline surging, I felt like I should now be Batman, jumping to the roof of the building across the street, swinging myself from roof top to roof top. Er, where is Robin, anyway?

Turning the corner, we re-entered the world of wet woolen socks on clotheslines, queues for showers, dripping candles, patchouli, and Reggae beats. One by one the rice paper lanterns dimmed, until all that I could see were the reflections of the glaring street lights through the loosely shuttered windows. Down the long hall, muffled sounds of coughing peppered the spongy air. I could hear the clanking of thermoses of *chang* downstairs, rising with wisps of tobacco smoke and laughter from the Tibetans below. I missed Phala and Amala and the family at the Kalimpong Café. Where is Moon Light?

Early next morning we found ourselves in the vacuum cleaner bag dust dunes of the public bus yard. Having been mysteriously absent for three days, Moon Light now reappeared and drew pointedly close to me. Da Duk prowled the ticket window, in a piqued fettle over the price of passage to Lhasa. The clerk at the grimy window was trying to charge him foreigners' rates. Why, wasn't Shigatse where his ancestors dropped their plows and tied up their horses? Wouldn't these descendants now come running to the Duk's clarion call? Moon Light looked at me, eyebrow askew. Ah hah! Da Duk's pretense now fully exposed, he hurtled abuse at both us and the Chinese. Mercifully, a great Khampa man suddenly appeared, threw our bags to the porter on the bus roof, and stuffed lightweight Da Duk in the back of the vehicle, wedging him between wooden boxes and overstuffed burlap bags. The bus instantly lurched, then roared down the now-paved highway towards the capital. We had finished with Second City.

Gyantse was really just down the road from Shigatse. But we were dredged and dusted by three hours of plowing through millions of years' worth of beige glacial flour, the bare soil upon which 100 generations of barley farmers with near-pathological confidence brought forth quite a handsome livelihood. We spent enough time on the road to cover every pore, every crease of our clothing, with a monochrome of grit. In the end, we all resembled one another, to the unspoken delight of both Tibetans and Westerners.

Frontiers of Experience

I couldn't shake the notion of extinction as we gazed at the panorama of Gyantse. From the dinosaurian ridgetop to the empty streets, all had seemed abandoned since remote antiquity.

The Chinese reapers had somehow missed Gyantse. It was as wild and woolly as Dodge City in 1870, complete with a saloon and a Miss Kitty Lobsang upstairs. The fortress town of Gyantse was where the Brits were halted in the invasion of 1904. The Tibetan officialdom held the line between sacred and profane at this spot then—not by a show of arms, but rather by a characteristic Tibetan bureaucratic obstinacy. Simply no one of any importance went to deal with the British forces under Colonel Younghusband. A displeased Tibetan, immured in a Buddhist ideology that disavows any overt display of anger, merely freezes you out.

We pulled into a broad U-shaped courtyard, framed by a two storey adobe inn. Long beams stretched along the front of the building—hitching posts. We were the only "group" at this rustic truck stop, but had really ceased being a cohort way back at Shigatse. It was just Jens, Moon Light, and myself, with the remora Da Duk clinging closely, as well as la comtessa Valerie and her friend Agnes. Our eyes lit up: In the center of the yard we spotted two water taps. We had long since abandoned any thoughts of privacy—here was a marvelous font with which our layers of Cretaceous grit could be banished in majestic ablutions. Moon Light dove first under the hose, merrily splashing water on his face and spraying his bare feet. After only thirty seconds, he reemerged as fresh as a dawn lotus. It must be in their genes, I thought, a wonderful physiological adjustment to centuries on the plateau. Tibetans have developed Teflon bodies and Pepsodent smiles. Despite the sticky filth of India and Nepal, the scouring dust of their

Chapter 4

homeland, and the deeply-staining brick tea, the most minimal of grooming seems sufficient to last Tibetans all day. With neither body hair nor odorous apocrine glands, they seem impervious to the physical adhesions of earthly *samsara*. We foreign sponges, in contrast, spent hours scraping raccoon faces, deodorizing, plucking, flossing, and rubbing aloes on our raw, sandblasted skin.

It was lunchtime in Gyantse. Moon Light and I wandered into the truck stop kitchen. The custom in Tibet seemed to hang around in the kitchen until you saw something that interested you. Then the cook would chop it up, stir-fry it, and hand it over, whatever it was. In the back room an elderly woman peeled new potatoes, while a granddaughter attended to the wok and another attended to the tables in the hall. The matriarch was regal in her old age. Her long grey hair had been tied back, flowing down her black *chupa* in a thin silver cascade. She invited me to sit with her for awhile, and spoke of how kind it was for us "to suffer such a great journey" to visit the Holy Places.

"You see, there is no difference with us. You are on pilgrimage," the woman continued. Speaking of Moon Light: "It is good to watch after these boys. I know you will take care of each other."

The granddaughter waitress caught my eye. Perhaps twenty, her cheeks were exactly the color of the red potatoes she was washing. I had the vision of a Tibetan bride, sweet and natural, from a good family, reliable and ambitious. A good family here meant pure and virtuous, not necessarily one of wealth or station. I could easily melt into this arrangement, and in two or three generations, no one would know of the lineage of Eric. I released that thought, and resumed prowling around the kitchen for edibles. In due time, I selected a few vegetables, an egg, and some bright red meat, and retired to the dining room. As usual, Moon Light nibbled at his food. He hadn't even glanced at the fawning waitress, his mind preoccupied by mysterious thoughts. Fortunately he was sport to explore the ancient town with me.

No sooner had we hit the streets than Moon Light ran off. A minute later he rode back through a cloud of dust on a small Tibetan pony. The next moment I found myself leading the reigns of this charger, Moon Light flashing strong white teeth. The pony ride through Frontierland took us through the broad dirt road of Main Street and eventually to the grand old monastery of Gyantse. I took several photographs of this returning son of the khan in the white Indian sweater. As the toothy horseman dismounted, I discretely slipped the horse's owner, a patient old man, a five yuan note.

We roamed the abandoned playground that once comprised Gyantse's monastery. Packs of dogs, unlikely Lhasa Apso and Mastiff crosses, trotted and yelped in territorial rows throughout the desolate courtyard. Their menacing presence was carefully followed by the eyes of the great mandala-shaped stupa of Paljor. Built as a layer-cake of 108 chapels, the giant Buddhist reliquary was unique in all the world. Unfortunately, someone had bolted it shut. Instead, we climbed a hill behind the main monastery hall. There I could see, far in the distance, the crenulated ramparts of Gyantse fort. Its massive walls clung tightly to the undulations of the peak—a virtual stegosaurus curled in a perpetual nap. Was this pinnacle accessible? As we approached the gate of the monastic complex, the yellow and red dogs, now sitting silently on their haunches, carefully eyed our departure.

By now the sun began to set, casting deep shadows across the furrows of spent barley fields. Moon Light and I walked back down to the city center. Local men crowded before one store front window and I walked over. Moon Light hesitated, then continued back to the truck stop. The shop seemed to be some sort of gaming hall. Smooth-faced young men acting tough played table shuffleboard, sliding red and black disks glided over concentric circles of red, blue, and white painted wood in glossy enamel. The room smelled of a woodsy, warm musk — none of the rank, stale beer and tobacco associated with bars in the West. Barely contained in their black plastic leather jackets and drinking cheap Chinese liquor, a couple of young men with wild, jet hair and flaming almond eyes threw their arms about and yelled in animated self-indulgence, spinning the disks across the table. Some sprawled glumly on benches in close units of threes and fours. Others engaged in explosive conversation, the boys dripping *chang* foam and unabashedly spraying saliva on each other. It was raw, this pack of young, indigenous males. I glided through the scene as a detached phantom. I thought of the vipers back in Dharamsala who would no doubt hiss of the indolence of a spoiled generation, the spawn of the Chinese occupation. As I completed my circuit of the bar, eyes slowly fixed upon me. Complete silence surrounded me as I made my way out of the den and into the descending ceiling of a turbulent, grey sky.

My buddy Valerie and I were up at dawn, blessed by another Dukless morning. Buckley and Strauss suggested in their tourist bible that the grand fortress of Gyantse Dzong could be scaled. The head of the trail was nearby, in fact. A Baba Yaga lived in a tin hut next to the gate, and she alone held the key to the massive padlock guarding the bottom reaches of the mountain. The travel writers were true to their words. The requisite five yuan note flung open the heavy wooden doors, leading to a narrow trail straight up the rocky hill and past heavy stone walls flecked with observation platforms. At the summit stood a chapel, brilliant in white against an indigo sky.

British extra-territoriality got no further in Central Asia in 1904 than this high perch. Beyond stretched the broad valley of the Tsangpo, the Brahmaputra River. This was the heart of sacred Tibet: the burial mounds of Tibet's first kings at Yarlung, and Samye Gompa, the country's first Buddhist center established by the deified Indian *yogin*, wild-eyed Padmasambhava. From the chapel, a sheer drop of 1,000 feet ended directly above the main bazaar of the city. In this crystal atmosphere, I could clearly see the Paljor monastery, its crumbling walls snaking away beyond the remotest hills. The city seemed designed to snuggle between the arms of church and state, *gompa* and *dzong*, by now as empty as the ether above our heads.

Valerie and I stumbled down the sharp cliff of the fortress-mountain and passed the elderly key warden, returning to find our public bus to Lhasa idling in sooty fits. Jens and Moon Light had already loaded our bags and were sitting tightly in their seats. Upon entering, I glanced around the large bus. Da Duk was on board! Through guile and charm, he had not only found the funds to continue on to the capital, but obviously relished in the audacity of accompanying us. To our further displeasure, Valerie and I were relegated to the heading-cracking back seats of the crowded vehicle, right next to Da Duk.

As the bus pulled out of the courtyard for the 12-hour ride to the Forbidden City, I caught a glimpse of our truck stop's momo-la sitting at the kitchen window, serenely peeling her endless mound of potatoes. Off we chugged due south, towards the northern boundary of Bhutan. As usual, Moon Light played junior fire chief in the jump seat of the driver's compartment, even though on this occasion the driver was Chinese. The city disappeared instantly, followed

Chapter 4

a short time later by the small barley farms. The vehicle then turned sharply towards the northeast and soon we were in the high country again, beginning a slow climb to another pass at 17,000 feet. A drooling, ten-year old boy next to the window continually fed me White Rabbit milk toffees as he stared unflinchingly at my arms. At 16,000 feet, according to the Belgian woman's altimeter, the vehicle began to asphyxiate. On the last grade to the pass, the engine stalled. Outside the bus it started to snow furiously. While the bus floundered, the driver kicked out all but five people and cajoled them to walk to the summit. The transmission was apparently missing a first gear. The driver managed to turn the vehicle completely around on the road, and threw the gears into reverse. In this position he backed his way to the top of the pass. Our Donner party eventually caught up with the bus, which had meanwhile righted itself for the journey downward. Onboard at last, we began a spiraling descent into the valley of Yamdrok Tso, the magical scorpion-shaped lake where carp as large as Volkswagens reputedly swim in its turquoise waters.

Jens and Valerie, clad in their homespun black woolens, slept quietly despite the dust, the rumbling and jolting. Da Duk and Moon Light kept warm in thin Indian sweaters, while I peered from under the fox fur of my Khampa hat at the white and beige landscape. All the foreigners had melded with the slow passage of Native and Chinese, the grey grit of the road blanketing every thought and experience.

We slowly encircled the bizarre valley of Scorpion Lake, groping through its sickly copper suphide glare. Along the shoreline, the eerie remains of villages and monasteries were strewn about, embedded in the salt-dunes like weathered driftwood. I searched the horizon for the ruins of Samdroling, the convent of the great Dorje Phagmo, the Diamond Sow. She was a female *tulku*, an avatar of Vishnu, credited with transforming herself into a sow and the nuns into piglets at the arrival of a Mongol army. But the venerable establishment was apparently no match for the hordes of the People's Liberation Army. Not a trace of life could be found along its desolate shores, no bird flew over its waters, no fish splashed.

For hours we revolved around the crenulated sea, darting in and out of reedy estuaries and open bays. Eventually, a long line of low wooden huts appeared and we began a slow glide to a halt. This was some sort of lunch break, another one of those rare experiences wherein the traveling West comes face to face with the country-folk of Tibet.

We had long since eaten all our Kathmandu provisions, the cookies, candies, and nuts, the cargo that made the difficult journey liveable. We were now parched, famished, and completely dependent on the *table d'hotel* of any isolated Chinese eating establishment we came across. A few of the men from the bus disembarked and wandered into the dining room. On one wall I saw a forlorn image of Mao Tse-tung, fat and smiling yet faded like some forgotten circus poster. After a few cups of a thin, rooty, leafy infusion, we beheld before us plates of an oozing green vegetable served over desiccated rice nibs. A temptation from Hell—the only food available was this platter of acrid, stir-fried chili peppers. In great agony, the desperate ate—drowning each fiery bolus with mouthfuls of the moldy, fly blown tea.

Its passengers writhing with stomach cramps, the bus resumed its journey to the capital, winding tortuously out of the valley of Yamdrok Tso. At the summit of the next high pass, we were greeted by a blinding meadow of white

Frontiers of Experience

The Holy Scorpion Lake, where once the abbess and her nuns turned into pigs to evade capture.

alyssum and pink crocuses. Looking down and ahead at the serpentine highway, now paved, the fertile valley of the Tsangpo and the cradle of Tibetan civilization unfolded towards the eastern horizon. Rows of mountains stretched with uncanny clarity for hundreds of miles, providing a vista unmatched on earth.

It seemed only a matter of minutes before we crossed the Tsangpo. The capital grew near—giant, multicolored Buddhas carved in the live rock began appearing. Lakes, streams, and orchards began to break through a yellowish haze. Reminding me of high school hillside initials, the slopes above many villages were covered with white rocks, arranged to spell out giant sized *mantras*: One read OM MANI PADME HUM ("Hail! The jewel is in the lotus"), the phrase evoking Chenrezi, who is manifested in all the Dalai Lamas and the righteous kings of old Tibet.

After passing a gas station and moving through a sharp curve, the spectacle which had humbled such august Western explorers as Harrer and David-Neel came into view. We had entered the broad valley of the Kyi Chu River. Fifteen miles distant, growing out of its own mountain, flew the golden parapets of the holy Potala Palace. I had expected the trumpets of Gabriel and a descent of the Seraphim, but there was nothing but the whine of tires. I fought in vain to express the appropriate emotion, but felt only the slightly embarrassing cliché of the moment when one sees an all-too-familiar tourist landmark. I felt cynical. To be honest, the Potala represented the end of a painful, butt numbing journey. It catalyzed a craving not for transcendence, but for hot showers, decent food, and comfortable slumber.

Da Duk began chanting, softly at first, then bursting into a self-congratulatory roar. Alerted by his nemesis' claxon, Moon Light finally spotted the Potala

Chapter 4

and began to run up and down the aisle, pointing it out to fellow travelers, should they have had any doubt by this time.

We entered the Forbidden City through the Chinese suburbs—long industrial rows of corrugated roofs on concrete block buildings. Hundreds of agile men and women on heavy bicycles flowed past lumbering, ancient green trucks coughing foul drafts. We shot through a park of willows and duck ponds, and past the very base of the maroon and white Potala. We ran a red light, and screeched to a halt at the Banok-shol Guest Hotel about a half-mile beyond the palace.

Hastily securing rooms, we stowed our luggage and ran the several blocks for the obligatory before-the-Potala camera shots. Moon Light posed, head erect and puffed out in his blue nylon wind-breaker as if in front of a trophy marlin. I stood in my red Michelin Man down parka, white teeth and red eyes beaming in front of the solitary fortress. It had rained that day. The dark maroon paint on the palace had run down onto the dazzling white, making the whole look ever so much like an immense wedding cake under hot studio lights.

Moon Light and I exhausted what remained of the day's energy flying through the circular maze of the Tibetan market. I was thinking wild thoughts: "Here he is, O Lhasans! I have returned your native son. Accept him, and do not cross me!" I was proud. Across the generations, I had brought him home.

5. On Dogmas and Cataclysms

> Being 'in the field' is real life. It's where I become more fully alive.
> —Ralph Bolton[28]

The Banok-shol had the ambiance of an Amsterdam youth hostel, a place one step beyond the high school gymnasium but hardly agreeable to most adult sensibilities. The bottom-end hotel was a shotgun affair where fuzzy nineteen-year olds came to learn the arts of primitive communalism. Brightly painted bilious green, with white and red cement pillars, the walls enlivened an otherwise cold and gloomy interior. Thin panels marginally separated the two hundred or so rooms splayed along three floors. Relentless dust of the plateau spilled through every crevice, covering all surfaces with a fine, silty grit. It was on your pillow, in your hair. It engulfed your toothbrush. Desiccated flies peppered the window sills. The hotel exuded a dimly nostalgic smell of a middle school cafeteria—of excess pepper, disinfectant, and asthmatic adolescents. But it was a Tibetan guesthouse, and that's all that mattered to most visitors. Here was the famous local where Ritz, Beammer, and the other Aussie Lesbians had bared their breasts and fought the Han invaders of the sacred land Even one anthropologist wrote a paper on gender based on her experiences staying here.

Jens and I shared double accommodations next to Moon Light and Da Duk. All the way to Lhasa, the Duk could not be shaken. How he had brow-beaten Moon Light into accepting the room arrangement was lost in the fatigue of the moment. But I, Eric, stood next door. I became Siegfried, posturing in a silver helmet of the Cuirassiers of the Guard, blocking and deflecting the evil around the precious one. I was also paying Moon Light's bill.

For one who knew very little of his traditional culture, it was strange to see Moon Light begin to act the part of tour guide here in Lhasa; he went around talking to foreigners, answering generally unsolicited questions. Did he believe the secrets of Tibet could be automatically recognized in him by his clients as some sort of biological inheritance? He was a Tibetan, a child of the Dalai Lama—that's all that seemed to matter in his eyes. His regular face and engaging personality attracted strangers like moths to the light. He became aware in Lhasa that high cheekbones and feather eyebrows were the marks of success in this netherworld of expatriots.

That first sharp morning, I felt compelled to burn an entire roll of my rare Plus-X film on this fleet Apollo, in the guise of Octavian, who repeatedly extended his arm in a pose of "munificent leadership" before the steps of the great Potala. I indulged his charade until he finally glanced over his shoulder and beheld his own wake. The fawning Moon Light's excess of self-infatuation could be easily shortcircuited, however, whenever Da Duk arrived. The street scraper jerked the ropes of every high-flyer. He could bring gloom to the brightest of landscapes and pull

Chapter 5

the Panchen Lama himself down from the heavens. However, during these mid-morning hours, Da Duk was busily sleeping off a hangover. I had no recourse but to wait patiently for Moon Light's self-congratulatory fit to subside.

Here I am, I thought, in Tibet. Here I am with the jewel of McLeod Ganj, hah! I triumphed in raw will-power; it was a first, wasn't it? Everyone traveling to Tibet wants to be exclusive: the first Westerner, the first woman foreigner to "do" or to "be"; the only outsider to witness this or that; the first European to know a Dalai Lama; the first American... Westerners want to be the first in Tibet following historical milestones, after 1950, 1959, or 1988. We hear tales of the first independent tourist, the first overlander from Kathmandu, the longest visa, the first to circumambulate Mt. Kailash in a rubber wet suit while eating a bushel of Belon oysters. Thus the fascination with Mallory and Heinrich Harrer: it is called summitteering.

The Potala resembled nothing less than Grand Coulee Dam in its immensity. It was a mountain, that being the original symbolic intent. The herculean efforts of the Chinese propagandists rewriting history were surely dashed upon this adamantine, native ediface. The Potala Palace is the greatest monument to independent achievement the Tibetan nation ever constructed, and not even Mao could destroy it. It is a message hardly lost on Tibetan nationals. Popular myth states that Chou En-lai, the more moderate of the founders of the People's Republic, personally ordered the protection of the monument. The Potala could never be symbolic of a "close cooperation between the Han and Tibetan peoples," as the Chinese propagandists were fond of proclaiming on the back of postcards. In reality, the building of the great palace by the Tibetan government represented a defiance to China. And still, the opium dreams of contemporary "Motherland" China glance off the precipitous, golden pagodas of the Potala, and fall as fractured mockeries upon the Chinese barracks and prisons surrounding it.

"Potala," which translates "Buddha Harbor," alludes to the lotus seat upon which Chenrizi, the God of Compassion with 1,000 eyes, looks down upon the earth. The Dalai Lama, as that very god, lived on top of this lofty peak—the palace of the Potala recreates the myth of heaven's anchor on earth. Another metaphor, that of an unsullied lotus bursting forth from the muck, constructs the palace's primary design element—the blazing white and blood red palace of 1,000 rooms organically unfolding from the granite rocks of Red Mountain, Marpo Ri. To this celestial lily pad Moon Light and I would return each day, every day, to wander through its labrynth of gold traceries and turquoise paving, its crimson silks and blazing butter lamps.

But today was only our first visit. The ancient path from the Banok-shol to the village of Shol at the foot of the palace ended abruptly in the height of mundanity—a ticket booth. Yellow-heads had to pay five yuan; Moon Light pulled out, under protest, the required half- yuan for locals. "They dare charge us—we're Tibetan! It belongs to us!" Moon Light stomped. The officials considered us Westerners ten times richer or ten times more naive.

The unvarying, one-way route through immeasureably long corridors led into dark rooms guarded by an army of questionable monks—the paid pious, as insincere as those found at Tashilhumpo. We went up stairways with the flocks of panting tourists, around the feet of gigantic statues arching above the pall, and exited cavernous rooms through the most miniscule of twisted passages. The scale

The Potala was a fan of nested boxes that spread atop Marpo Ri on the west side of Old Lhasa. Old and young pilgrims struggled up and down the endless runs of steps, past massive walls of plastered masonry.

Chapter 5

was too large; so unreal as to bring on thoughts, in this American, of comedic fantasy. The Potala was beginning to remind me of the silver mine at Knott's Berry Farm. Perhaps this is intended by the Chinese—a pedestrian passage for tourists through the subterranean world of some Asian Niebelungen. This Potala exhibition seemed to have been arranged by the conquerors as a reminder to the troglodyte society they had liberated. Any mural, *thangka*, or other artifact that showed historical cooperation with China was prominently displayed. Oddly, though, the Dalai Lama's robes were folded and placed in the center of the thrones with his photographs stuck on top. It suggested he might be dropping in at any moment, or that he never completely left.

We popped out of the Potala on the north side, several hundred feet below its golden summit. Out of the burnished purple gloom and into blinding sunlight, we headed down the hill and off to the ancient city of Lhasa proper that spread out before us.

In an excess of urban planning, the Chinese had attempted to spice up the flavor of the old capital by replacing many of the traditionally sloped adobe and peg-beam Tibetan buildings with dour cinder block and concrete. A space had been plowed open in front of the formerly cloistered Jokhang, the pivot of Tibetan religious life. The cathedral was the grotto, the *sanctum sanctorum*—a rambling, flat edifice built over a dark lake containing a myriad of water spirits. Now, the new plaza was not only filled with prostrating pilgrims, but souvenir hawkers and tea shops, turning what had been a tight nautilus spiral of ecclesiastical mystery into a provincial Tiananmen Square.

Moon Light wanted to visit all the shops encircling the Jokhang, and gaze at all the shoppers. In his methodical probing, he discovered a vast network of fellow Dharamsala Tibetans. He found fourth and fifth cousins, old classmates, acquaintances of friends of friends. One smile from his 150-watt mouth and the most aloof strangers became his lost brother or sister. On the eastern flanks of the bazaar known as the Barkhor we walked into an electronics store. With a few words muttered to an unknown chum, Moon Light and I were soon sitting among a small circle of Tibetan cronies passing around an electric razor. In his turn, Moon Light proudly but furtively rubbed his hairless face with the buzzing novelty. We were as apes grooming in the sunshine.

We continued our broad circuit of the Jokhang through the Barkhor. Tibetan school girls from Mussorie in India were making the scene dressed in neatly tailored pastel cottons. They all seemed to know Moon Light, of course, becoming flustered and giggily as their young idol approached. How he worked the crowd! It was as if he was returning from a golden Tibet of the future—a clean, free, polished, white bread version of Holy Tibet—a Westernized Tibet. In leather, chrome, with jaunty, straight locks, a button nose, and the affectation of one bright red fingernail on his little finger, Moon Light gracefully proclaimed his particular message of self-hybridization as much as the surgeries, bleachings, and depilorizing had with Michael Jackson.

Bright star, shining, gliding down the path of shadows with my friend, beyond differentiation. I have become part of the crowd, belonging to the group—a *nang-pa*. To watch Tibetan men, women, and children running off in all vectors to important business, I felt no different. The streets of Lhasa constituted a real place for me, and I was a functioning component of it. Around the corner, over boxes, side-stepping dogs and pushcarts, we plunged into back alleys and residential courtyards, laundry fluttering from wires, wet felt *chupa* steaming in the

Parking on the streets of Lhasa was really quite easy.

thin, dry air. I had always been here, in the center of my own sacred landscape along the Kyi Chu quay. We were blazing, careening through the peopled landscape, past blooming lilacs, through drooping willows.

My fugue came to an abrupt halt. A martyr's breath! In an instant I felt the ragged iron drain pipe scrape my skull, my body propelled backwards with brutal force. Hitting the low overhang of a store front roof, I fell resoundingly into the dung-filled center of an alleyway. Moon Light must have pulled me out, for my next memory was sitting on the curb, my left arm covered with the foulest muck and my right temple wet with blood. For fear of horrific infection, I could not touch one with the other. As the stars of the concussion subsided, I saw Moon Light moistening a soft, clean handkerchief with his saliva, and patting a wound of unseen proportions. Adrenalin poured into my blood stream, I felt I had made the first sacrifice!

"I'll take you to the hospital!" Moon Light exclaimed.

"No! The Chinese can't do anything. I've got to wash my arm!" I fussed, fearing infection that would surely end my work, "Then we have to go to the Jokhang. Just the Jokhang!"

"But you're bleeding—so much blood." Moon Light looked at the darkening red splotches on the white cotton cloth, lifted it off my forehead, and turned to me, "This I will keep forever. For sure, forever."

Chapter 5

My friend carefully folded the talisman and placed it in his shirt pocket. I suddenly became Tsar Alexander II, blown apart by Nihilists in front of the Winter Palace, peasants running forth to soak their scarves in his imperial martyr's blood. With this first bloodletting, I had become a St. Sebastian *in contraposito*, fettered by arrows, my Western essences assuming a cultic dimension in a distant march.

Moon Light's saliva had a miraculous healing effect. My scalp laceration closed in a matter of seconds. He ran over to an adjacent apartment block. The residents inside, who became besotted by his unrelenting charm, were turned into yet another batch of cousins. A minute later I washed my arm at a courtyard tap within the residential compound.

Splattered with my own blood, I felt fit for presentation to the Wrathful Deities at the Jokhang. After all, some pilgrims tore themselves from the comfort of their families and trekked for months across the icy deserts in pursuit of the temple — the guilt of our taking a taxi to Tibet had been atoned for. Death and resurrection had been in the hands of the delicate Tibetan boy.

We walked out through the narrow passageways of urban-most Tibet, and soon found ourselves back on the Barkhor, the broad circle, the inner-most ring, the center of the Tibetan pilgrimage. The Jokhang temple itself was thronged with scores of prostrating pilgrims, who over the centuries, had worn the entrance flagstones completely smooth. The great bronze prayer cylinders flanking the doorway were as polished gold, rotating slowly at the impetus of its supplicants. Courtyards within courtyards led into the smoky, incensed gloom of the great temple, illuminated exclusively by thousands of butter lamps.

I walked past the forty-foot statue of Padmasambhava, God of Shamans, through the dioramas of a myriad of deities, to the solid gold image of the Jowo himself — reputedly the only true likeness of the Buddha, having been cast during his own lifetime. The Jo represents Siddhartha at the miraculous age of 16, that brief, weightless, aquamarine inflorescence between the end of physical growth and the beginning of decay.

While Moon Light stood outside, I hesitated at length within the airless chapel of the Protectors, hoping that they would acknowledge my wounds – *benedictus qui venit in nomine Domini, et donum fac remissionis*. Here stood the great statue of the King of Nechung, the deity of my teacher Nechung Rinpoche and of the State Oracle of Tibet, wearing his woven sun hat and riding a wild horse. The holy relics were incongruously, though simply, isolated from the masses by a chicken wire screen. I met face to face with the screaming eyes of the Protector. My body became red hot, my eyes filling with fire, the air crackling with thermal auspices. Juniper smoke began to burn holes in the dark brown veils. In an instant the spell was broken by the ripples of Moon Light's cool voice.

We quickly re-entered the blazing glaze of the Tibetan market. Leaving the inner circle, Moon Light and I walked to the main thoroughfare. Long blocks of multi-storied flats represented yet another Chinese attempt at modernization. These buildings, though constructed of industrial concrete, were softened in traditional Lhasa whitewash and trimmed with black, green, and red on window and door frames. Inexplicably, Moon Light ducked into one of them, pulling me inside.

Surprise! It was the house of another of Moon Light's cousins. I had been with my friend ceaselessly since our arrival. How did he know these people? He spoke with such familiarity to this unknown Lhasa resident. The bespectacled, middle-aged cousin lived alone in his apartment. He spoke to us in perfect refugee English, inviting us inside a large room filled with sturdy Chinese furniture, an *art moderne* television, and a streamlined radio from the days of the Andrew Sisters. We were immediately presented with offering of food: tins of *tsampa* with a generous parcel of dried, shredded yak cheese, a plate of nuts and dried fruits, salted tea with *drimar* (yak butter). As Moon Light talked about his family, our host brought bars of Cadbury chocolate. I sat on rare Tibetan rugs, my arms propped up with numerous cushions like a Turkish vizir—old Heinrich Harrer in Austria had had it no better. Despite the urban sophistication of the Lhasans, Moon Light was the only son Johnny, fresh from the war in Europe. The boy had returned to his jerkwater hamlet in the deepest Ozarks where everyone who had ever lived there was related. It seemed the same with him wherever we went. He formed the epitome of adaptability and lived solely by his charms and guile.

The waning hours of the woody afternoon were spent with Moon Light, who by now ricocheted from house to house like a pin ball. Genealogies, both fact and fictional, spun forth as names dropped like ripe apples. And so he attempted, wattle and daub, to slather up a foundation of birthright to Lhasa, the Holy City. He had carelessly returned to a disintegrating ideal from which his father had fled. With the youthful absence of enmity born of historical memory, alliances were easily formed, evaporated, and reformed.

We walked slowly home. The russet beams of a setting sun glanced off crystal facets, the window panes of Shol, muted here and there by thick dustings of grey Lhasan dust. Would there ever be another, as the knight of hearts plunging into the darkness, so reckless and righteous?

Moon Light disappeared into a gang of pseudo-cousins, now also mushrooming around Da Duk back at the Banok-shol Hotel. I walked past my door and out to the flat rooftop, attracted to a flitting commotion like caddisflies around a boathouse lamp. Several benches had been laid out as a common lounge for residents of the tourist camp, and they were covered with young drifters attired in bright gauzes. Here sat an animated Zig-zag man, dressed in a long grey caftan. Stoking his straggly beard and making broad, sweeping movements, he seemed like the old Hills Brothers coffee man. Moth-like women and rat-faced men loafed at the feet of this Mosaic patriarch wearing a single scimitar-shaped silver earring. Reggae music blared from a tinny cassette as gossamer-haired girls in thin cotton hareem pants performed a disenthralled tarantella.

As a disembodied spirit, I walked with wide eyes through this loose tribe of expatriots. The Hills Brothers' *imam* was some sort of entrepreneur, I gathered, and a dictator among his band of neo-hippies. I called him Dr. Zog after the bizarre king of Albania from the 1930s. I snooped into the storage room adjoining the rooftop lounge. The drifters were making their own cheese, a starchy grey, pasty concoction dripping from cloth bags. Added to locally obtained tomatoes, sprouts, and round loaves of Tibetan bread, the group had set up a lively business selling sandwiches to the laziest 10% of Westerners in the Banok-shol. After all, who knows what dog or cat carcass went down at the local Chop Suey, eh? Besides a cheese cake, today's buffet line of *inji* favorites included sawdust bread slices with homemade mayo (¥3), "Bavarian" potato slop, and a salad bar of turnip greens with the *fromage du jour* dressing (¥3). It was a combination of Club Med and Woodstock, with pretension to the former but lacking the gaiety of the latter.

Chapter 5

To add an extra relish of insult, the moon children advertised their fare on pretty, multi-colored card stock, obtained at the local Friendship Store. Emblazoned with the yellow and red seal of the People's Republic, the colorful "writing paper" was actually official award certificate blanks used normally by high school teachers to reward scholarship. Displayed prominently on the lobby bulletin board:

> Tired of the mysterious yak burger hassle? Try a sandwich of fresh, home-made cheese and garden veggies. Only ¥5.00. Golden Himalayan Sandwiches, Rm. 435.

Dr. Zog's marketing approach had given me an idea for Moon Light, stage mom that I was for his debut in Tibet. The Chinese tourist industry in Lhasa had fallen short of visitors' expectations. So clueless, it seemed, that the Chinese had failed to grasp the necessity of providing the most simple amenities. You can get tanked oxygen at the fancy Lhasa Hotel to settle your imported Scotch, but try finding razor blades in the shops of Lhasa. Whether the Chinese viewed the foreigner as so completely alien that old fashioned Chinese pragmatics could never suffice, or they simply didn't care, a giant vacuum of Western-oriented services remained for any would-be yuan-maker.

Tourists didn't expect the Ritz—quite the opposite. Tibet maintained its historical appeal largely because of its difficulties. Inconvenience, hostility, and suspicion were expected in the Forbidden Land. Fluffy white sheets, oxygen-enriched air conditioning, color television, and flush toilets available at the CITS flagship Lhasa Hotel were incongruous with the Holy frontier image of Tibet that the followers of David-Neel and Lama Govinda had come to expect. But the modern traveler, even the most daring and care free, still tethered themselves to the world on the other side. Even Dr. Zog, the Hills Brothers coffee man, had to travel fast, speed-dreaming through the plateau before his visa expired. They needed film and post cards, writing paper and batteries, simply to prove where they had been. They needed ethnic clothes to show each other that they were so Tibetan they could pass through the country undetected. These were the necessities on the journey to Otherworld.

I visited every tourist flop, and meticulously scanned every information board:

> Wanted: Ride to Mt. Kailash—have hiking boots and/or loom to trade.
>
> Need black hair dye. Leave note for Mondi at front desk.
>
> An Evening in Old Tibet. Lecture by the world's leading expert on travel in Tibet, Eddie Mintz. Lhasa Hotel, 3 May, 19:00, ¥ 10.00.
>
> Wanted—someone to take me to a Sky Burial. Gill, Rm. 405.
>
> Tibetan lessons by real Tibetan for Westerners.
>
> English lessons by inji man.

For *injis*? Lets get real here...Tibetans don't have any money. Perhaps the Chinese tourists officials thought some impenetrable language barrier drove foreign tourists away from the large, government-built hotels. It seemed more likely the failure of Chinese central planning to move beyond simplistic propaganda: Did Chinggis Khan really set out to unify the Great Motherland of China? We knew from a certain Venetian that the fearful *kumus*-drinking horsemen of the steppes were substantially different from the lilac-powdered *literati* sitting behind their lotus silk screens in far-off Cathay. Westerners' own presumptions of how Tibet should be, populated by happy herdsmen living in the twelfth century, further infuriated foreigners against the modernized Chinese. A sign of quiet desperation, it seems, that free-spirited, independent Euro-American had to provide requisite services themselves. The tourist world of Lhasa had thrown open its doors to all sorts of drifter-bourne hucksterisms. It was time the locals cashed in.

I met Andre and Pam, an American couple who well represented the young middle class traveler. New to Tibet, they traveled close enough to the land, but far enough to require an immensely long supply line to back-home comforts. For me, Andre was a source of precious film. I long ago exhausted the 30-40 rolls I had brought with me for fieldwork documentation. Andre pulled out his suitcase, opened a Tupperware, and produced five rolls of beautiful Fujichrome! It turned out that he was an attorney, and really quite up on the situation in Tibet. Like so many other Westerners, he had just been in Dharamsala, so appreciated the privilege of being among the first handful of foreigners to be able to spend much time in Tibet, freely and without supervision. Andre and Pam, so ordinary they could have walked out of the *Reader's Digest*. Each of their features were so plain they would have been hard to describe. It was disappointing to meet them, for they represented the rapid approach of mass tourism in Tibet. While the freaky vanguard of the old Overland Asia Trail was expected to make its debut in the country as soon as general travel restrictions were lifted, it seemed outrageous for suburbanites from Spokane and Des Moines to flood the sacred land.

Moon Light came over to my room one afternoon. His first job in the homeland would be as a culture-broker-gopher-errand-boy for lazy New Agers. I'd be his agent, his manager, the request went. I felt game—after all, we had the experience of organizing our own tour from the Nepal border. Moon Light would have no problem. His charm worked overtime. No doubt it would overcome his ignorance of the Chinese language. He wanted to be a guide, he said, so he could tell tourists the truth about Tibet. Official Han Chinese tour escorts, he argued, knew nothing about Tibetan culture, didn't want to be there, and generally despised the privileges and wealth of the foreign visitors.

Moon Light seemed immensely excited over the idea, as he was with anything novel. He suggested I immediately write a bulletin board posting offering his services. I thought of buying a broad brimmed hat and wearing gold chains under an open collar polyester shirt. At 8:00 p.m., while the most of the hotel guests were scouring the town for yak burgers and cheap Chinese beer, I quietly placed a carefully lettered card on the board downstairs.

At first nothing materialized. Over the next week I watched how the tourists had set up a pharmacy in an empty room at the Banok Shol—band-aids, Tylenol, tampons, rubbing alcohol, bottles of Maalox and Metamucil. The least ghoulish of them had finally set up a notice not to visit Sky Burials, as Tibetans "might resent" having strangers watch vultures gobble up Granny.

On Sunday morning a man called Moon Light to Room 322 for his first assignment. A few minutes later he left. I did not see Moon Light all that afternoon. He finally returned to Room 322 in the early evening with a small package.

Chapter 5

A moment later Moon Light came over to my room fuming—he'd earned a grand ¥10 finding haemorrhoid suppositories for a tender overlander just in from Kathmandu. Da Duk, standing just down the corridor, was besides himself in laughter.

Another idea came to mind as Jens, Moon Light, Da Duk, and I visited the Tibetan shoe factory in east Lhasa to order custom boots. I had remembered Alexandra David-Neel's words:

> The boots which I had bought from Kham showed, as well as the peculiar material of my dress, that we hailed from that province and provided me with a certificate of Thibetan nationality.[29]

In this one-room sweatshop, twenty women sat on huge mounds of colored felt and dried yak hide. We were surprised that the traditional foot-gear was still being made, having never seen these on the streets. Instead, shiny black leather boots with high heels brought over by the Chinese had been de rigeur for years. In the airless room, embroidered, boot-length felt uppers were stitched onto tough hides to form colorful, boat-shaped moccasins. A special grass could be stuffed around the foot to fill out the shoe, the uppers secured around the leg with ribbons woven of brightly colored cotton. And like all traditional Tibetan clothing, sumptuary custom dictated who could wear what. Lamas once wore maroon and grey felt boots, while the lay-folk were content with black or red. Nobility, both secular and lay, wore the same style, but of black velvet with elaborate silk applique. We decided on the maroon and grey.

Jens and I had our feet traced on paper for the custom-making of our shoes. The boots were splendid, indeed, despite the fact that the special dried grass was unavailable, which made the experience of walking seem reminiscent of slogging about in oversized junior pajama bottoms with vinyl-soled foot covers.

Back out on the streets, Jens and I discovered that no Caucasian wanted to be without a pair of these tribe-identifiers. Predictably, we were mercilessly hounded: "Where did you get them?" "How much? Custom-made!" We would momentarily keep silent, holding the suspense. In a rare show of cooperation, Moon Light and Da Duk then would explain that no tourist could possibly survive the wilds of the Inner Asian circuit without nomadic knock-offs.

After similar encounters with frantic tourists, we decided that I would walk about the streets of Lhasa and refer all inquiries to Room 315 at the Banokshol. The two Dharamsala boys would take the required measurements, and forward them on to the boot factory, collecting a hefty commission along the way. Da Duk had arranged a ¥5 commission from the boot shop proprietress. I maintained this "march of the clowns" for the next few days, trying my best not to laugh too hard at the scene we had created.

In less than a week the brilliant venture failed. An eager tourist had simply followed Da Duk to the boot factory at the edge of town. The word went out and the monopoly was broken.

We'd have to do better than this, if Moon Light was to set himself up as the paragon of the new, Dalai Lama-following Tibetan entrepreneur/nationalists being encouraged to settle in the homeland.

Early the next week Moon Light and I returned to the Potala. This time Da Duk accompanied us. He had slicked himself down to play guide to four *injis* he had picked up at the hotel. He smelled something lucrative in the ironic guide training I had been providing to Moon Light. Tenzin, the young man who accompanied us from the Nepalese border, was eager to try anything for a job. He tagged along too.

Once inside the palace, I left Moon Light and Tenzin at the main entrance and positioned myself within sight of Da Duk's party winding its way up the broad steps. From chapel to chapel they trod, disappearing into the gloom, then reappearing into the bright orange flames of butter lamps. In sweeping gestures, the Duk spoke of the work of the gods, the miracles of the great Fifth Dalai Lama, and the evils of Chinese occupation. What he didn't know he ad libbed. Two in his group yawned while he rattled off in his glib English slurries of fiction mixed with fact. His affectations reminded me of those perfectly poised female Intourist propagandists in the Soviet Union of the 1960s, with simulated Oleg Cassini miniskirts, spit-curls, and dome-shaped white and blue hats with wings, endlessly extolling the virtues of utilitarian socialism. It was red and white peppermint swirl Coca-Cola marketing.

Da Duk's American slang was so polished he could slide any damning phrase past most English-speaking official guides in the Potala. He spoke with the type of hyperbolic sincerity born in the streets, but he remained a stranger in his own land. As I left to find Moon Light and Tenzin, three of the tourists wandered off like ducklings. Others were backing away, like customers from a too aggressive car salesman. Two used feline displacement techniques, studiously preoccupying themselves with other matters.

Eric is not a prodigious expert on Tibetan iconography, but for Moon Light's purposes, I became the font of all knowledge. On those many days we spent at the Potala, I carefully explained what I knew about this or that image and the history of the various Dalai Lamas, and spoke about the ancient days of Tibetan kings who ruled from the top of the peak, now the center of modern Lhasa. In each chamber, a lama-caretaker spoke to Moon Light in polite Lhasa Tibetan. Gleaning a bit from the conversation, I added my own thoughts and presented a somewhat more synthesized picture to Moon Light. Tenzin stood by silently, looking confused as usual.

On one of these sessions at the palace, I suddenly became aware of another's silent presence. An ear stretched across the room, straining to pick up my conversation. Da Duk's sensitive bat sonar received my exegeses, processed them, and relayed information directly to his clients. My words to Moon Light would be broadcast in Duk-ese a few moments later at the other end of the chapel to Western tourists. After that, Moon Light and I launched a concerted effort to distance Da Duk from ourselves. In fact, the intrigue-ridden shadows in the Potala were ideal for vanishing. We descended rapidly through the labyrinth.

With each level downward, the rooms grew larger, as did their statuary. The gods inhabiting the intimate apartments of the Dalai Lama at the pinnacle were seldom more than two feet high. Those residing in the chapels a few floors down were life-sized. The images discovered in the foundations of the 14-storey edifice were massive. With Tenzin and Moon Light at hand and Da Duk several hundred rooms behind, we stumbled upon a long neglected room at the base of the palace. Here stood a large, rectangular hall with high ceilings. A row of twenty massive, gilded bronzes with bulging eyes stared down upon us—Tsongkhapa, Thupden Gyatso, Padmasambhava, Chenrezi... all the stars of State, burnished in radiant fire. Absolutely insignificant we seemed, trivial in our daily pursuits. As if by some imperial design, the exit to the palace was tucked behind the last Titan, the door a mere mouse hole leading into the raucous world. Did we grow larger during our ascent to the sacred realms and smaller on our descent to the earth? The phenomenon reminded me that Tibetan architects did not design the Potala for tourists, but to replicate the celestial hierarchy.

The old gold and deep musk disappeared in the fluorescent white flash of noon on Marpo Ri. A cobblestone road, curled in a long spiral, slowly spooled its way down the peak to Lhasa and the neighborhood of Shol. We were buffeted by clean breezes from the distant valley of Sera. Tattered strips of generations of prayer flags flew on the bare bones of gnarled junipers clinging to the hill. The rags represented the offerings of departing visitors. Strips of clothing or even hair had sufficed. At once, Moon Light and Tenzin each plucked sturdy black locks from their scalps and tied then to the brittle branches. With a certain trepidation, I followed suit, the wind catching our black, golden, and black banners on a grizzled branch of ancient juniper. Clothing snapping in the wind, I looked out across the plain of the Kyi Chu, and saw the budding path of willows tracing a path to Drepung. In the roiling turbulence, I was struck with a hollow sense of foreboding.

> We the spirits of the air,
> that of human things take care,
> out of pity now descend
> to forewarn what woes attend.[30]

Like some mild, middle-aged German tutor, I was glowing, satisfied with Moon Light's lesson. He seemed the type of young student that had to be tricked into learning: it had to be effortless, non-authoritative. Education also had to be immediately applicable — more specifically, relevant to earning fast money. And cash generated further adventure. I had bags of surprises.

We had passed all the holy gate-keepers on our descent from Marpo Ri, the genuine mendicants and the ancient canines, and entered the village of Shol. A busy noodle shop had sprouted up along the main street, wedged between an electronics repair shop and the ruins of the ancient triple gate of Lhasa. The ingenious shopkeeper had named his kitchen "Rambo-bar," and proclaimed it with a giant sign of bare-chested Stallone toting a machine gun. A bit shy of the Gandhian type of liberation promoted by the Dalai Lama?

The restaurant was packed with animated young Tibetans, a Lhasan Café du Monde. As I glanced at the menu, an array of noodles with increasingly hotter components, Moon Light had turned his hartshorn velvet eyes towards a giggling waitress dressed in purple and yellow silk. He commanded the moment — Tenzin and I became mere foils for his banter with the girl. While Tenzin withdrew into muddled passivity, I struggled to regain control over the important business of ordering lunch. I shot a vectored shaft of fire at Moon Light, singeing a few notes off of the symphonic performance. With a slight smile, Tenzin and I were quickly brought back into his reality. The Easter egg waitress immediately presented us sweet, hot milk-tea. Ms. Eyelash followed with bowls of red pepper-garnished wheat noodles. I proceeded to eat my lunch demonstrably, as the fading alpha lion gnawing the fallen gazelle.

Leaving the restaurant, I set up my camera on the other side of the street and waited to catch tourists looking silly. As hoped, two care-free young Western men soon appeared, laughing and pointing at the sign hanging above the Rambo-bar. I squeezed the shutter. It was perfect with the Potala shining behind them.

When we returned to the Banok-shol, Tenzin drifted off to his room. Moon Light disappeared into his room next to Jens and me, one that he inexplicably shared with Da Duk. The latter was sunning himself on the roof, in the company of Jens, who had spent the day exhaustively circling the shops of the Barkhor with the "French suite," a group of young Europeans who often hung out together. Here Jens met Pia, a lymphatic waif from the dank moors of Jutland. Her long hair was as transparent as her skin. She floated up to Jens with self-possessed grace, the likes of which had not been seen by the Danes since the days of the princesses Alexandria and Dagmar. I knew my comfortable surroundings were soon to change. We Scandinavians of the French suite were all blessed with autumnal golden hair, and became the objects of attraction where ever we went in Lhasa.

"I would be well to be rid of Jens." The vicious thought jumped into my head. Like a celestial object of considerable mass, he disturbed the delicate balance of tensions that existed between Da Duk, Moon Light, and myself. I never could be sure who he was or why he was here. Yet he presented an ingratiating spirit, one without agenda. I hoped limpid Pia would remove him as surely as an expired visa would. For the moment, Jens remained, crowding my room with the goofy energies of a Flemish madrigal.

Moon Light started making large sums of money, which he entrusted to me—500, 900, 1,300 *renminbei*, that I tucked into a folder underneath my mattress. After few weeks working in the Potala, CITS made Moon Light an official guide. He began to develop an efficient routine. He'd leave the room next door that he still shared with Da Duk, and head for the laundry sink located in the hotel courtyard. While road-wrinkled young tourists hung up their faded cottons, Moon Light washed his small feet, one toe at a time, in the great white basin. In one quick motion, he hosed down his hair and splashed his apple-cheeked face. He often wore heavy Indian woolen trousers and a cheap, button-down shirt. By first light, he skittered down the road, reporting to work at the Chinese agency.

I stoically endured my long days writing nonsense in the colorful schoolboys' notebooks I had found at the Friendship Store. I watched the afternoon winds depositing veneers of grit on my red painted table, and the lazy flies squeezing themselves around the windowpanes. Looking out upon the main street of Lhasa, I spotted a farmer bringing a yak into town to sell, and observed Khampas swaggering through town.

One day I saw an older maroon-robed monk and two familiar faces approaching from the east. Tanya and Greg from Nechung Monastery in Hawai`i strolled past my window. This meant that the reincarnation of Nechung Rinpoche must have been found here, and T&G were here to retrieve the child. I read that these things had to be done in the deepest of secrecy, even in the days before occupation. I imagined that smuggling out the *tulku* of the State Oracle institution would be an act of greatest opacity. Here they were in broad daylight, on the main street of the capital. I bolted downstairs, and headed around the block in the opposite direction in order to surprise them from behind. Denied being privy to great secrets, I crashed the mystery by ambushing my friends:

"I know what you're doing!" I taunted as I ran up to Tanya and Greg.

"Eric! Say, you do get around!" Tanya cried, rolling her eyes.

Chapter 5

"Be kind, you guys. When did you get in?"

"Just yesterday. We're up at Nechung at Drepung. First chance out," Greg related.

"What are *you* doing here? Who're you with?" Tanya asked me, laughing.

"You know, the anthropology game. I brought two Dharamsala boys with me. I'm over there, that window."

"It was a rough, hard trip, wasn't it?" Greg questioned with a sigh.

"Not too bad. We got a minibus. No trouble with the Chinese. How about you... I had no idea you would be here so soon."

"We've got to take Lobsang Tenzin to the doctor. Why don't you come up to Drepung and visit us. No problem. Bring your friends. How about noon on Saturday?"

"Oh, yeah? I would love it. We'll get bikes. Okay, then?"

I watched as the Dharma cadre disappeared down the street and into the Barkhor, then returned to the Banok-shol to watch the sun go down. Perhaps Moon Light would come home a bit early and we could share dinner.

A befuddled Tenzin walked over to my room.. He didn't seem to know what sort of job he wants. He claimed he's sick. Stomach and skin problems? Maybe—he seemed to be confused most of the time, but was making friends. It didn't look like he had much money; his clothes were a mess. But today he brought me a Dalai Lama blessing cord, a *srung-dud*. Often he bought me tea, or brought beer and chocolate. Sometimes he treated me to noodles at one of the nearby restaurants. Many times Tenzin waited to meet me down at the General Post Office.

Moon Light came home quite late. I saw him briefly. He handed over a wad of red and green *reminbei* notes for me to hide, and went in to his room. I saw that Da Duk was very ill as the door closed slowly. I stared at the shadows on the ceiling. Jens was gone—up in Pia's room no doubt. I could hear the Reggae sounds of the cheese factory crew several doors down, and the whisperings of the Tibetan women changing shifts on the wood fired hot water heater. The Bank-shol was the only budget hotel in town with hot showers. No one asked where the huge logs came from—ancient cedars, juniper, maple.

Moon Light and I had breakfast in the morning at the corner greasy-spoon: eggs fried in mustard oil, hard toast, salted tea, dried cheese.

"Eric," Moon Light asked, "I saw an *inji* man in the shower this morning. His back was covered with hair. I saw it through the steam clouds. It was much black hair, like a *migyur*."

"Yeah. Pretty gross, huh?" I smiled. "A wild yeti."

"I also saw this other man once and he had little brown dots all over his skin. It looks so strange. Is it normal?"

"It just goes with the yellow hair."

Moon Light seemed satisfied with that answer. Finishing the runny egg, he picked up his bag and headed off to the tour company.

I sat in the painted wooden chair by myself. To capture the moment of conjunction and mutual conquest, I envisioned Moon Light and me having a photo taken back in India. We requested a formal studio portrait, posed in the stiff Victorian idiom that has never been lost upon contemporary Indian portraiture. I couldn't fail to think of the infamous portrait of King Ludwig III and the actor

On Dogmas and Cataclysms

Joseph Kainz, audaciously sitting in the presence of his standing sovereign. Our print was to be sepia toned. CNN style correspondent Elsa Klensch described the shoot:

> Sitting rigidly on a high-backed chair, Eric is clad in magnificent if ponderous nineteenth century Tibetan robes. The inner shirt is cut from naturally buff colored raw silk from Assam. The sleeves and collar are trimmed with deep, forest green mulberry silk from Varanasi. Over this is draped a blood-red tunic of weighty silk, which fades to deep black according to the play of light. The grand outer robe is an antique silk *chupa*, thickly padded and golden. Running dragons festooned the entire garment as silver piping trims the hem. The stiff high collar depicts bamboo stalks with leaves; a sky-blue brocade lines the collar and sleeves with woven phoenixes. The sleeves of the inner tunic extend beyond the outer shirt, which in-turn project beyond the sleeves of the robe. The same layering is produced at the collar—a sequence of dark green, cream, red, blue, and gold stripes are formed from the overlapping layers in a manner reminiscent of Imperial Japanese coronation *kimono*. The five primary Buddhist colors are thus represented. The robe is gathered in careful pleats and secured below the waist with a red, white, and indigo homespun woolen belt. Maroon woolen trousers of fine *shema* from Shigatse are tucked into Manchu-style black velvet calf boots trimmed in turquoise and built over white kid clogs with black leather uppers. The boots are secured with rainbow colored ribbons of woven cotton tied snugly around the upper calf.
>
> For accessorizing, Eric sports a red silk sash over the left shoulder, which supports a silver amulet box inlaid with turquoise and red coral. He fills the *gau* with fragments of initiation strings and *khatag* personally received from the hand of the Dalai Lama. Around his neck he suspends a pendant composed of a miniature *vajra* scepter studded with alternating diamonds and rubies, a marble of fine turquoise, and several beads of extinct Red Sea coral. Eric wears the headdress of a Amdo nomad headman—a red, blue, and silver brocade cloud with appliquéd geometric patterns of multi-colored felt. The dramatic hat is lined with red Himalayan fox fur, turned up in the front and sides forming a wide band with lappets at the back. These are secured with long ribbons of more forest green mulberry silk. Eric encircles his left wrist with a sandalwood rosary with skull counters carved of bone and punctuated with strings of purple silk. He wears dark glasses. Between the kaleidoscope of silken draperies and the wisps of red fur, Eric's golden moustache and smiling eyes shine through.

In my vision, Moon Light stood slightly behind the throne occupied by the neo-mandarin, left hand lightly resting on the chair back. He seemed as artificial as myself, surfeit with hard-won trophies. Ms. Klensch resumed:

> Moon Light constructs a broad fashion statement with a blue t-shirt imprinted with the images of Kellogg's Snap, Crackle, and Pop, and Frisky, the winking, chopping-licking dog food icon. The shirt is labeled with a clever jive phrase, "jimmi smak, riddim jack, funky hustlin daddy mac." Over his hip t-shirt he is clad in a Turkish black leather jacket cut to a young Michael-Jackson-cum-Japanese-gang-boy format. Over this, Moon Light pins a large Dalai Lama photo button. A green baseball cap imprinted with "Hawaii" covers his head—one shiny shock of black hair shoots forward from the band. His Levi's 501 button-down jeans are terminated with an ultimate symbol of Western consumerism—a pair of day-glo green

Chapter 5

and white Nike running shoes. Around his neck our model wears his protector's rhullite quartz crystal, mounted in silver with a garnet stud. A bracelet of seven phosphorescent plastic beads strung with nylon fish line decorates his left wrist. A fashionable Swatch digital watch on his right wrist completes the image.

Grainy focus, with a murky back screen of the Vale of Kashmir, our tableau could be entitled "Lord Curzon with his Sherpa Man-servant," or perhaps "Merlin meets the Atomic Clock." The portrait is a quartet — a twin icon with two dimensions of exoticism. Spacial distance is represented in the crossed motifs of Western and Eastern exotica. Time represented is bipolar. For me, it portrays an unspecified period in the archaic past, nothing less than the ethnographic present; for Moon Light, it is an expression of contemporary self with a future projected on an unspecified "anywhere." We were archetypes for each other — souvenirs of worlds and times once experienced and still yet to come.

The image lingered as I finished my sugary tea. Then I slid the small chair under the table. I glanced down the road now bright with the 10:00 a.m. sunshine. I paid the bill with a green ¥ 2 banknote and a little red one. Without the need to meet schedules and deadlines, but to simply record what I wanted to document, I was freer than the feather-duster dogs that trotted down the sidewalks of Lhasa, and even the dozens of doves that perched on the telephone lines above me.

I wandered back into the Barkhor, past the smoking juniper furnaces, beyond the reddened tables of the open-air yak meat vendors. In the center of a small intersection stood a cluster of about seven or eight young Khampa traders. Someone suddenly grabbed my arm from behind and he hauled me strongly into the center of the group. I thought they were going to try to sell me something. Instead, they simply were passing around among themselves bits of red coral and turquoise, amber beads and chased metal cases. I felt two or three arms around my shoulders, then waist. One held my hand, then another took his place. They began passing me around like an exotic toy. I could feel the rough texture of woolen *chupa*, and thick canvas cloth, and smell the yeasty tang of *chang* and the buttery *drimar* saturating their smooth brown faces so close to mine. In the middle of the intersection in the market, we were a ball of textures and colors — red tassels, black wool, flashes of blue and yellow, strong white teeth. I was firmly but gently held, like a cub in the mouth of a tiger. The aggressively friendly Khampa tribesmen supported me, my feet did not touch the ground. And then it suddenly broke off. I found myself in front of a yak meat stall, a hairless orange goat head looking up at me. The Khampas had vanished. Testosterone still raging and heart pounding, I could still feel the strong grip of the nomads, of my body being deftly handled. Dazed, I impulsively brought two kilos of dried yak strips, and several strings of dried cheese. Talking with the vendor had the effect of putting my feet firmly back on the lightweight soil of the street. I looked around; I ran my fingers through my hair and dusted myself off.

As they settled into Lhasa life, Da Duk and Moon Light began to take an interest in the local disco, a notorious former truck stop that played bootlegged tapes on Saturday night. Those late hours were reserved for Moon Light and Da Duk. I had unbridled access to the most esoteric traditional chapels in Lhasa; yet the Lhasa disco was the one place strictly banned from my entering.

Evidently, no Westerner had ever been invited to the parties held at the disco. The locale stood as a strictly private, *nangpa* place of reconnaissance between refugee and native Tibetan youth, providing a place for the youth of either sex to meet. I imagined dripping red lights in a smoky, hot atmosphere. Tall young bucks dancing with their arms in the air, white shirts buttoned down, sleeves rolled up; tight jeans with black leather belts covered with carbuncles of shiny chrome studs; hips gyrating; flowing rivulets of sandalwood scented perspiration—it all worked against my image of wholesome Tibetan continence.

Even at the disco in modern Lhasa, girls danced with girls, boys with boys. The time for mingling and flirting was during brief dance breaks. Fights between the glossy expatriates and the non-defecting "true sons" of the land were frequent and bitter. Competition over the Lhasa girls served as catalyst. "Real" Tibetans were those who remained with the Dalai Lama; "genuine" Tibetans were the toughs who chose to stay and stand their ground against the Chinese. The "Tibetan Question," in all its dimensions, has everything to do with who or what is considered authentic.

The Khampa studs grew white with jealously at the verve of Moon Light and Da Duk, with their EuroAmerican muscle shirts and Nike sneakers, their money, their knowledge of Western popular dance and fluent English, the language of mobility. I'm not sure what Moon Light and Da Duk thought of my disappointment at not seeing this part of life in Lhasa. I was too young to park my big SUV outside the high school gym, engine running, waiting patiently to bring the kids back home.

I returned to my little room at the Banok-shol. Outside the window along the courtyard stood a bench. Tenzin sat there, his legs warming in the late afternoon sun. I threw my bag on my bed, and came out to join him. We ordered a thermos of tea. It became an opportunity for Tenzin to practice his English. He relentlessly asked me questions about cars in America, and about skyscrapers in New York. It was engaging, sitting here in our own sunbeam. He was stroking the hair on my arm. "I'm a monkey," I told passing Tibetans, who quickly burst into laughter.

Presently, Moon Light came out of his room, spoke a few words, and ran downstairs to the lobby. A moment later, he sprinted in front of us and back into his room. Then a few minutes later he repeated the action. Da Duk promptly marched out of their room and disappeared down the hall. Irritated, I left Tenzin sitting on the bench and went for a walk, just around the block. But it became another block and then three more—aimless, agitated. I looked back at the Banok-shol from across the street, and felt an odd foreboding. I caught a whiff of something gone dreadfully awry. The anxiety weighed down on me like a merciless sun at noon. At least an hour went by before I returned to the hotel, where I found Da Duk standing on the balcony.

"Moon Light is in our room with a *pummo*," he proclaimed. "I've been evicted!"

"A girl?" I said, choking back my racing heart.

"Yeah. He met her last night at the disco. Guess that's how he's going to spend his money."

"Wha…? You mean he's paying…buying girls?"

"What do you think of your loyal friend now?"

"I don't believe it! Not him."

Chapter 5

Dazed, I gingerly returned to my bench in the sunshine. I sat there a moment, my head spinning. A hundred conflicting emotions arose and fell back. I grew nauseous. I entered my room, and laid on my bed. It was cool. The silk comforter had been changed while I was out. But there was only a thin wall between my room and Moon Light's. I could hear quiet conversation. Then it ceased. I had to get out, back to the bench in the hallway. I wanted to flee the hotel completely, but was somehow attracted to staying. Perhaps a curiosity. Perhaps it simply wasn't true. Focus on something else, I told my bolting mind. Across the courtyard Tenzin and I watched the *inji* take their turns at the shower room. Middle-aged women professors with towels wrapped around their heads were followed by lanky German adolescents; semi-naked Israeli soldiers in khaki shorts stood around talking with young American women in tie-dyed t-shirts as steam rose from the cracks in the windows. Soon, Moon Light's door opened wide, on its own, as if Linda Blair was mentally controlling it. He emerged with a beaming smile, coming directly to me, and smelling vaguely of cheap vegetal cologne. He laughed as he moved a fallen lock of raven black hair across his forehead.

An instant later the woman appeared. He introduced me, but I only caught the first instant of her smile. I could only look down as she greeted me. I stepped back into my room as the couple began to depart, the progression of time unbearably long. First Moon Light stepped slowly out into the veranda, his Nike-clad left foot eventually disappearing from view. Looking out of the doorway of my room, I saw the young woman marching away. She wore a tiny brown silk dress and had a large gold watch on her wrist. She carried a black leather handbag with a wide strap. A peach flowered scarf was tied loosely around her neck that fluttered as she continued to move away, swinging her arms. I heard her tall platform shoes make an arrested, staccato cadence as they retreated down the wooden floors. I saw her vinyl heels, striped like a garish Jell-O dessert. She picked up speed as she retreated further. She rounded the corner, business end first, followed by her legs and shoes. Finally, each stripe of her heels disappeared like an accelerating coral snake diving into a rocky lair. Orange slithering, then red, yellow, purple, lime green—gone! I stepped back into my room, and immediately lit three sticks of incense. I chanted the mantra of Manjusri, sitting down on the bed, my eyes starting to fill with tears. A minute later a beaming Moon Light returned. As he looked into my face, his radiant smile turned to concern, then anguish.

"But she's from a good family," Moon Light nervously rationalized. "Ngari, or someplace like that. I forget the name just exactly. Don't worry, Eric. Her father and mother are good people!"

"Right, it's a great relief that she is from a good family," I said as my rage boiled. How could Moon Light be so stupid as to bring her over here! The nerve, I thought, to even have introduced her to me! Is he that naive, that dense,...uncaring! My eyes burned at Moon Light, but I could not speak. A few days later, Moon Light moved downstairs with his fellow Dharamsala schoolmate Racoon, who had recently moved to Lhasa. Since Moon Light considered me an inviolate Westerner vis-à-vis the Chinese, he still kept his money with me. I stashed it in a saddlebag that a friend had given me, and stowed the bag rather disingeniously under the bed.

On Dogmas and Cataclysms

Sunday mornings had become a special time of solitude for me, following the riotous Saturdays in the big city. All the reveling Tibetans in my own little family lay soundly asleep. With time on my hands, I tended to slip into an idle tourist mode, hanging out with Jens and Pia and my friends of the French suite. I rapidly become a European expatriate, drinking Uzo and smoking Galloises, On this warm Sunday, I planned a great escapade — I would sneak past the army base and climb the Chakpo-ri to visit the ruins of the great Tibetan medical college.

I had to be clever. Thinking I would be invisible to earth-bound sentries, I donned a pair of buff-colored pants and a turquoise polo shirt. Beyond a row of pig pens, there stood a small public access road just to the left of the army base that led to a tiny monastery carved into the side of the 900-foot Chakpo-ri hill in the middle of Lhasa. There were no lamas here, just boy caretakers who hounded the occasional pilgrim or tourist for pens and sweets. The chapel lay deep within the mountain, carved out of the live stone. A tunnel led into solid rock, its floor of granite slippery with centuries of butter offerings. In the rear of the temple, monks had built an altar consisting of a goat's head sculpted of dough. They surrounded the effigy with butter lamps, offering bowls of water and paper flowers, incense, rock sugar, and Chinese coins. I skated around the altar; sliding, I aimed myself at the portal. Outside, I bypassed the road and scrambled over a small gap in the rock cliff, up and onto a small path. Here I met two scrawny dogs, too weak to bite me. I continued my upward ascent of Chakpo-ri, and came upon two ruined houses. Perhaps the smaller had been a storeroom, judging from the abundance of ceramic shards. I also found bits of oxidized copper and iron, like shrapnel. I could now see across much of the Lhasa Valley. Straight down stood the army camp. I saw about 15-20 men in bright green uniforms walking between the blockhouses. I envisioned them shooting at me, and began to slink as I moved among the rocks. Happy to be agile and unchallenged.

The peak of Chakpo-ri still loomed about 300 feet higher, but the path did not seem too steep. Directly beneath the new television tower were the ruins of the medical college. I could see that part of a pavement remained. Surrounding the site of the famous school were concrete and stucco rubble and broken rocks. Pottery shards had been strewn about everywhere. I found dozens of clay *tsa tsa* Buddha images. I walked about the site, collecting a few fragments of exploded shells and pottery. These will go to Professor Bessac, I thought. I scrambled over to the west side of the peak, keeping out of sight to those below. I headed nearly straight down to the road the encircled part of the mountain, a section of the Holy Ling Khor, the outer pilgrim's path around Lhasa. That was it! I got away with tweaking Big Brother Parrot In no time I melted into the throngs of prostrating nomads doing their arduous circumambulations around the Chakpo-ri Hill. I was off across the plain to an ancient willow grove with its own gods and secrets.

The light wind of victory made everything I encountered immensely pleasurable and funny. In fact, I had a premonition to turn my head while walking along the Ling Khor. In that instant a woman's hat blew off her head and rolled down the street, landing underneath a dog who was peeing. Everyone stopped in their tracks and laughed uncontrollably, including the hat's owner and even the dog. A few moments later I walked past my money changer. These were usually young men who hung out around tourist destinations offering to facilitate the exchange of the burdensome government foreign exchange certificates for real *ren-*

Chapter 5

minbei. Instead of his usual chant of "Change money! Change money!" the young man blurted out "Sex! Sex!" I laughed under my breath, then tripped on a rock.

I continued to follow the course of the Kyi Chu River, which formed the southern boundary of the municipality, eventually coming upon a suspension foot bridge festooned with hundreds of prayer flags. Here stood the famous Turquoise Bridge mentioned in Western travel literature of the early twentieth century. The ancient covered span once sported name-sake blue tiles on its roof, but these had been removed and the whole structure replaced with a modern steel cable suspension. It led to a long, wooded island in the river, a picnic ground. Some Tibetans were doing their laundry on the river banks. Some men sat on blankets drinking *chang*. They raised their cups to me as I passed, smiling broadly. I noticed through the willow trees two youngish women stretched out on a blanket. They giggled as they caught my attention, then began to wave. One held up a tea thermos and smiled.

I wandered back into the inner circle of the Barkhor. Through the clouds of juniper incense, I saw a face shining back at me. He smiled, burning through the haze; I looked for an escape.

"Excuse me," he said in clear English. "Don't I know you?"

I recognized the face, but that was all.

"Weren't you in Dharamsala many years ago?" "I remember you as Karma Tashi Dorje," the man said as his eyes grew brighter. "Eric?"

I looked intently on this portly man, with one gold tooth and thinly framed eyes. It was Sonam, the little guy who had been my middleman in the rug business in the late 1970s. He was that scruffy street boy, eager to please, hard-working, not too clever. We walked over to the nearest restaurant and ordered tea.

Now Sonam was a wealthy merchant, he said, with Rs. 40,000 in the bank. I had difficulty believing that the well fed man before me had emerged from so distant a past, in a space of such profound exile, into the immediate hazy sunshine of the Barkhor. Since the rug days, he had been taught handicraft work in Dharamsala and other H.P. towns. He had difficulties: a foot had been amputated, his parents were gone, his brother sick. But he told he how wonderful it was to have a wife, who lived back in Simla, Himachal Pradesh. He managed a whole tribe of "How much?" women, the elaborately ornamented strolling Khampa who sold jewelry directly off their bodies to fascinated Westerners. Most of the merchandise they sold was newly made in Nepal and imported for sale in the tourist markets of Lhasa. The models who paraded the populated paths of the Barkhor wore a disconcerting combination of heirloom jewelry and cheap knock-offs. They teased their customers and each other, and reveled in the good-natured fun of the trade. And it seemed so profitable.

I felt uneasy. I remembered when Sonam lost one of my rugs off the top of a bus in Pathankot when he ran into the station to use the restroom. Upon returning, the rug had vanished. I remembered how he waited months for my payments. I remember the detailed, plaintive letters expressing the anguish of having nothing and willing to run all errands. Kip, with whom I had maintained contact, was all part of it, serving as an unpaid buyer and agent of the fledgling "Central Asian Carpets, Ltd." that had the blessing of the State Oracle and the acknowledgment of the Dalai Lama. This baggage was all bound up in the plump man sharing tea with me. I felt a bit embarrassed; he had become a success despite me. I tried to bury myself in the sunshine streaming through the dusty windows of the Barkhor restaurant. Sonam, on parting, looked into his bag and gave me a wonderful silver ring, with a large red coral set in the center. He followed the next day with a packet of biscuits and cans of Pepsi, all placed in a new leather bag.

My friend Alan finally arrived in Lhasa from Dharamsala. Alan was an attorney from San Diego who had become quite the activist during his tenure in McLeod Ganj. He eventually knew everyone I had met during this extended fieldwork session, thus served well as a foil and sounding board for my myriad problems. He traveled with a Tibeto-Canadian activist, Karma Dorje, a tall man with long, straight black hair. Karma Dorje quickly demonstrated his exceedingly daring nationalistic prowess. He openly carried a day pack with a Tibetan flag sewn onto it. He handed out Dalai Lama photos to everyone who asked. He had carried in hundreds of pamphlets with the Dalai Lama's March 10th speech printed in Tibetan. In short, he quickly found himself in a very privileged position among local Tibetans. Although ethnically Tibetan, he remained a citizen of China-friendly Canada — the worst that could happen to him would be a short detention involving a "self-criticism," or perhaps a ticket home. On the other hand, a local Tibetan caught with such "splittist" propaganda could be executed for treason. Karma seemed hardly Westernized. Rather, he evoked the type of heroic Tibetan male whose open defiance of the Chinese is as much an expression of macho bravura as of patriotism. Many male Tibetans, in the homeland as well as in exile, display their dominance within their group by overtly defying assimilation. The key to Tibetan male prowess seems to be the ability to tweak the noses of the Chinese, much like the American Dakota or Crow Indians did in "counting coups." Indeed, Karma mildly complained that nubile young women threw themselves at him. Ironically, most of them were Western women.

The three of us found ourselves in the square in front of the meat stalls, about two blocks from the Banok-shol. This was the same place where the Khampa traders came to toy with me, the place of their rough house macho and silky strong arms around my chest. Today the Khampas and their "How much?" walking jewelry stores were nowhere to be seen. Instead, black-garbed pilgrims from outlying villages choked the clearing leading to the Barkhor. They were all moving toward the Jokhang Temple in the center of the neighborhood.

"Eric, look at these Tibetans," Karma Dorje intoned, watching the mass of pilgrims file into the narrow streets leading to the Barkhor and the Jokhang beyond. "They are like sheep, and follow any bright and shiny object."

"No, I think you're wrong. They have some pretty strong convictions about who's who," I reflected.

"Yeah, why do you say that?" Alan added.

"When you're desperate, you loose discrimination," Karma followed, " for anything that's not Chinese, at least."

"We should go up to Drepung tomorrow," Alan offered.

"You know Tanya and Greg from Dharamsala are there," I said.

"Wow! They get around. What are they up to?"

"Looking for the incarnation."

"So soon? How are they going to pull that off?" Karma questioned.

"Do you know anything about this, Karma-la?" I asked.

"Maybe we'll know more out at Drepung. Let's go!"

Just at that moment a group of three pilgrims appeared — two old bald women and an old toothless man. Judging from the clothing, they had been on

Chapter 5

the road for several weeks. Their faces were beaming with the pleasure of finally having arrived in the holy city. Karma Dorje reached into his finely crafted leather satchel and pulled out three fresh Dalai Lama photographs. He placed a snapshot in the folded hands of each of the elderly pilgrims. Each face lit up like the first rays of the sun hitting the distant hills. There were some tears, mostly whispers of thanks. Karma-la told them where we were from and that we had all had the fortune of meeting the Dalai Lama in person. One woman grasped her bosom.

Why I chose to wear a yellow shirt and maroon windbreaker on this day is lost to the spirits of the winds. While we still waited to pass through the crowd, I saw a mischievous glimmer in Alan's eye. Then his face crinkled with mirth. Used to the histrionics of the court room, Alan pointed to me in my yellow shirt and maroon jacket, and announced clearly to the pilgrims:

"He's a lama! He's a lama! Lama!"

"What are you doing?!" I shouted.

"Lama, lama, lama, this one, here." Alan continued, raising my arm. The pilgrims immediately turned on me and began to bow, throwing their folded hands above their heads, then to their mouths, then to their hearts. I stared at Alan in utter disbelief. The ghost of Alexandra David-Neel loomed:

> Years before, when we travelled in the northern country and I wore my beautiful lama robes, it was I who was requested to bless the people, blow on the sick to cure them, and prophesy about countless things. I performed a few miracles, chance, the faith and the robust constitution of those who were benefitted making it difficult to abstain from working wonders, and I had some gratifying success as an oracle.[31]

"No, no. *Ma re! Ma re! Nga lama la ma re*," I cried, grasping the pilgrims' hands.

"Alan, you creep! Why do you have to disappoint them? That was so bad," I implored.

"But *I* thought you were a lama, Eric. Just look at you!" he laughed. By now Karma was bent over in laughter. The pilgrims smiled but looked confused. Still, they were immensely happy to gaze at the face of the Dalai Lama. The mendicants slowly moved on to the Barkhor, holding the photos we gave them in front of them.

I now determined that Alan needed a certain amount of indoctrination. I took him directly to the Potala. It seemed that on this day, the Chinese monk supervisors were off duty, leaving monk guides who were exceedingly friendly and open. In the private apartments of the Dalai Lama, the Eastern and Western Sunshine Halls, the guardian monk gave us thumbs-up on the photo badges of the former resident that we were wearing. In one of the chapels in the Red Palace, a dour guard-lama panted "Hurry up! Hurry up!" as we entered the throne room of the 8th and 10th Dalai Lamas. We were both a bit put off by the rough treatment as the monk proceeded to give a very cursory explanation of the room's contents. But as the three other people in the room left, the monk's face brightened, "Take a picture! Take a picture now!" I proceeded to knock off four or five shots of the precious treasures, each photo would have required a "processing fee" of 100 FECs had the Chinese been there. "When Kundun returns, there will be no more parrots," the monk said with a beaming smile, "No more Chinese!" Then he quickly escorted us out of the chapel.

Dong Lin

Pilgrims often walked hundreds of miles to visit the Jokhang Temple in the heart of Lhasa.

Chapter 5

We next stopped at the throne room of the mischievous 6th Dalai Lama, the one who loosened his robes to chase women and carouse on the streets of Shol. Handing the monk attendant a Dalai Lama photo, we asked if we could throw our *khatag* upon the Dalai Lama's throne. Deed done, he immediately replaced our *khatag* with fresh ones, which he placed around our necks. No more parrots. We roamed through Songsen Gompo's chapel, above which hung a huge blue and gold plaque in Chinese, Manchu, and Tibetan, "Blissful Soil Nourishing Miraculous Fruits." We quickly moved down to the main chanting hall, the most spectacular room in the entire palace. The awesome hall was used for the main throne room of the Dalai Lamas, from the Great 5th to the 14th. On the western side stood the thirteen-step dais, behind which hung a mirror and a photograph of the current exiled leader. A path led around the Snow Lion Throne to the tombs, the stupas or *chorten* of the Dalai Lamas. Alan started to wobble as we entered the dark hall. One by one we passed the tombs containing the mummified bodies, each one fashioned from solid gold plates, and covered with turquoise, coral, agate, jade, and diamonds. Directly behind the throne of the Dalai Lamas stood the massive golden *chorten* of the Great 5th, nearly 15 meters high. It seemed to pulsate with energy.

"Can you feel that?" Alan exclaimed, holding his hands in front of his body. "Look at it!" The room was devoid of air; Alan began to stagger. "It's actually hot," he said, hairs bristling, "I can't believe it! I can't take much more of it."

"Wow! It's like a nuclear reactor," I said, feeling the throbbing center of the Potala radiate every cell of my body.

We left that great and holy place, and wandered down to the chapel of Padmasambhava. The monk attending Guru Rinpoche's shrine spoke only Tibetan, so I translated his story to Alan. And then, like before, we ran out into the scalding bright light and down to Shol, past chai shops and t-shirt stands.

It was still early in the morning when Alan, Racoon, and Karma Dorje were finally ready to rent bikes for the trek to the great Drepung Monastery and its neighboring temple, the holy Nechung Gompa. The old man's bike shop in the Banok-shol Hotel seemed a place of great antiquity, like a blacksmith of old Manchuria. Here one could rent one of the sturdy Chinese iron bicycles for almost nothing per day.

We had been "in it" for a couple of weeks now, at a great altitude and out of most of the earth's atmosphere. Lhasa valley is set at nearly 12,000 feet., twice as high and then some as the tip of the great smelter smokestack set upon the windswept plateau of Anaconda, Montana. I still remembered how the stack peered over the ridge of the surrounding mountains as my family drove out of Butte. Here in Tibet, we were all now acclimated enough to pedal a bike, and do so quickly through the Lhasa streets clogged with traffic. This morning wore a blue sky with spring green sprouts turning the beige hills into a soft mat of feathery tendrils. The first rays of the sun shot out across the clear hills, hitting the golden roofs of the Potala as we passed directly in front of it.

The flood plain of the Kyi Chu River through Lhasa being as flat as a billiard table made biking through the countryside a breeze. In no time we had passed through the old gate, past the Chakpo-ri with its military base and radio station, past endless blocks of monotonous Chinese buildings to the edge of town. Here willow trees formed a bower across the road, highlighted with blooming lilac shrubs. It led to a bright white wall and a gate guarded by green, red, and white snow lions. This was the Norbulinka, the summer palace of the Dalai Lamas. The road led on up to the right, following a small canal. Out in the countryside, it was peacefully quiet and perfumed, with little black birds singing. Occasionally we came upon a busy farmhouse with a yak or two, a tractor or an old truck. We sped through the 12 miles to the site of what had been the world's largest monastery.

Finally, we came to a broad, rock-strewn alluvial fan. About 500 feet up from the road and the valley floor were the ruins of the great monastery of Drepung. It showed evidence of substantial reconstruction. To the right of the monastery was a patch of light green and a few white and maroon buildings: the original Nechung Monastery. The sacred juniper grove of the protector deity appeared just behind the *gompa*, in a shallow ravine.

Alan, Karma, and Racoon went ahead. I stayed behind long enough for the quiet of the natural landscape to return. Now, all that could be heard was the flapping of prayer flags in the monastery village. In that instant, I felt a shock wave pass, a sharp pressure. A vectored vortex, an ordered wind, moved at incredible speed from the banks of the Kyi Chu River and disappeared in the sacred grove at the bank of the monastery. I felt a snap, like the crack of a whip, and for an instant in my peripheral vision I saw the leaves of the distant trees shake violently. The grove looked mysterious, in keeping with its oracular reputation. Gnarled junipers of great age grew between massive granite boulders. A small spring emanated from the rocks just above the wood, its crystalline sound providing a melodious background to the profound silence of the sacred place. I wanted to stay in this place forever, melding with the rocks and becoming covered with lichen. I wanted to remain in the warming sunshine and be soothed by the fragrant breezes of the juniper forest. But as I saw my friends pass over a ridge leading to Drepung monastery, I picked up my bike and pedaled furiously to catch up.

We were sadly disappointed at what had become of Drepung. Once holding 10,000 monks, pigeon-holed in several colleges, the monastery was now a ghost town. The two great iron tea vats next to the kitchen had now filled with rain water and algae. Only a handful of monks now kept some of the more important buildings open to the occasional tourist. I saw their laundry drying in the wind just outside of the main chapel. The majority of the buildings were without roofs, merely abandoned shells. I found it hard to envision that this was once the great institution from which the spiritual lineage of the Dalai Lamas arose. Until the end, it remained one of the three royal monasteries of the capital. But then I remembered that nearly two generations of Drepung monks had reestablished a great monastery in Mundgod, India. Here at the original place, scavenging dogs roamed the streets where hundreds of monks once hurried to their studies and to their ancient rites. We quickly left.

We walked our bicycles up the narrow path across the hill slope to Nechung Gompa, and parked them just outside the walls of the complex. A tiny village of three or four households huddled around the eastern side of the modest sized monastery. We entered the gate and walked into a small anteroom. Tanya and Greg met us there and introduced us to a small, middle aged monk known affectionately as Lama Chung Chung (little lama). They first ushered us into the main chapel, where I presented a bolt of yellow silk and red brocade I bought at the Barkhor. Tanya and Greg disappeared into their office. The lama showed us

Chapter 5

what remained of the precious Nechung treasure. A stump of juniper wood stood in one chapel. This was the tree where the oracular spirit, the messenger of the protector King Pehar, Dorje Drakden, flew out of a box being transported along the Kyi Chu River. In the form of a swift red arrow, he shot into the tree in the grove at Nechung. When the Great Fifth Dalai Lama established the Potala Palace in the seventeenth century, he ordered a monastery to be constructed at this spot in the sacred grove. Here would be the official residence of the State Oracle of Tibet who Dorje Drakden spoke through. Many sacred objects had been carted off by the Chinese in the early years of the occupation, but the most valuable had been successfully sent to India with the exodus of Nechung Rinpoche in 1962. Rinpoche brought with him a 1,200 year old vessel in which the deity could reside without the agency of any medium. Also leaving for exile after the People's Uprising was Lobsang Jigme, the late medium of Dorje Drakden.

Lama Chung Chung showed us sparsely decorated halls, leading to a three-storey room. Somehow surviving the Lhasa Uprising and the Cultural Revolution, a twelve-meter statue of Maitrea, the Buddha to come. In front, lay pilgrims had gathered to receive the *tsok*, the remains of the offering to the gods. Red grains of rice and little, dried *tsampa* balls were handed out to the enthusiastic crowd. Karma judiciously handed out a few Dalai Lama pictures. Alan and I had a bag of about 40 or 50 *srung-dud* cords blessed by the Dalai Lama. The mob swarmed us. Old women wept. Bare-headed Khampa men smiled, and touched the cords to the top of their heads. It was a well-animated communion at the lotus feet of the giant Buddha.

Our pockets loaded with holy *tsok*, we left the sanctuary for the rooms of Tanya and Greg. We had tea and exchanged pleasantries. But Tanya and Greg really did not seem to fit into this monastery, the home of their institution. They seemed strangers to the place, just as much the tourist as we were. Yet, despite their overwhelmingly alien appearance, they were very much in charge. I knew their business, but had not shared my knowledge with either Alan, Racoon, nor Karma. It was an awkward time.

Thinking I could provide a light moment to the conversation, I sought out Greg's opinion of the two boys who accompanied me to Tibet. I had always liked Greg for his honesty.

"Those two street rats?" Greg explained. "They are just two little hustlers on the make."

I was immediately taken aback. Sure, Da Duk was a pain in the neck, but even he had a pure heart. As for Moon Light, no one had better say a bad word about my white rabbit.

"But Moon Light's certainly not bad, Greg, he had to get away from his family. They were dragging him down. He's a good boy!" I argued.

"Eric. Can't you see they are taking advantage of you?" Greg continued. "Both of them. They're just no more than street kids trying to cash in on the first reasonable Westerner who pays them any interest. As for that Moon Light guy, he's just a smooth shark."

I was knocked off my feet. I had known Greg for ten years. He stood by me when Rinpoche gave me his profound and subtle teachings. Greg had almost been a confidant, one to whom I could express my fears and doubts easily. He had helped me in so many ways, his reassuring smile, his getting me access to the highest lamas. But this? It seemed that he completely misunderstood my two companions from Dharamsala. How could he say such things about Moon Light? He doesn't understand how or why Moon Light reaches out to me.

I realized that Tanya and Greg had grown distant since our years in Hawai`i. We weren't the young kids that we had been, amazed and entranced by the world of high lamas that was all around us, the swirling maroon and orange colors, the deep chants and the meditations. I felt T & G had failed to grasp the reality of the modern Tibetan world. It wasn't all monks and incense, after all. It was a world of passion and pain, of delight and great beauty, of struggle and victory. And Tanya and Greg were in the middle of it. The Chinese occupation, the radical changes in the everyday lives of Tibetans, surrounded them. How could my friends have such narrow minds?

Fortunately at that moment, Alan, Karma, and Racoon looked anxious to leave Nechung Monastery as well. I glanced at Greg incredulously for one more instant. Lama Chung Chung brought us out to the door where our bicycles were parked. As I put the metal key in the bike lock, a wind kicked up from the West, blowing sand in my eyes. Tears rolled down my cheeks and evaporated immediately in the dry thin air. By now it was getting late in the afternoon, and the shadows of the willows stretched for endless distances towards the city.

In no time we were at the outskirts of Lhasa, stopping in Lhasa Hotel for a yak burger. It looked like a slick Western chain hotel — it was a Holiday Inn, after all. It had the ambiance of a small airport in the Midwest, rather stark, with a lot of glass, but not quite Bauhaus. This premier guest accommodation in Lhasa seemed more like a Georgia O'Keefe painting, with strong blacks and whites muted by an occasional pastel. Management has filled the gift shop with overpriced Chinese cloisonné and vermeil, silk hankies, crude Norbulinka postcards, and Gillette razor blades. The saleswoman was particularly rude. In the cold marble lobby we discovered Da Duk, nicely dressed in a white shirt and black pants.

"Fancy meeting you here!" said Da Duk.

"Wow! What are you doing at Holiday Inn? I mean, do you have a job here?"

"Sort of. I have a small tour coming up, and they wanted to talk to me."

"Like an interview?" I said. " Do you mean with CITS? The Chinese agency?"

"Right. The big time." Da Duk clucked. "The audience is captive. Chinese want to keep the *injis* here for three reasons. One, the transportation is difficult--too embarrassing. Two, the hotel is for Westerners who can't use anything other than Western toilets. And then, it's for Westerners who can't use chopsticks!"

"That's great! You think you can handle this office?" I cautioned.

"Oh, no problem. Just talking and walking."

I actually felt concern for Da Duk, and pleased he was finding some regular employment. He wasn't a bad influence on Moon Light, or anyone else. I wondered if he had been my friend all along. It was nice to see him again after what Greg had said.

"Best of luck, Speedo!" I said, giving Da Duk a big hug.

"La Sooo! You go now and eat yak burger. See you back home."

Alan, Racoon, Karma, and I retrieved our bikes and rode with the setting sun back through Lhasa. Thinking about Da Duk, I began to realize that might be seriously in trouble. Rumor had it that he had faked his CITS identification card.

Chapter 5

And the Public Security Bureau told him that by failing to get an official red visa stamp on his Overseas Chinese passport, he could not leave China. Since discovering the disco, Moon Light had been taking an interest in Da Duk, perhaps even befriending him. Moon Light even worked with him to help arrange our driver friend Lopsang's jeep and minibus for last minute tours. But Da Duk continued his great frustration, losing his temper all the time, drinking too much. He became very sad when the "How much?" girls and the "Change money?" boys approached *him* in the Barkhor. He didn't want to buy cheap souvenirs of Tibet made in Nepal. He wasn't a tourist—he was a Tibetan! As a consequence of this series of affronts to his identity, Da Duk seriously began to rethink his gringo look, the t-shirts, Nike sneakers and baseball hats.

That night I never noticed if Moon Light returned or not. I heard a commotion down the hall at about 2:30 a.m., and assumed it was Da Duk returning. The next morning Alan and I continued our exploration of the city.

The Norbulinka palace at the western side of Lhasa provided a summer home to the Dalai Lama and his court. It seemed easy to visit—just a short bicycle trip down the flood plain and across a small patch of marsh flanked by lilacs. The entire palace complex, perhaps six acres, stood in a state of great disrepair and neglect. The "Jewel Park" of the 14th Dalai Lama is actually quite unique in Tibetan architecture, something different, eminently strange. Here we found buildings with Western porticos and double grand staircases, furnished in Chinese rosewood furniture and tightly woven Tibetan rugs. The frescoed walls of the 14th Dalai Lama's main reception room, the Traktrak Migyur, were painted in the striking photo-realistic style popular in the last days of Tibetan independence. The work at the right side of the throne, perhaps painted by the great state *thangka* painter, Jampa Tseten, showed the center image of the Dalai Lama flanked by foreign emissaries, including the British agent Hugh Richardson. The work was softened by a golden glow, in stark contrast to its overriding hyperrealism.

The palaces of Norbulinka are very small by Western royal standards. The furnishings are stylish 1940s—overstuffed mohair couches and purple arm chairs, floor lamps with shades, and smooth walnut tables that would go nicely in Kate Smith's home. The god-king's bathroom had gleaming white tiles and a porcelain toilet imported from America. Representing some unknown rite of offering, the claw-footed bathtub was filled to the brim with barley, coins, and Chinese currency.

A skeleton crew ran the palace since most of the buildings were closed. Ironically, the zoo, the menagerie of the Dalai Lama, still stood on the north side of the estate. While a few monkeys seemed to be having a good time, a forlorn sun bear paced in his small enclosure. A few deer tiptoed through the willows while peacocks strutted on the lawns. Geese, ducks, and a crane waded in a small pool. One temple to the west of the reception halls seemed a miniature of the great chanting halls of Drepung and Sera monasteries. Despite its size and its condition, I had the feeling that Norbulinka had been a very private place. Perhaps here one also can get a sense of the life of the 14th Dalai Lama when he had the luxury of time and calm. Then he lived as student being prepared to lead an ancient country, a time before the harsh reality of colonization and exile of his people.

Poor Moon Light seemed pooped today, lying in the sun with his contented little smile in the courtyard of the Banok-shol. He's been teaching Tashi English three hours per day. I wonder if he is charging him any money.

Since I kept Moon Light's money with me, presumably away from his roommate Da Duk, I noticed that he was spending significantly more. Moon Light played around so much right now, seemingly disconcerned with the future. Seeing him doze in the early morning sunshine, I devolved into a pique of righteous indignation. If he doesn't straighten up fast, he will be in big trouble. Does he think he can sell his charms forever? As soon as I felt the red heat rising up through my spine, Da Duk came over to me.

"You know, Moon Light shouldn't waste his time on running around and spending money on girls."

"You're right, of course." I said, feeling like Amala and Phala of the Kalimpong Café.

"Victory, first...pleasure later!" Da Duk exclaimed. "We can't waste time. The enemy is in our country. We are here to learn the truth and let the Dalai Lama know."

It seemed ironic to hear such wise words coming from Da Duk, and soothing words for my shattered self-image. Was he really being a friend? Is he still trying to break me away from Moon Light's protection?

Da Duk and I left the Banok-shol and headed for the Barkhor. Thousands of Tibetans were celebrating a great festival for Buddha's birthday. The gigantic incense burners on the eastside of the Jokhang Temple burned like blast furnaces. The bazaar was dense with beggars of all types: from quiet *sutra* readers to extraordinarily aggressive children dripping with snot and encrusted with mud. One Shao-lin type pilgrim made a *khor-la* encirclement of the Jokhang, not by prostrating along the length of his body, but by its width. He carried a large, silver *gau* containing the image of the 14th Dalai Lama, and an even larger silver *vajra*. He slid his calloused, shirtless body forward through the dust of the street, and intoned a *mantra* with a powerful, deep voice. I found Jigme inside the sanctum sanctorum of Tibetan Buddhism, the Jokhang Cathedral.

I first met Jigme in Lhasa at the Snow Lion Hotel, a competitor to the Banok-shol. There he had been hired as an interpreter by a Western physician, a trekkers' doctor who operated out of Kathmandu. I doubt Jigme had the experience of a seasoned tour guide, for like Da Duk and Moon Light, this too had been his first trip to Tibet. Here in Lhasa, with his camera, Western clothes, mannerisms, and fluent use of idiomatic American English, he stood in marked contrast to local Tibetans. Foreigners perceived him as an "authentic" Tibetan back home in Kathmandu, however, enough so to be hired by an *inji* as guide to Tibet. Here in the homeland, however, residents treated him just like another tourist. When Jigme spoke to local residents in flawless Tibetan, they gaped in perplexed amazement.

For Jigme, trying to be a Tibetan in his homeland seemed disheartening. Many times in front of the Jokhang he was besieged by the "How much?" saleswomen selling spurious Tibetan jewelry and gemstones. Jigme, in his embarrassment, told me the women thought him Japanese.

In the Jokhang I found Jigme sitting alone in apparent despondency and frustration as endless queues of homespun-clad Tibetan pilgrims filed past the ancient statue of Jowo, the lodestone of the nation. Glumly, he resumed a close orbit of his Western friends.

I brought him out of there quickly and into the brilliant light of the Barkhor throng. The two of us walked past stalls of gaudy Tibetan-like carpets

Chapter 5

from Nepal and tables covered with brightly colored plastic combs and mirrors, finally stopping at a vendor selling souvenir Tibetan jackets to tourists. Jigme tried on a cheaply made black cotton jacket with a bright blue polyester lining trim—clearly a poor imitation of the beautiful *sheema* wool homespun with it s silk brocade lining worn by middle class men in Tsang. Eventually in the stacks of ready-made, Jigme found a coat that fit. Immediately donning it in front of the mystified saleswoman, Jigme proudly proclaimed, without the slightest conceit or sarcasm, "Now I am a Tibetan!"

We walked back to the tourist hotels, passing many French, American, Danish, and Italian men and even an occasional Western woman clad in the same black jackets with polyester trim. Jigme showed a studied indifference. Should I bring it to his attention? He succeeded in meeting not local expectations, but the expectations driven by tourist modes of authority. It was a reality of Tibet engendered by the Shangri-La of Western popular culture. I could not interfere without destroying his dream. A few days later Jigme returned to Kathmandu, having demonstrated for himself, at least, an idea of what it means to be Tibetan.

The summer sun in Lhasa got stronger and the dusty flies born of the spring moisture had disappeared. I had settled into a very comfortable routine of doing next to nothing but slowly breathing the thin air and watching the window pots burst into color. Here in Tibet, Moon Light and Da Duk were now discovering the world of the affluent traveler. I sensed that soon I would be asked to pimp tourists to him, with the overflow going to Da Duk, Racoon, and even Tenzin. One evening as I was sitting in my little room in the Banok-shol, Moon Light walked into my open door.

"Eric, I want to ask you about this tour job," Moon Light said, rather breathlessly.

"A tour?" I answered with a twinge of sarcasm.

"This American woman. There is this very wealthy American woman who wants to go to Kailash. She will pay anything."

"Mt. Kailash! That's a long ways away, Moon Light. Are you sure you can do it? It's not easy to get to Kailash. Where are you going to get the vehicles?"

"She's extremely grateful to me and very kind. She had bad luck with CITS and no good experience."

"So she's throwing herself on you? I guess it makes sense."

"Eric, Tibetans should be guides in their own land, don't you agree?"

"Sure."

"Not only that, we speak English and are offered great courtesies by other Tibetans. Remember the monks and the servants in the restaurants?"

"Is she by herself?"

"Yes. And she's going to pay me $50 a day above the cost of the transport, food, and driver. She's very wealthy!"

"Do you realize how much money that is? That's more money than Chinese make here in a month. Are you sure you can get all the permissions?"

"No problem, Eric. I have a friend at CITS and he can list my tour on his own record."

"So you're sure you're not working with the Chinese?"

"Not to worry."

"Okay. Well, let me meet her first. I understand these American matrons. I don't want you to get into trouble. She might just be exaggerating. Some of these *injis* are just full of ridiculous dreams."

I thought he really might be on to something. How infinitely better it would be on a tour with Moon Light than some officious CITS parrot who you knew would be reporting back to superiors. He was motivated and indigenous — what a great combination for success. Still, my Moon Light did not express himself as a hearty man, one of those sturdy nomadic lads hardened by daily exposure on the high Chang Thang and used to the bumps and jolts of the rocky roads outside Lhasa. Rather, he affected the form of a thin and spindly hot house flower.

That evening one Moon Light called me from downstairs. An old wealthy lady waited at the front desk, according to Moon Light. She was raising a ruckus with the manager over her bill. Could I come down and reason with her? I had expected to see some dottering dowager with a floor length anorak and pith helmet. As I ran down the stairs following Moon Light, I heard her exasperated comments grow louder. But as I got closer, the screams and shouts turned into laughter. Rounding the corner, Memsahib's stiff tweed collars turned into a floppy braless tie-dyed T-shirt. Here stood Veejay, as she called herself. She had become lost somewhere in the 60s, and never stopped seeing herself as a free-wheeling hippy chick. The vision in front of me had long, thick, coarse greying hair, reminding me clearly of the witch with the loose hairpins in the old Rocky and Bullwinkle cartoon. I saw a cloud of blue eyeshadow around her trail-reddened eyes. Her fingers were stacked with rings of every possible combination of lapis, turquoise, and coral silverwork, and her feet were wrapped in sandals. The manager was smiling at me.

"As I was telling Moon Light here, I figure it will take about 15 days to get to Kailash and back. Do you think he can do it?" Veejay fired off.

"Yeah, sure. Why not?" I looked at Moon Light with a smile.

"I can get the Land Rover, " Moon Light enjoined.

"I can pay $50 a day. In U.S. dollars. Can't seem to get the Chinese or anyone else around here to understand that, at least until I met this polite young man. We've got to move! I've been waiting all my life to do this, and now I'm here. So let's go!"

Moon Light was all teeth, from ear to ear.

"Moon Light won't cook for you or anything like that. And he needs a driver," I negotiated.

"Oh, you two just work out the details," the flower granny belted, "I only have two and a half weeks left on my damned visa."

The back slapping Molly Brown here was certainly going to be a handful for the lithe Mr. Ocean of Moon Light. But he'll do okay, I thought. Jeez, I'm sure going to miss him.

"So it's arranged then? Moon Light inquired.

"Well, you two need to work out the details," I told them. "You'll need some money up front to secure the vehicle and driver. Where will you stay out at Kailash?"

"Oh, I have friends to take care of that. It won't be difficult," Moon Light intoned, conjuring up resources that didn't exist.

Chapter 5

"Hah! Don't worry about that! I can sleep under the stars. Just so we get there and back. It's a pilgrimage, you know, not Club Med!" she cackled.

Fortunately, Alan came by as we were finishing and spirited me off to the hotel a few doors away for a yak burger. Down the street, I could still hear the jingling of Veejay's Nepalese bracelets in the lobby of the Banok-shol. To leave Moon Light with the *inji* woman seemed sad, as I reflected on my own expiring visa. In fortnight, I too would be looking for a bus, jeep, or truck to trundle me away down south and over the mountains into India.

Alan and I sat at the restaurant's long table where only Danish was seemingly spoken. I perched there silently, watching the globules of fat flow from the yak burger patty in front of me, congealing on the cold plate.

"God, this place is smoky," Alan uttered as acrid blue clouds rose behind the metal hut outside the dim window. The waitress and the cook floated silently around the restaurant, like diaphanous cords of fog flowing down steep redwood covered hills. The normally in-your-face Alan was distracted, too, intently watching the European couple in the front cooing at each other. I thought of the old American woman and her new sidekick Moon Light traipsing across the gravelly Chang Thang. I saw her wearing a red lama's hat while riding her sturdy little pony. Leading the reigns was her elegant groom Moon Light, and in the distance stood the snowy Mt. Kailash itself, silhouetted by a glorious yellow sunburst setting behind it. Alan started talking something about postcards—we could make postcards of the sights and market them to tourists.

Moon Light told reception at the Banok Shol that some *injis* didn't like the Reggae music blaring at 1:00 a.m. Other *injis* had been complaining that the hotel provided very little hot water in the shower rooms. Every morning at about 5:00 a.m. one of the hotel sisters would fire up the titanic steam boilers, using huge cords of firewood from Tibet's last remaining forests. In reality there had been plenty of hot water. Moon Light and I made a little English sign stating that you have to let the water run awhile for the full effect. "Hot! Hot! Hot! What do they want?" Aja-la said in exasperation, "To get cooked?"

The next morning developed into a glorious day. At dawn I went to the Jokhang and up onto the roof through the chamber of Palden Lhamo. The sweet child monk I met there seemed very helpful, but wouldn't let me in to the chapel of the wrathful deities. After leaving, I bought dried yak meat and more silk in the Barkhor. Went to the modern art gallery, too. Contemporary paintings of clouds and meditating monks, high pastures, doorways. I was feeling at home in the city. People were starting to recognize me, and even the street hustlers left me alone now. The road to Kailash was blocked today, so Moon Light took a small group out to Shigatse and Gyantse. It will be a four day trip and should bring him over ¥700. Quite a golden boy.

Never once did I worry about Moon Light. The next few days I mused over his accomplishments. He had learned a trade; he did extraordinarily well. Nightly, I saw his huge pile of *reminbei* and FECs under my bed. We originally planned to stay in Lhasa throughout the summer, then return to Dharamsala as the winter approached and the tourists left. The activity in his homeland launched him out of the routine back at Kalimpong Café and into the world of adults, relationships, and decisions. He doesn't need me any more. If he required help, here were all his cousins and Tibetan friends. Jens would be in Lhasa a month or two longer, and so would Alan. Tanya and Greg were semi-permanently located up in Nechung. I can leave now. Yesterday Moon Light took a small group out to Ganden monastery and negotiated guidework for the next seven days. He will make 100 FEC a day. He secured a private vehicle and also gets to see the sites himself in comfort. He bought a brand new suit jacket, and even had an "assistant" now. This was Kelsang, an older Indo-Tibetan. He's new and will take the old *inji-mo* to Kailash and back when the road finally clears. Turns out that Veejay would only pay $200 for the trip, not the fortune Moon Light had anticipated. He appeared very happy in dumping the aging American hippy on the neophyte Kelsang.

It burned well into the summer now. The kindly Lama Yeshe Zopa and 25-30 Western disciples had finally arrived from Kopan Monastery in Kathmandu. They took over most of the eastern part of the hotel, including its large meeting room. The freaks were squeezed out on the western side. Moon Light and Racoon were in the basement. I'm not sure where Da Duk stayed.

I faded from sight in my room with the bright window and oversized bed. Soon, even the hotel manager didn't know me. I am paying six times more to stay here just for being an *inji*. Even competence in the language doesn't seem to help much. I am an object. Under the "money for natives" program, I am ignored. Even my sheets at the hotel haven't been changed for over three weeks. Tourists were leaving. The forlorn bulletin board had a single posting—socks were lost by someone in room 231. By now, grafitti appeared all over the defunct freak cheese factory enterprise. The Chinese police saw their advertising on official government award paper stock, and closed them down. Dr. Zog and his groupies had vanished.

At the Jokhang, a Western nun and monk and their teacher prostrated and chanted in front of the large statue of Padmasambhava while local Tibetans circled the outer perimeter of mani-wheels. The Caucasian monk whispered to Kelsang Rinpoche, "It's good letting them see Westerners practice their religion." On the street I saw one 30ish Western man dressed in a sheepskin in the manner of the Chang Thang nomads. He had shaved his head and was red all over from exposure. His hands and bare feet were filthy and his lips were blistered. He carried a knife and fork hung from a rope belt around his waist. Although looking like a lost Neanderthal, he garnered barely a glance from the locals.

Alan planned to leave later and we all needed exit visas. So Alan and I made the best of it in our little trip down to the Public Security Bureau a few blocks east of the Banok-shol Hotel. The police station was in one of those new courtyard buildings built to vaguely resemble traditional Tibetan buildings. No sooner did we enter the gate that we were shown to a comfortable reception room and invited to sit on overstuffed armchairs. Immediately, a waiter brought tea. Then an officer arrived with one aide. Smiles all around, the officer pulled out a pack of Marlboros and offered Alan and me cigarettes and a light. The low coffee table contained a ridiculously large, 12-stall ashtray, like the ones popular in America in the 1950s. The Public Security Bureau struck me, somewhat incongruously, as a very hospitable place. The officer then asked to see our passports, and those papers known as "Alien Travel Permit." The thin, green clad man opened mine first, and quite suddenly dropped his smile. He stared at my Chinese visa, the one that had allowed three months visit in Tibet. He hit the document with the back of his hand and looked over to his aide in exasperation. They mumbled to each other for a few minutes. Alan and I just kept quiet. The officer finally just shook his head and waved his hand to a clerk in the window. He stood up, grew a forced smile through his red face, and bowed slightly. Then he handed over our passports to the clerk, turned on his heels, and disappeared with his assistant. The clerk handed us each a slip of paper with a great red ink seal—our exit visas. As we walked back down the street, I leaned over to Alan and said, "I don't think they wanted us to stay here three months." We broke into a great laugh.

It was 5:30 a.m. I sat in the lonely bus by myself, waiting for the driver and the rest of the party to arrive. The time had come to leave. It was ironic, but I had managed to get the same driver and bus for the long trip back to the Nepal border. As I was putting my bags in the back, a bright voice shouted from outside. "Eric! Eric! Could you let me in?" Moon Light exclaimed. I opened the door. Moon Light picked up my bags and put them away in the rack. "There. I help you."

He sat down next to me in the cold darkness, and held my hand without saying a word. In the quiet, I offered him a cigarette, the flame briefly lighting the streamlined planes of his face. Smoke rose and spread out in a flattened pall in the silent confinement.

"I'm just going away to renew my visa in Kathmandu, to get some more money wired over. Then I will be back," I promised.

"Don't worry—I'll be okay. My money will be safe now in my room with Racoon."

"Is there anything I can do for you? Anyone to contact?"

"No, I'll be back to Dharamsala after the summer, maybe in October, but you'll be here."

"Can you say goodbye to Racoon and Da Duk, then? Tanya and Greg. I haven't been able to get up to see them."

"Sure. I will!"

Moon Light reached into his jacket and pulled out a pure white *khatag*, and placed it around my neck. I reached over the rack and gave him my saddle bag. I filled it with all the turquoise I had purchased, plus Stephen Bachelor's guidebook to Tibet.

"Here little brother, this is for you."

"Yes. Thank you. I will miss you, Eric-la."

In that instant the bus door burst open. The tranquil smoke clouds were flushed away as the driver and the rest of the passengers clambered aboard. Dawn appeared and Moon Light was gone.

6. Götterdämmerung

> When you come back, come back to stay. I will build a room for you and Moon Light to live in.—Phala

The rolling dawn was mirrored in sleet-soaked sheets of grey as the minibus eased itself out of the hotel courtyard and glided around the boulevards of the new Lhasa. We passed the hulking Nechung and Drepung monasteries cloaked in a rare low-lying fog. Like a biblical prophet, I did not look back. The Tibetan capital receded, secure in its braided river plain. We effortlessly passed the rock-carved Buddha at the western end of the valley. The last night's rain had softened all edges, transforming the hard hyperreality of the crystalline Tibetan landscape into pointillist canvases. Bold streaks sliced down the granite domes in the Kyi Chu canyon, the torrents finally spreading out upon entering the endless tracts of the Yarlung Tsangpo River. Rain droplets on the vehicle's windows bent images into wavy fields of rose, silver, blue, and mint green.

All held quiet on this bus of strangers—their adventures over, their funds depleted. For the first time in nearly a year, I existed without my Tibetan friends. Again our driver was Lopsang, and only he showed any signs of life as he drove from village to village renewing his social contacts with his buddies and his girlfriends. Down across the Tsangpo and up the switchbacks to the weird banks of the turquoise lake Yamdruk Tso, all painted desolation as we drove down and back into the valley for a night's stop at Gyantse. Gone were the apple-cheeked girl and the wizened Momo-la who had attended the small restaurant several months ago. After the front desk staff had gathered up our money, the passengers were stuffed into two small rooms on the second floor. I seemed in danger of becoming an *inji*, I thought.

In the morning we had a few hours to visit the mandala-shaped Palden Chökhang. The sun and a brilliant blue sky had broken through as I wandered through ruins of a tantric *gompa*. The sight of murals depicting creatures with detached eyeballs and flayed skins painted in stark colors brought me to a heightened sense of my own fragility—the message as intended, no doubt.

Back on the bus, we were surprised to discover that Lopsang did not seem in a rush to get to the night stop, the army base at Dingri. He actually welcomed side trips and photo diversions, which we all took full advantage of. At the village of Sakya, about 20 miles off the main highway, we visited the thirteenth century monastery where Phagspa Rinpoche ruled Tibet under the graces of the Golden Horde of Khubilai Khan. The imposing maroon monolithic chanting hall stood tall, nearly all that remained of the elaborate monastic complex that once extended through town, across the stream, and up the side of the hill.

Inside the *gompa*, about 50-60 monks were very busy going about their offices. The monastery had an extensive library, and maintained various throne rooms for the mythical return of the current Sakya Lama from his exile in Seattle, Washington. In the main chanting hall, shelf after shelf of priceless Yuan dynasty ceramics were sitting as casually as in grandma's living room. But the informality was deceptive. Despite several clearly written signs in English, one tourist couple attempted to sneak a picture of the building's interior. The flash immediately attracted an angry monk, who pointed to the sign and demanded the exposed film. When the uncomprehending tourists started to walk away, the monk grabbed the foreigner's camera strap. Amid the shouting, I calmly walked over to another lama and handed him a Dalai Lama picture. Beaming with smiles, he promptly took me to an upstairs gallery and showed me rarely visited parts of the complex, an institution that has probably not changed much since the days of Khubilai himself.

We traveled over the Dingri Plain for hours, seemingly days, watching in silence the beige dust devils rise from the gravel beds and sweep off to the east. In the haze to the south the unmoving Everest massif floated above the moraines of the Ronbok Valley. Mile after mile, the high plains sailed by, peppered here and there by wild black yaks and white pools of slightly carbonated spring water.

As the sun began to set, we arrived at the timeless PLA camp about 60 miles west of Dingri. It was here that Moon Light and Tenzin had played baseball with Jens while Da Duk threw a tantrum in front of Chinese enlisted men. It seemed so long ago. For now, however, we were served a simple meal of cabbage and rice, and herded into a single dormitory room for the night. Unfortunately, Lopsang had taken a fancy to one young American woman in our party. She had been suffering acutely from high altitude malaise, and the driver's amorous overtures were the last thing on her mind.

I can't stand this place!" she finally screamed, "There's no air, no decent food. I can't breathe!" Her flailing about began to annoy several others sharing the cramped room.

"Can you make introduction?" Lopsang said to me, oblivious to the woman's anguish.

"I think you'd better sleep in your bus." I answered quietly. "The *pumo* is not feeling well."

"Does she need a doctor or some medicine? I can ask the army men."

I looked over at her while she kicked her suitcase, "I don't think she needs anything except to sleep. Altitude, you know."

Poor guy looked dejected. He picked up his bag and slowly left the room. By now the woman was sitting on her bed, frantically going through her purse. She never looked up, nor showed any inkling of acknowledgment of Lopsang's ardor. Then I looked into my own bags. I had but a single can of pineapple chunks left in my pack. And I was out of cigarettes! Only a couple of days to go now, and we would be back to the world of plenty down below.

That night the stars came out on an absolutely clear black void. So high is the Dingri plateau that there is no atmospheric distortion—the stars do not twinkle, but shine as steadily as if we were in outer space. The broad stretch of the Milky Way extended from horizon to horizon, Mars glowed a pert red dot hanging above a setting Jupiter. The starlight illuminated the grand Himalayan range to the south, each peak backlit by occasional flashes of lighting from the thunderheads lying *below* the ridge on the opposite side. The electrical pyrotechnics were a reminder of the start of the monsoons in South Asia, of the season of unbearable heat followed by drenching rain, mosquitoes, and disease. Although it was late in June, a heavy frost covered the stratospheric PLA camp in the early morning

Clouds and glacial ice brought forth lively springs of pure water for the wild yaks and me to drink. The tourists on the bus did not care to try it.

Chapter 6

hours. After a fitful sleep, all the *injis*, Lopsang, and myself piled back on the minibus for the last leg of the journey. For the next hour, we slowly climbed to the great, flat continental divide. At 17,500 feet, we stopped to place offerings of cloth, paper, and again hair at the colorful stupa erected to the gods of the wind. Lobsang then put the bus into neutral and cut the engine. We quickly drifted down through Nyalam and into the steep Dud Kosi Gorge, nearing falling two vertical miles in 37 horizontal ones. Finally, at about 1:30 p.m. we coasted into the border town of Zangmu. Lopsang kept his bus on the uppermost switchback of the vertical village. The turns were too sharp for even a minibus.

As the passengers piled out of the vehicle, I quickly said farewell to the ever-horny Lopsang, and grabbed a tall Swiss man I had befriended that instant.

"Gunther," I whispered, "we have to get down to Kodari while there are still enough taxis."

"I'm a good runner," he quipped with a twinkle in his sky blue eyes.

"I had imagined so. This is going to be fun."

Zhangmu, I recalled, hangs over a tremendous gorge at 8,700 feet, the Nepalese town of Kodari at about 5,000 feet immediately below it. These borderlands are cast in a 90-degree world, a densely occupied up-and-down realm a bit like the cliff dwellings of Mesa Verde, or like a set of children's blocks, stacked without any apparent order and vulnerable to the steady pull of gravity. At Zhangmu, we got off the minibus on a terrace that looked down a neighbor's stovepipe. Just beneath that cottage stood an old Chinese auto, and straight down from that parking deck was a munching goat. It looked up at us, its pupils narrowing in the sunlight.

That is about all we could see, as Gunther and I synched our packs tight to our bodies and jumped down the first retaining wall. Boom! We hit the spongy earth in someone's backyard, and quickly ran around a drainage ditch to the front, knocking over a stack of cans. Boom! We crossed the next switchback on the road and stumbled down the curb, jumping about five feet to someone's front yard. Here we quickly ran past a Chinese woman hanging laundry, and bounded over a little barking dog. As we continued down the side of the steep hill, Gunther and I started picking up speed and agility. We flew over fences and careened around bikes and trash bins on our way down the mountain. Our feet rarely touched the ground as we rode on a cushion of air with arms outstretched. Twelve, fifteen terraces went by, and we were still gaining speed. We felt no pain, only exhilaration, as we plummeted towards Kodari at the bottom of the valley. Having lived at high altitude for so long now, we were both supercharged by the sudden intake of rich oxygen here in the valley. Our heart and lungs were far stronger than our muscles — endorphins poured into our systems and overrode all sense of restraint. We were euphoric as we streaked around the west side of the Chinese checkpoint on the road. In the corner of my eye, I saw PLA nightsticks shaking in the air at us, from guards too lazy to chase or shoot us.

Beyond boxes, through restaurants, past trucks lumbering up the switchbacks, over roofs, we slid down the grass and gravel to the camp of the dwarf porters and finally into the woods deeply cut by a raging stream. We sprinted across the Friendship Bridge and out of Tibet to the Kingdom of

Götterdämmerung

Nepal. Gunther and I started to apply the brakes, but still charged past one Nepalese guard sleeping in his shack. A second was out in the customs house garden, urinating. We slowed substantially as we approached a line of six taxis parked on the road. We looked down at the little cloud of dust gathering at out feet as we ground to a full stop. Indeed, we were the first to secure a ride to the capital. As Gunther negotiated a very cheap price for the ride into Kathmandu, I looked back to see our party far up on the Zhangmu hill, gingerly stepping down the steep trail paralleling the winding road.

"Ja. This is good," Gunther laughed. Having secured a taxi, we relaxed and waited for about 20 minutes for the next two Kathmandu-bound travelers to arrive. They were German men, exhausted but happy to find our taxi waiting for them. The four of us then loaded up the car, and sped off down the road.

The air was freshly washed. Gunther and I stretched out in the back of the cab. The young Swiss man took off his boots and red woolen socks and propped his large feet out the window of the speeding vehicle. His strawberry blond hair sparkled in the dappled sunlight as the wind whipped through the car. I could smell the clean cedars and long-needle pines as we passed the hot springs of Tatopani and smoothly rolled down the asphalt road to Kathmandu. I dozed serenely under my woven Thai hat, opening my eyes to catch the gentle flight of a blue butterfly in a field of wild mustard. Fifteen-foot hemp plants wafted in the breezes, and fluffy white clouds specked a faultless blue sky. It was well accomplished.

I feasted my first night back in the tourist mangers of Thamel. Gunther and I headed straight for the Rum Doodle for a grand pizza and beer, and then to the "Bee" Restaurant (so called for the hordes of wasps attracted to the bakery) for a cinnamon bun and tea. My legs were extremely wobbly from the fugue down the mountain, yet I somehow managed to navigate through the narrow streets filled with backpackers and porters. As always, I had ensconced myself in the tattered Blue Diamond Hotel between Thamel and Ratna Park. Since I could barely walk, I sat for hours by the open window and looked out on the city.

A grey early monsoon blanket was smothering Kathmandu, and tourists were leaving as rats on a sinking freighter. The sluggish hot rains had begun, melting the clots of offal and mire in the street. Depressions filled with fetid algae in vacant lots and choking clouds of black smoke belched from overcrowded buses on the swarming streets. A black crow hovered for an instant over a squatting woman in a stone blue sari. Above, I saw the wing tips of Thai Airlines Airbus slice through the heavy clouds for a moment, then disappear again into the saturated mists.

I had already made a futile little trip to Tribhuvan University. I first went over to the Thamel travel agency and picked up Sangay Lama, my miniature Tamang friend. We stuffed ourselves into the tiny thuk-thuk for the winding and bumpy excursion to the south of town. There I was met by a surreptitious secretary at the Research Office who was trying to find an excuse why my research permit was still pending. He slowly leafed through 30-40 thick grey files lying on top of a battered black filing cabinet.

"Sorry. I cannot seem to find your file," said Asok the Clerk, flipping and scanning in vain in his stuffy office.

"Last time you had me go to the American Embassy for a certificate," I argued, "You should at least have that!"

I stared at Asok. Perhaps the dog ate the file, I thought. Does he want a bribe?

Chapter 6

"Hmmm. Let me look over *here*," he said as he looked behind a dusty storage box. He immediately produced another 20-30 thick grey folders.

"Ah, here it is!" Asok said, pleased, as he saw my name on the top file. He looked through the pages, finding them all in order,

"We should be able to have the decision soon. Why don't you come back in two weeks."

All smiles and handshakes, I left that office, knowing full well the permit would never be issued. I went out to the courtyard and found Sangay Lama. As we drove back to town, I had the satisfaction of knowing that I had finished my fieldwork, and then some. I had gone to Tibet and back without the burden of Tribhuvan University's dubious assistance, and felt pleased to have joined the ranks of "unofficial" scholars in this land of byzantine bureaucracy. Documenting modern Tibetans moving back and forth across the Himalayas, I gathered data for a different sort of ethnography from the village-centered studies typical of much of the anthropological enterprise. Was their activity so much different than during the old days of the transcontinental salt, silk, and wool trade? If Tibetan identity had rarely been centered on a fixed "place," where was it located? Was being Tibetan merely a state of mind? If so, were *injis* playing Tibetan a part of Tibetan society? The youth of the diaspora seemed to be using the Western model of Shangri-La to construct their own fantasies of homeland, and were utilizing Western agency and trope to pursue and articulate those ideals.

Sangay and I trundled back through the darkening skies to dinner at the little Tibetan restaurant close to the Blue Diamond. We both ordered *thukpa*, a thick soup with noodles. I sat there looking at Sangay's great golden earring. His short hair and stocky body made him look ever so much like a tiny Mr. Clean. He was disconcertingly staring at me.

I looked into his ardent eyes and sang to myself, "Mr. Clean gets rid of dirt and stains and grease in just a minute…" I really couldn't go on any further. He wouldn't get through my young bodyguards at the Blue Diamond despite my insistence. The boys there were very caste conscious, and Sangay was a porter. It wasn't fair, I rationalized, and it would give him no end of embarrassment. Sangay then invited me over to his hut, I gathered somewhere in the rat-infested old quarter of the city. I declined, but could not make a clean break. Having disappointed myself, I made an awkward adieu to my ageless little Tamang friend and headed out into the gloom of the descending evening.

The strange thing about Tibetan *thukpa* is that it can never fill you up. It's a bit like tea, salty, with the meanest of substance. I was soon hitting the streets of Kathmandu, on the prowl again for food. I remembered the little grocery near Pierre and Lulu's house. Here it stood, next to a pharmacy with which to stock up on antibiotics. I saw a welcoming tin of Danish ham staring at me, white and red lettering over a dark blue litho tin. A small pink ham embellished the label, with a tiny bowl of pineapple to the side. Danish ham, I thought, how much I have missed this rubbery little treat. I quickly purchased the somewhat dusty can, and threw in a box of Indian cookies.

I stopped in to see if Lulu and Pierre were home at Mosquito Manor. They seemed to have adapted well to life as aid administrators in Kathmandu, and were growing fat. We chatted for a few minutes, then Pierre became very serious: "We heard through people coming from Dharamsala that Moon Light's family are anxious to get their son back."

Götterdämmerung

"Doesn't surprise me," I said cynically, having been somewhat taken aback. "They need him to run the restaurant, and won't let him do what he wants. You know, he is 21 already."

"Well," said Pierre, "I'm just passing what I heard."

"He was in great shape, making a lot of money. He'll be okay. Besides, I will be back in about three weeks, then will bring him back in October."

"Oh, I see..." said an unsmiling Lulu.

I stayed only long enough to drink a fast chai in this awkward and morose atmosphere. I said goodbye to Lulu and Pierre, and quickly trotted off to the Blue Diamond Hotel with my precious ham in hand.

It had grown very late now, but that did not stop me from opening the canned ham with my Swiss army knife. I placed the gelatinous cylinder on a plate, and cut it into nine equal slices. I ate two cookies with hot tea, then proceeded to savor each round of ham until the whole was gone. I thought of fruit pastries with red and white flags, of little butter pats embossed with crowns, and rich green split pea soup. The ham might suffice instead. It had a wonderful feeling of richness and caloric soundness. Too long had I sufficed on the meager diet of *tsampa* and salted tea. I drifted off to a sound sleep.

About 2 a.m. I awoke to a ringing in my ears. It was not the clanking of brass and aluminum cooking utensils on the rooftop tap of the neighbors, but a roaring scream that sent my head spinning. I tried to stand up, but stumbled and fell to the floor. Foul humors rushed forth, but were held back by cramping abdominal muscles. My stomach was rigid as wave after wave of nausea set in.

Yak Thukpa

Ingredients

2 1/2 cups wheat flour
3 eggs
1 pound yak meat
1/2 teaspoon salt

Beat eggs lightly and mix it into the flour in a large bowl. Knead it into a small ball of dough, cover it with a damp cloth and allow it to stand for 10 minutes. Again knead it for 5 minutes and sprinkle the top with corn meal. Roll out the dough on a floured board until about 50 cm wide. Fold it into several pleats, allowing about 2.5 cm unfolded. Cut across pleats with a sharp knife, hold the unfolded portion and shake out the noodles. Boil three litres salted water in a large pot. Add sliced yak meat and cook for 15 minutes. Add thukpa noodle dough and cook an additional 5 minutes, making sure the noodles do not stick together. Serve with a little green onion on top if desired.

Chapter 6

The clock slowed. The ham! It must be the ham, I thought. I have food poisoning!

By now the room spun at an alarming rate. I plastered myself against the bed and could not lift my head. Cold sweat beaded on my forehead. The clock slowed even further. I could think of nothing but the fetid ham festering in my stomach. I struggled into the bathroom, and lay on the spinning cold floor tiles for what seemed like hours. Finally, my stomach and intestines began purging, each in turn. I could not stop. Every time I attempted to return to bed, I was greeted by a new round of malaise. As a protection against choking, the mind does not let you fall asleep when you are nauseous. I desperately wanted to sleep, but each time I started to doze, a set of severe cramps would begin. Food no longer in my body, I began to discharge water and mucus. I knew this to be serious, as neither cramps nor feelings of nausea abated. I sat on the toilet, my head between my knees.

Finally, after an eternity of minute tortures, I managed to drag myself across the floor to the bed. There I saw blue and green flashes of light swimming past my eyes. Suddenly a gust of wind broke through the window. A great wrathful deity, a red Mahakala with three heads, each with three eyes, appeared and rushed past me, clanking and spewing fire. It stopped about seven feet away and turned. In its left hand it held a jingling trident, with tiny bells in the shape of skulls. It ominously moved its right arm in a broad sweeping gesture; two sparks flew from its hand. The sparks orbited my head twice before hitting the ground in front of me, growing into a pair of dancing skeletons. Brandishing swords, the *citipati* danced around my withering body. Various other spirits flocked in, troop after troop, some oxen-headed, others antlered with serpent-tongues; manifold-eyed monsters with projecting fangs appeared, their heads crowned with tiaras of human skulls. "Dragon-faced fiends, naked save for tiger-skins about their loins"[32] ran about with eyes filled with blood. In a terrifying moment the skeletons turned on me. Taking razor sharp instruments, the apparitions cut deeply in my skin, and began to strip the flesh from my bones, consuming it. Finally with my consciousness lingering ever-so-slightly, they disarticulated my skeleton and lay the bones in a heap on the hotel room floor. A large yak-headed creature then appeared, and with a great mallet crushed the bones and flesh into a homogenized pink mass. The room disappeared and I perceived myself upon a moon-less desert plain. The Tibetan syllable "ham" appeared, looming above me. In a blinding instant, the matter that had been my body was turned into a fine powder. It caught on the strong winds blowing from the north, and dissipated into a swirling cloud high over the rippling sands.

The night slowly turned into day as I lay in bed, and back to night. On the next morning, I was able to phone downstairs for a pot of tea. Although I would lose 90% of the fluid, it was enough to keep me hydrated, I reasoned. Three more nights passed with little sleep, and four more days went by without so much as looking outside. Finally, I ordered toast, and spent four hours eating the smallest of morsels. I kept that down, at least most of it.

That evening I ordered fried rice from room service. This time I had managed to open the door and sign the check. I don't remember how the tea had gotten in previously. Simple rice, with vegetables, peas and carrots, not a speck of meat—that was it after several days. I revolted at the mere thought of the taste of ham. I thought of Moon Light—about ten days must have passed since I left him in Lhasa. He would probably be now on the Chang Thang visiting the nomad camp with the German man he contracted with. I saw Moon Light laughing and swapping jokes with the *Brogspa* herdsmen right now. Did it seem right that he was so isolated? I shook off that image.

On the fifth day of my ordeal, I felt somewhat better, and met a grad school colleague of mine in the Blue Diamond's restaurant. Judy Weinstein labored well into her fieldwork on women's health issues in Kathmandu, and brimming over to talk about her experiences with someone from home. I wobbled into the restaurant at about 10:30 a.m. She had already arrived. I had told her on the phone about my illness, but nevertheless she seemed shocked by my appearance. Judy was a substantial, dark haired Jewish woman from New York in her early 30s. As I drank my orange juice, she rattled on endlessly about her grants and projects, about village life in the valley, and gossip to take home. Take home? That's right, I had mentioned to her that I had decided to return to Honolulu, to gather up my strength and recharge my batteries. The summer heat bore down, and soon the monsoons would make the continuation of the South Asia foray counterproductive. I would return to Tibet in the fall, maybe in October. Moon Light would be finishing up the tourist season then.

"Yeah, it was either dysentery or a shamanistic initiation," I said.

"Let me book your flight for you. No, it's no problem. I know what dysentery is like. Be sure to take Lomital and your anti-nausea drugs before you get on the plane."

"They're not expecting me back at the university," I said.

Judy sipped her cocoa, "Don't worry, there's plenty to do. Maybe you can start writing up or teach for a semester."

"Still, I have certain responsibilities."

"Well, you could, er, for USIA right here…you know, teach English. The Tibetans will still be here when you get back."

I know she didn't mean to be offensive. Tibetans would still be here when I returned, but not my friends. I handed over my Singapore Airlines ticket to Judy as she got up.

"Okay. Fine, then. I'll take care of it and bring it over tomorrow. I'll call you first thing."

That meeting took all the day's energy. I returned to my room and shivered the night away. I kept my window curtain open, though, and looked out on the middle class apartments and red brick houses of outer Thamel. I watched as each light in every window went dark, and the funky city in the Himalayan foothills grew ghostly quiet. I saw the orange glow of Swayambhu fade to a single red light in the inky blackness. Then that too went out.

A litany of ideas plowed through my mind. Well, it's hot and messy. I'm tired and have just enough money and energy to go home. It's been nice and I have just begun to fly. The falcon taught me to dive quickly, silently, with no notice. It's just in and out with the kill.

In the morning, Judy brought the ticket over as promised. The next day I corked up both ends with heavy prescription drugs, got on the plane, and left South Asia. I do not remember the 18-hour stopover in Singapore, when I left the aircraft, where I stayed, what I ate — nothing at all, except the eerie blue glow of St. Elmo's fire on the wings of the 757 as we plunged through endless monsoonal storms.

Chapter 6

I arrived at customs at Honolulu International a walking skeleton, and completely unprepared, disheveled, and disoriented. The blast of scented, warm tropical air hit me like a plunge into a steam room, making me wilt even more. I passed the drug-sniffing dogs, the fresh meat-sniffing dogs, and even the fresh fruit-sniffing dogs with flying colors. "Where are you going?" the customs agent asked politely. I really had no idea. I had given up my apartment; I didn't know where my friends were, and all would be working at this hour, anyway. To my surprise, he let me through.

The only thing I clearly figured out was that I should report to the university. It had, after all, a nice quiet lounge to sleep in if need be. So, I gathered up my luggage and secured a dollar in coins for the bus. I had less than $53 on my person. Somehow, through dozing and snoring, jolting and lurching, I managed to make my transfer to the university bus downtown, and I eventually arrived in Manoa. Like a trained pigeon, I made a straight shot for Porteus Hall, third floor and found Ethyl, the department secretary.

Ethyl was an elderly Japanese American woman, and a chain smoker. She had a soft spot for struggling students, especially those returning from the "grand initiation" of anthropological fieldwork. Ethyl took one look at me, put her cigarette down, and opened a drawer in her desk.

"Here." She handed me a key, "Why don't you put your stuff in Room 345. There are three students in there now, but two are never there. So they lose it! Hah!"

"I look that bad, huh?"

"Eric. Look at you. Look how much weight you have lost!"

"Yeah, I sort of got sick. Had to come back to recharge."

"Do you have enough data to start writing up?"

"I'm not sure yet. Maybe. Maybe I will start working on it and see what else is needed."

Enough data? The thought of staying hadn't entered my mind, but Ethyl might be on to something. After all, the office looked welcoming. Everyone spoke English, the weather was pleasant, and my data was here.

I threw my bags in the simple, windowless office, and called my former housemate, Fishhead, who had taken over the lease when I left. He said I could spend the night. After another long city bus ride, I arrived to a wooden floor and a blanket. It was cold that night, but I hardly noticed. I fell into a deep sleep, and work up the next day to roommates having breakfast around me. Fishhead made it fairly clear that he was not about to give up the lease. In fact, this house had never been on the rental market. It passed from the owners to tenants and succeeding renters from friend to friend for years. It was clear that I was out of the system.

I called Maui. Sure, Kalani and his girlfriend would be happy to have me visit for a couple of weeks. Great, a place to rest with beautiful flowers and deep quiet. Kalani was a professional chef, so I might be able to get my appetite back.

It was a brilliant blustery day when I took the Number 19 bus to the airport and flew to Maui. The Hawaiian Air flight took just 25 minutes, fully stocked with bumps and great downdrafts off the slopes of the Haleakala volcano.

I was well taken care of in Maui. Kalani the Chef made every meal with thought and care, to please the most assaulted palate. Good wines, roses form the ample garden, soft trade winds—but all had changed. Friends' faces had distorted;

relationships had moved on. I was acutely out-of-phase. My mind, my soul still resided high up on the plateau. My thoughts were frequently with Moon Light, hovering like a nimbus around an angelic head. Still, there seemed no way to fly this emaciated body back to Asia, no resources for another round of battling the menacing demons affecting Moon Light's life of discovery.

On the seventh day of my recuperation in Maui the phone rang. I wouldn't have answered it, but Kalani and his girlfriend were both at work. I put down one of Jacques Pepin's cookbooks that I had been reading. It was Penny Moblo in Honolulu, a fellow grad student. She needed a housemate. The old one had apparently stormed off, leaving a cloud of bills. Would I be interested in moving in?

I guess I had no choice. Before I left Honolulu for Maui, I had dropped off an application for the single, hotly contested teaching assistantship at the Department of Anthropology. There had been fierce competition, with only 8 slots for 24 grad students. Perhaps I should accept Penny's offer. If my T.A.-ship cames in, it would be a nice source of income for the meantime; on the other hand, it would essentially commit me to staying in Hawai`i and beginning to write up my dissertation. Indeed, I had already been asked by both Chaminade University and the University of Hawai`i's Continuing Education program to resume my part-time teaching duties.

Yes, I told Penny. I would move into that rickety old house up on Sunset Drive, high above the university. After three more days of endless servings of *tarte au pomme* and truffled squab, I said goodbye to my Maui hosts and moved right into a tiny bedroom in the termite-eaten cottage. Such a deep sleep.

For the next few weeks I had the unnerving feeling of watching a video of my own existence. Peering out of my eyes, I saw the world in grotesque distortions. Familiar faces were odd and elongated, the colors were off. Food tasted too salty, and the excess sugar in everything made my energies peak and crash throughout the day. But finally I began to gain some weight. I began to read, and I began to write. On August 10, I heard the superb news from the department chair that I had received a teaching assistantship for the coming academic year. And I would be teaching one freshman extension class that fall. I could be set to finish the program. Well, finish if I had enough data. I think I do have enough, enough to at least get started. Should I try...? It was enough, I rationalized. It was enough.

I began to settle into a bit of a routine of going into the office and arranging my notes. At lunch I would be sure to get a chocolate shake from the student union. It all became a comfortable retreat. I stood free to dive deeply, exploring concepts and theories, and meshing them with my data.

Providence rendered a perfectly still day. The oxygen hung in the trees like great puffs of sweet vanilla. I looked out on the lawns of the university campus from my snug office on the third floor. With my promotion to T.A. from a mere grad student, I received a window and a phone! Ethyl even let me smoke in the tiny shared office, simply because she hated my officemate. Summer had set in, and I could watch the boys throw frisbees across the quad. Then I would sit down at my desk. Fred, my advisor, came in and said, "Just write. Start to write." I started in the middle—chapter 6. I started and continued. I did not stop for at least four hours that late afternoon. I printed out my material and put the initial work on my desk—there! It was happening, the years of life in the

Chapter 6

Himalayas were being put into a frame, and abstracted from the quickly turning days of the present. I felt a swelling of pleasant humors, which flowed through me like a headlight along a dark trail. I became grounded to the resumption of student life in Honolulu. The mental winds were passing quickly.

The carillon struck nine as I headed out of Porteus Hall and down the upper campus to the city. I went grocery shopping for the first time since returning from Asia. In the beans, rice, and pasta aisle I carefully examined the display of Chef Boyardee Beefaroni cans, now on sale for 89¢ each. I filled my cart with all sorts of American delights—chocolate, potato chips, strawberry ice cream, pickled herring, brown sugar, Campbell's Golden Mushroom soup, Froot Loops, and a giant can of Hills Bros coffee.

I walked back to my little cottage on Dole Street. (Penny got evicted a week ago when the toilet fell through the termite-ravaged floor boards, and she spoke out to the landlord). I brushed my new roommate's four Siamese cats off the kitchen table and counted my innumerable blessings. It was done! It was finished! I had managed to get into Tibet to do my fieldwork and get enough data to start writing. I left my little brother Moon Light in a happy state, well employed and well-fed in Lhasa. Even Da Duk worked at a real job. Tourism was bringing unprecedented wealth to the country. Would economic success in the homeland end the Tibetan diaspora? But how would I know if matters were stable? Communications were difficult. Neither Moon Light nor Da Duk would risk their somewhat precarious positions by writing to me directly. And what would motivate the boys to go through the effort of calling me from the central telephone exchange? No, I would have to get by without any direct knowledge until I managed to get back to Tibet.

I envisioned, therefore, a world where Moon Light was steadily growing more wealthy and wiser with experience. People were listening to him; his command of English constituted a tremendous asset in a developing Tibet. The reformers back in Beijing couldn't be more delighted at Tibetans such as Moon Light. Could this cadre of young returnees break the impasse that had existed for so many years between the Dalai Lama and the PRC officials? I contemplated a Tibet liberated through tourism. The naive Westerner would be in a position to peel back the accretions of historical dissonance that had built up over the generations. Once the outside world saw the truth there can be no turning back. I snuggled into the white sheets of my tidy bed in my mango-shaded cottage, six blocks from the anthropology office, dreaming of the empires of the future.

In late August I saw a pale blue Indian aerogramme in my box in the student lounge. It had been sent from the Kalimpong Café in Dharamsala. It was not from Moon Light, but his Amala. I slowly walked back to my office and sat down at the desk:

> Astonished to learn about Moon Light's not being with you and it was indeed sad too. He's the only property of our house and you know well, he's the inside and outside for us. Since the day he parted from us there's been a downfall in our small Café, e.g., Amala is the only one who'll have to cook, to be waiter and cashier and what not. So you can imagine what condition our family is in—four children are enrolled in school. So please do let us know about Moon Light.

Götterdämmerung

> Yes, the day he got the letter from you he never sat a minute and was always engaged in making passports and all. And I was told that Eric was responsible for his condition. Maybe he'll take Moon Light to USA and help his poorer brothers and sisters. So, we trust you and let our child go but today, when we heard from you, very much upset to know because we didn't expect you in such way. Now where is he?

The tiny Sherpa woman who wrote the letter, once supported her family of six small children and a husband by cooking and selling food on the sidewalk at the McLeod Ganj bus stop. I couldn't see how the family had come to be so dependent on Moon Light. The pressures on him not to leave, for Tibet, USA, whatever, were enormous. My mouth became dry. I walked down to Ethyl's office and poured myself a coffee in one of her little styrofoam cups. My heart pounded, and I trembled as I returned to the letter:

> Moon Light is in a bad condition, so please do search for him and let us know.
>
> Actually, it is very natural that you should ask his parents first and then start, but you haven't. Anyhow, never ever commit such mistakes in future or never snap the ties between parents and their only child. Before, we are very relieved for we got a letter from Moon Light in the month of June and today, your letter makes us feel sorrow, sadness. You know, Moon Light, he sacrifices all his relations and even his poor parents for your sake so, we think it is your responsibility for our missing child.
>
> A mother can't stand her child apart from her sight. So you know well, he's a girlish type of nature and listens to other's words within no time. Eric, which is the place you parted from Moon Light, 'till where he is with you? Leaving aside our decrease in the Café, we are scared to know where he is and in what condition. He may not be getting full nourishment. Yes, I've gone too far in making you feel rage. If so, then I apologize for my mistake. That's all for now. Love from our family, Amala

I hadn't encountered such rancor from a parent since 20 year-old Eric took 18 year-old Debbie camping in Glacier National Park during a rainstorm. Now, I was angry. It seemed to be just the words of a hysterical, over-protective mother. I pretended not to understand. Moon Light would return when he wanted to. He had achieved 21 now, an age of emancipation for Americans. He made more money in a day than his whole family made in a week. Moreover, he was largely his own boss. He didn't need me, that's for sure. But over the next few days, the letter nagged at me. The guilty foreigner. The heartless *inji*.

The hot months of the Hawaiian summer were elongating towards the rainy fall. Classes had started and the gentle hum of the academic routine had set in. It was a tremendous relief to see that I could function after all, that I could teach and write. But always upon returning to my little bedroom in the shaded cottage, I stepped into a darkened void of measureless amplitude. Save the 60-70 lbs of cats and a passively hostile roommate, there appeared to be nothing at all here. The mango cottage bore zero resemblance to a home, someplace to dig my feet into.

I wrote a long letter to Amala to tell her she had little to worry about. Three weeks later another blue aerogramme appeared in my box. At first I

Chapter 6

thought that Moon Light had managed to get a letter out of Tibet. But instead, it was another letter from his mother:

> Hallow Eric-lak. Before I add nothing special let me say an unpeteenth sorry for making you unhappy. Actually I have no earthly right to blame you as you know and mentioned 'he is grown up'. Anyhow, he made with a word of leaving to America, so I thought, one of our children should be there, but today I found his words were untrue so once again I feel sorry about it. I was very much glad to learn about your feelings and the words 'your eldest son' still reckons in my heart. Really! There's no bound for my joy on account of hearing the words. Can't imagine how lucky am I to be a mother of seven children including you as eldest.

Her letter reminded me of an old crank ranting at the television set. I disassociated from the message. Missing was the living presence of Moon Light. Amala and I were going on and on, round and round about her son, and neither of us had the slightest idea what he really did these days in Tibet. If he had cared so much, wouldn't he have at least written his mother? So I have become the eldest son to replace him?

Amala's letter continued:

> Eric, in my previous letter I mentioned the ups and downs of our family but never be so serious about it for I have managed two labourers from Orrisa. Moreover, I'm able to save some amount to pay the school fee and have no financial problems except missing our child. Knowing well that Moon Light and Phala were the main actors of this play, so lacking of the main actors really it is very hard for heroine to complete such play. I mean Phala is quite recovered but couldn't lend his hand to help me for doctor ordered him to take a rest for more than a year. So you must imagine. At Lhasa Moon Light can collect some work through teaching or tours and fill up his belly as insects can. But it seems unfair from us to let our child go to Tibet at this moment due to the absences of H.H. the Dalai Lama. Sooner or later we must go on getting our freedom, but not before that. You'll see what our government will say! So please do address him as you being the eldest son and hope he'll not turn down your words.

Amala ended her letter with humility and an apology for previously sending me that blockbuster:

> Recently we received a chit from Moon Light along with few snaps and were glad to know about his well being. In my former letter I've written some hurting words for you—actually I have no intention to do so. Really, I've become somewhat cracked. So again I feel very sorry! To end up, first try to know me really as there's no difference with your Amala to an animal except for one's food. With love from our family, especially from Amala.

It was a relief that Moon Light had finally sent a letter fromTibet. He probably had it passed from hand to hand and out of the country to S.E. Asia, to India, all the way to Dharamsala. Of course he would be okay. He was a man, not a boy now, that much seemed clear. He's doing the right thing taking on responsibility for himself. He was liberating himself. I felt very proud of him.

Götterdämmerung

On September 23, I arrived at my office at about 6:45 a.m. and began to type. Emerging from a cloud of smoke and coffee rings about 10 a.m., I taught my first class of the day with Dr. Dewey. At 2 p.m. I went down to get the afternoon paper. On the front page appeared a story that the Dalai Lama had presented a major peace initiative to China through his address to the U.S. Congress. "Five-Point Plan for Peace," the headline proclaimed. Congressman Lantos from California and many others were already acting vigorously in its support.

The Chinese embassy in Washington was incensed. I sat up late that night scanning the news channels for the latest news of this possible breakthrough. Imagine Tibet turned into a "Zone of Peace"! The Dalai Lama's idea, an amended version of his famous Strasbourg proposal, seemed reasonable and considerate to the Chinese. This is something Beijing could tolerate, I thought. Everyone could come back. Tourism would continue to flourish; monasteries would be rebuilt. I dreamt of yellow flags waving in the dark blue sky, like Heinrich Harrer's golden locks in the windy sunshine of the Chang Thang. Moon Light would be out riding his pony, and I would sit snuggly next to the charcoal brasier writing my next book.

The very next day the Chinese Central Government issued a strident denouncement of the Tibetan leader. Harsh and abusive, it did nothing but arouse Western sympathies for the Tibetan cause. China shot back insisting that the Dalai Lama worked in collaboration with "foreign anti-China forces determined to split the Motherland." Worse, they began to use the most insulting language to discredit the Dalai Lama. Not only was he a traitor, they alleged, His Holiness conspired to revive feudalism for his own benefit. His very existence toiled against the interests of the Tibetan masses, they claimed. I thought it outrageous—the Chinese were becoming laughingstocks of the world.

I was convinced that, over the long haul, the Chinese could not get away with their propaganda campaign. There were too many tourists in Lhasa should the Chinese try to do anything overtly. Only by slowly removing the foreigners while increasing surveillance on native Tibetans could the Chinese have a chance of succeeding. The volatile situation on the familiar streets of Lhasa, which I had so recently left, would have easily supported a "tourist revolt" if China did not come to reason. The senile old men in Beijing seemed to have missed the point— the Dalai Lama was strongly revered in the country and increasingly around the world. The simple reality of the 1950s lacked the instantaneous communications of today, especially in such isolated regions as Tibet. Nowadays, the Chinese simply couldn't get away with an operation similar to their backyard invasion of 1951.

The Dalai Lama addressed Congress. I thought back not less than ten years ago when he had substantial difficulty even getting a visa to visit the U.S. on purely religious matters. I remember writing my senator, and getting a supportive reply from Sen. Daniel Inouye saying that he would look into the matter at the State Department. I had also written my representative, but she ignored my letter.

Across the Pacific and beyond the deep interior of China, monks from Drepung Monastery in Lhasa were upset at the Chinese induced slander of His Holiness. The words of 19-year old Jampel Tsering:

> We wanted to tell the world community that the Chinese propaganda was wrong, that the Dalai Lama was right, and that Tibetans were not happy inside Tibet.

Chapter 6

> So we decided to demonstrate. We had precise aims and reasons to do so. After a long discussion, my friend Ngawang Phulchung; my brother, Ngawang Delek and I made the initial decision to carry out a peaceful demonstration. We then went about round up participants...we were twenty-one people.
>
> If we were arrested, we felt that it would be very embarrassing if they asked us our reasons for taking part in the demonstration and we didn't have anything to say. So we had discussions on what to say, so we could be ready with the reasons. We decided that the points we should keep in mind were the historical facts about Tibet being independent from China, and that we were denied basic freedoms such as the right to religious freedom...We explained to each other how we would tell the Chinese that their restriction on the admission of monks and nuns into monasteries and nunneries in fact violated their own statements concerning religious freedom. The final point was that the Chinese government intentionally discriminates against the Tibetans, that we are treated differently than they treat other Chinese.[33]

Saturday morning I drove my moped down to Ala Moana Center and picked up the *New York Times* and a few other papers. The Dalai Lama was being lionized by the Western press for speaking on the transformation of Tibet into a Zone of Peace. I closed my eyes and saw a flurry of Dalai Lama pixs tumbling across the void before the Jokhang Temple. Pilgrims snatched them out of the air and held them tightly to their breast. I saw happy smiles and twinkling eyes.

On early Sunday morning, September 27, twenty monks boarded tractors at Drepung and left for the center of Lhasa. At ten o'clock the clerics began a demonstration, holding three homemade Tibetan national flags and circling the Jokhang. Hundreds of Tibetans gathered and watched as the monks headed for the TAR government offices. Suddenly, as they approached the gates of the office, scores of police descended on them. Bound with ropes, they were beaten, and all taken to Gutsa Prison, one of many in the Lhasa Valley. A great hush fell on the crowd.

The news arrived on CNN. Mike Chinoy reported the incident late Sunday afternoon, Hawaiian time. I was eating dinner. The sound on the t.v. was off, but I knew immediately what it meant. They showed a map of China, highlighting a red Tibet Autonomous Region. A tapering black arrow pointed to Lhasa. China will kill them all, I thought. I felt myself falling off a cliff. What was I doing here in the shaded tropics? What was I doing sitting on this soft brown velour couch, constantly pushing away overfed Siamese cats kneading my stomach? Why did I sit here in Honolulu trying to encapsulate the nationalistic struggle of Tibetans into a dissertation while this reality unfolded? I plummeted, all the blood flowing out of my head. I stared at the phone...Moon Light! Oh my God! He's in great danger.

I stood up and paced back and forth. The phone had a nimbus around it. Who could I call? Moon Light has no phone number. Besides, I'm sure the Chinese have cut the lines to Tibet. My heart raced in panic. The cats hid under the bed. My fat roommate asked me what was wrong as he ate pork buns. I didn't respond.

Götterdämmerung

All I could think of doing was to head for the mountains behind the university. Climbing Punch Bowl crater, I looked out over the sprawling city of Honolulu, the isolated metropolis in the center of thousands of miles of inhospitable blue ocean. I soundly reprimanded myself, a soul-less hungry ghost seeking shelter and the warm comforts of the student life. My bank account could stand the strain of returning to Lhasa now, even if I somehow managed the unlikely occasion of securing a visa. Guilt overwhelmed me, I felt myself shrinking, my body feeling as disgusting as a wriggling maggot suddenly exposed to the brightness of the open air. I went back to my office and wrote a letter for assistance to Amnesty International. I wrote another letter to the Red Cross. I felt a great vacuum, a void. No air, no illuminating visions of Moon Light going about his business in Lhasa. It all stopped suddenly. It became worse, very bad, very quickly:

Wednesday, October 1 – Chinese National Day. From what I could gather from news sources, a protesting crowd had gathered before the Jokhang Temple on this important Chinese holiday. Several hundred everyday Tibetans were joined by monks for the Jokhang, including the outspoken monk, Jampa Tenzin. No one organized the demonstration. The point of defiance was the occasion of the Chinese National Day, which few local countrymen and women wished to celebrate. The protest escalated quickly. Twenty to thirty monks from Sera Monastery joined in the chanting for independence in the square in front of the Jokhang. Still the swirling masses increased. The crowd headed down the street to the Public Security Bureau, chanting that Tibet was free, and that the Dalai Lama stood as their leader. It seemed too much for the skittish Chinese police; they attacked the Sera monks. Pouring out of the police station, they publicly beat the monks with whatever was on hand – belts, pistol butts, and shovels. Great hordes of green cotton-clad police flowed into the middle of the rally, and carried bleeding, bound monks back into the station.

The mass of people really began to grow then, as hundreds of everyday Tibetans left their houses and shops to show solidarity with the imprisoned Sera monks. They demanded the immediate release of the young clerics. Someone threw a rock at the Public Security building. Then another, and another. The police motorcycle and handcar parked outside was overturned, then set on fire. Soon, the entire police station started to smoulder. Shots rang out from broken windows on the second floor – people fell, children fell. Burning furniture was being thrown out of the windows onto the street. From the photographs that the American Steve Lehman took and were being flashed across the world, I could see a charred coffee table and what looked like a large 1950s ashtray sitting outside the shattered ground floor window.[34]

Soon, the burning station was abandoned by the police. Jokhang monk Jampa Tenzin and others ran into the conflagration to rescue the monks left inside. He was severely burned. All the newspapers and news broadcasts featured the Uprising. It would be among the largest in Tibetan history. Ten people died, and over 40 others were wounded. More photos were published by American Blake Kerr and his friend John Ackerly. News anchors stood in front of their cameras, wringing their hands. Moderate protests were issued from governments around the world, "We deplore the actions..."

Deplore the actions! I faced a gaping crater. Everything that I had witnessed and participated in the last year suddenly vanished. Like slamming a door on a rising souffle, the trepid, delicate attempts at restoration of Tibetan con-

Chapter 6

sciousness in the homeland had fallen. This seemed not just the end of tourism to the top of the world, but of all the gain and hopes over a generation and a half. Moon Light, Da Duk, Tenzin, and all the others would lose their jobs and be swept away into the morass. Who could tell me now? What has happened to Angela, Karma Dorje Gyatsen, Tanya and Greg Retro and their attempts to find the baby Nechung Rinpoche? What about the old Amalas who told me about the life of Sera Monastery in the grand old days? At school, my friends and professors sadly shook their heads. In a few days, the news reports faded from the screen. I continued to stare.

I must have been in shock. I remember nothing more than waking up on the brown velour couch, the soft yellow green tropical sunshine filtering through the mango tree. It was 76 degrees, cool for Honolulu. The cats still slept in the roommate's bedroom. A calm chirping from the crickets was all I could hear, except for the white noise from the nearby H-1 highway. It must have been morning, maybe evening. Still here? I thought. The room no longer seemed familiar. I looked up at a cheap replica of King Tutankhamon's funerary mask (Franklin Mint™). What was I doing here? Was it Monday morning or Saturday? I didn't know. I looked at the pen on the table. I could write... who would I write? I stared at the phone. It didn't ring.

Eventually I got up, dressed, and walked briskly down McCully Street to Waikiki Beach. I stared out at the sea with its gentle waves. I looked up and watched the fluffy clouds sail along on the trade winds. I watched an endless procession of 747s head to the Mainland. I examined the bleached skeletons of old coral heads wash back and forth in the surf. The tide slipped out. I lost myself with the retreating surf until the sun had set in a dull green flash.

On the way back home, I drove past Nechung Rinpoche's old house, now occupied by students. They stood out on the driveway washing their car. Then I slowly drove past Lama Rinchen's center, prayer flags and all. Someone else was burning Tibetan incense.

Despondent, somehow I got the strength to return to the university early the next morning. Now it was certain I had to finish my project. It seemed easy. I couldn't write a classical ethnography — rather I documented a finite epoch in time, a history. In a few weeks I received letters from Amnesty International and the Red Cross. They both indicated, albeit with empathy, that there were too many individual problems around the world to attempt to deal with each case. They would monitor the situation, however, etc., etc.

Open Tibet had always been an oxymoron, and now it was finished. Was I among the last outsiders to witness the final closing of the door? I went back to writing its history with a greater intensity than I had ever experienced. It seemed important to get this material published as soon as possible, to help spread the message about the cyclical horrors of the occupation. Therefore, as I finished each chapter, I quickly edited and sent them out as individual articles for the academic and popular press. It kept me very occupied.

In the tropics, there is little change of length of day from summer to winter. In Hawai`i, the temperature cools slightly, and substantial rain begins to fall. I kept a minimalist lifestyle — the four walls of my office, the late night returns to the termite-eaten cottage inhabited by the wormy cats and the grumpy Pillsbury Doughboy roommate. I thought of Moon Light in his spotless white turtle-neck. I dreaded what the Chinese would do to his flawlessly symmetrical face in prison.

Götterdämmerung

During these wet months, I sent letters to Lulu and Pierre, Judy Weinstein, and Thinley in Kathmandu, asking them to let me know immediately if they hear of anything from Moon Light. I wrote to Tanya and Greg who were now back in Dharamsala.

Ackerly and Kerr published their photos everywhere, and even testified in Congress. Still, deadly silence screamed in Tibet. I lay surrounded by a darkness so deep that even the bright tropical pastels and the balmly mists of Hawai`i could not lighten my soul. I continued to write, everyday, 14, even 15 hours until my eyes could no longer focus and endless cups of coffee had soured my stomach.

Christmas passed and the year changed with barely a flicker. Finally, on January 15, I received a short letter from Thinley, the Kathmandu carpet maker. Moon Light had been found! He was staying out at Bodhanath, just to east of Kathmandu. Thinley didn't let on how Moon Light escaped from Tibet. Thinley wrote, however, that Moon Light seemed in critical need of money. Alarmingly, he said that Moon Light had taken to hanging out with Western girls in Thamel in order to make money. I didn't know exactly what that meant; my mind raced. Was he charming money directly from their purses, or doing a pole dance in some dingy Kathmandu disco? The keepers of the pure flame in Dharamsala are not going to take to kindly to this. His mother is really going to kill me.

Now it was clearly my responsibility to take it from here. Remembering that Thinley still owed me $100 from when I lent him some capital to expand his fledgling carpet business. I dashed back a letter:

> Please go find Moon Light. When you see him, please give him the US $100 that I had lent you. In dollars if possible.

The funds wouldn't go too far, but it might keep him out of trouble and back across India to Himachal Pradesh.

Another extensive period of silence followed Thinley's letter. Alan had long ago returned to San Diego, beginning a voluminous correspondence with me that culminated in a co-authored article on Dalai Lama photograph exchanges in Tibet. Angela had returned to the East Coast. She too had published an article on the role of tourism in Tibet during the experimental year of relative freedom and openness. Her experience had been harrowing. In Shigatse, she had been caught possessing several copies of the Dalai Lama's March 10 speech. The Chinese arrested and detained her at the local Public Security Bureau. When the police found out she was an English major, they ordered her to write an essay confessing her "crimes against the State" and the "promotion of splittist attitudes" among the local population. They kept Angela for 24 hours, then sent her packing on the next bus to the border. The purple-faced Chinese, I thought: If they had actually deposed the Dalai Lama in 1959, why would they get so incensed? Indeed, no one talks about the "former Dalai Lama" like one would the kings of several Balkan countries. He remains the Dalai Lama.

I wrote many letters to Moon Light to be forwarded through Thinley. They all went unanswered. I received a few cards from friends passing through Kathmandu, some of whom related sketchy, second-hand and anecdotal information about the mercurial boy. Then I heard about dark, ominous clouds brewing in Dharamsala in the aftermath of the recent Lhasa uprisings.

On a slate grey afternoon in a chilly Honolulu, I received a holiday greetings card with a photograph of beautiful roses on the cover:

> Dear Eric. Please do me a favour by sending this only card till Moon Light—for we don't have his address. To add more, do address him and tell to write us. Today, we received your letter which is for Moon Light. Till today, you're doing everything what one real brother can do. So, please do continue till end. For me, there's no difference between you and Moon Light. So please this year we all are missing Moon Light a lot since he celebrated last NewYear with us.
>
> So, this is the card for him. To let him know that his Amala is always remembering him in my dreams—the next day for me was full of joy and happiness.
>
> We are very sorry for we couldn't reach your note till Moon Light due to not having his address. To end up. Please be gentle with Moon Light and I am sorry for his childish misbehavior. Love again, Amala.

Götterdämmerung

In early March of the new year, demonstrators again hit the streets of Lhasa, during the Monlam Chenmo festival, the Great Prayer. This time, martial law was proclaimed and PLA tanks were deployed. Guns were again turned on the crowd who demanded freedom. Scores of monks, nuns, and civilians were arrested, tortured, and killed. This time tourists had long departed, the event poorly covered in the West.

Time dragged on into early spring. I couldn't imagine how Moon Light survived hustling on the streets of Thamel. The situation in Tibet exploded into global outrange, but it would soon be eclipsed by broader discontent in China — Tiananmen Square appeared just around the corner. Soon the green tanks would be pointed on their own people, in the capital, with the world looking on.

Finally, a thin aerogram arrived bearing an orange stamp and the cancellation, "Macleodganj:"

> April 16, 1988
> Dear Eric-la:
>
> Here I am back home. Thanks a lot for your kind letter plus two t-shirts. It is very nice and I want to wear it today. I am very sorry I couldn't write you earlier than this because I didn't have a good address. Now I already decided to stay at home at the Kalimpong Café at my proper address. When are you coming to India? I will tell you my whole story when you come to India.
>
> Please pay my warm Tashi Deleg to your family. Tell them I am one of their sons in India, but different as he is Tibetans. Please do take care of your health.
>
> My mum is very happy I have returned home. My mum is requesting you to send the book that you wrote about Tibet. She said congratulations to you. Dearest Eric-la, I shall be glad if you send me some pictures that we took at the roof of the world. I am dying to see those pictures. Will you please send me as soon as you can. Thank you. Your brother Da'od Gyatso.

Not a word about his great escape from occupied Tibet. Soon, another letter arrived from Himachal that gave a few details. From what information I could gather, Da Duk, Moon Light, and others managed to continue to conduct tours in Central Tibet for a few days after the October uprising in Lhasa. Perhaps this provided an expedient way for the Chinese to get the foreigners out of the country. No big deal if one returning refugee disappeared in the process. Moon Light related that he simply signed up for a seven-day escorted Lhasa Hotel tour to the Nepalese border with about five Westerners in tow. Again the mini-bus; again with Lopsang the randy driver. Moon Light told his supervisors in Lhasa that he would deadhead back to the city and await further instructions. Instead, he simply grabbed his bags at Zhangmu, walked across the border, and caught a taxi with his party. It couldn't have been simpler. Needless to say, the 8½ pounds of turquoise in the leather saddle bags that Moon Light kept for me never made it back. It had been left in the little room in the Banok-shol. More sinister, though, was that all of Moon Light's money disappeared. And he never received my $100.00 in Kathmandu, for he had left before Thinley had a chance to turn it over,

Chapter 6

July 17, 1988

Dearest Eric-la. Today I received your letter. Thanks for all your helping me in my troubles in India. You know very well about my hurt in my heart. Now, I really don't like to stay in India. It's really a poor and dirty place. People really have big mouths. It is raining here in Dharamsala too. I'm sad you are lonely in America. I understand what was feeling in your heart, "especially about me." I already confess in Tibetan government office that I said I am your assistant as a translator in your research. Now, they knew me very well and I don't have any problem from the government-in-exile. But, I still want to make audience with His Holiness the 14th Dalai Lama of Tibet. Kundun knows the truth very well as our Lord of Compassion. Now, I am bit relaxed because of your secret copies that I received today. We have to continue our communicating in letter and it's nice if you visit India. We will clear it up. Please indicate if you have received the Free Tibet button and Tibetan national flag button which is packed.

Sometimes comes full of tears from my eyes that we are 10,000 km away. Last night I dreamed of you. We both were playing in the ground of America. Also, you were teaching me how to use a computer and when I woke up I saw my head was just crossing each other and still in India. In just laughed at myself and went off on my usual duty. I'm always helping for your research and always for ever. When we are together I wish to teach you Tibetan language, how to write U-chen. I will try to bring more books on Tibetan history. Please write me and send sponsorship declaration form soon then I can start my passport. That's all for today, With all my love to my God brother Eric, your God given brother Da'od Gyatso.

In November of that year I received a strange letter from Junko, a young Japanese woman who I had met briefly in McLeod Ganj, and had befriended the Kalimpong Café's family. How odd for her to write me, I thought. I opened up the crisp white envelope and began to read the neatly written blue ink:

Here in McLeodganj I every day go to Kalimpong Café to eat and talk with them. So I know all fact and details about Moon Light's affair during this time.

Today Moon Light received the documents from you which guarantee his staying and studying in U.S.A. About these documents we had to think over the part of "Tibetan refugee" which was typed in as his identification. Then his mother asked me to write and explain you about that part and I thought its better to write you a little bit more as outsider. (I mean I'm not real family member who are suffering).

Five Tibetan who have created false story against Moon Light are still trying to kick him off and acting with ill-will. Again and again those people continue to put up posters which are written "Moon Light is a Chinese spy, so don't go and eat at Kalimpong Café." Still now. Moon Light and his family did and also are doing to show and proof his innocence. People who know Moon Light and his family had will to help them, but nothing became good. His family often went to explain their circumstances at spe-

Götterdämmerung

cial office whose work is to listen the problem from people and talk and help to improve it.

During all this time, the family had been keeping all the patience because they really know the fighting between Tibetan is worst and nobody wish it. But still nothing improved despite all their efforts and patience. At last the family found that Tibetan official didn't do any help and didn't have any will to help. The family was so distressed to have known it and mother lost her weight very much. People who suffer continuously can easily have diseases. People who have ill-will were also disturbing family's life (mind and health), including Café's business.

The letter dragged on, a stinging indictment of my lack of ability and coming from someone outside of the family. It was like fingernails on a chalkboard, and it made me feel even more helpless than anything that had transpired before:

As you know, India gave a place for Tibetan refugees, so the security people and police who really control McLeodganj are Indian. So Moon Light and his father had to go to the police station many times because police asked them to come and explain this affair. Everything was too much. And the family was forced to think about their certain ground to help this painful circumstance. This all forced them to become Indian. Here in India no Tibetan refugee can kick them as Indian off.

Moon Light and his family didn't want to become Indian because they take much pride as Tibetan and their spirit and all are purely patriotic Tibetan. Of course Indian citizen means just a paper. So now Moon Light is an Indian citizen.

I hope you don't mind to make extra letter which is typed the reason why Tibetan refugee is an Indian, or to remake new papers as you think is proper.

I'm hearing your name "Eric, Eric-la, Eric-la" from Moon Light many many times. He and his family are grateful for you everything and completely trust you. Your friend, Junko.

Moon Light kept writing me that he wished to wait until I arrived back in India to tell me the entire story. But I blanched to learn that the town of McLeod Ganj had started a witch hunt aimed at destroying Moon Light and his family. It did not make sense why the villagers had singled him out. After all, hundreds of other refugee youngsters entered Tibet during the last few years, and returned with important information on conditions there. Moon Light had some difficulty, but he successfully escaped an occupied Tibet. He found himself a double refugee. Da Duk, I had heard, was offered money and an apartment to stay in Lhasa by the Chinese. There could be no comparison. Moon Light had assured me that he kept a low profile during the uprisings. He just walked across the border when the coast was clear. No daring escape, he just walked across the border.

One attribute of Gandhian non-violence used as a tactic of ethnic survival by the Dalai Lama is its individually. The Tibetan body itself may be emblematic of defiance. Hunger strikes are examples. Now I learn, as Moon Light's village pillory continued, his appetite disappeared and his health slipped away. From a photograph sent to me by a that a mutual friend, I could see Moon Light surely wasting away. Were the villagers in McLeod Ganj jealous of the fact that Kalimpong Café seemed so much more successful than most of the other establishments? In the previous decade, I remembered the haughty dowager's tea shop, a former duchess running a noodle stand. What a strong woman, I thought, to adapt to that great change in status, serving the likes of me and the other spiky-haired dandies of the late Disco Era. The family of the Kalimpong Café, on the other hand, were parvenus, arriving only in the 1980s. Their energy, youth, and six kids succeeded as the older émigrés' pretensions faded. I saw no reason for the elderly Tibetans to attack the first born of this family.

At least he had returned, and safely at that. I looked at my bank account and I looked at the progress I was making writing my thesis. It would have been the right thing to at least have been in Dharamsala for Moon Light's return. Such a heroic act would have been splendid—to plunge into occupied territory and pluck the distressed lad from the claws of the enemy, like Batman and Robin or T.E. Lawrence and Daod. But there were academic committees to serve, papers to grade. There were landlords and student loans to placate. The best way I could aid the Tibetan cause was to know its history, know its people, and pass on the knowledge. That was the only realistic route to action.

Upon getting Moon Light's letter, I took the initiative and promptly removed myself from the dark green plantation cottage with its flea-infested Siamese cats and tubby roommate. With two female graduate students, one husband, one four year-old boy, and one reasonable cat, our motley tribe moved into a modern split-level in suburban Kane`ohe, on the remote north side of O`ahu. In its own isolation, it seemed such a bright sunny world!

The house was comfortable, with its polished wooden floors and redwood siding. After the first night in the new house, I got up at sunrise to go to school. I walked three blocks to the bus stop on Kamehameha Highway and sat on a concrete bench. In front of me lay the turquoise Kane`ohe Bay, ringed by a grand semi-circular arc of verdant mountains, with the Mokapu Craters on the right and the Ko`olau Range on the left. In the center of the broad bay, tiny Coconut Island popped up. The small volcanic center of sunken Ko`olau Crater had been terraformed in the 1930s into a private pleasure estate by Fleischmann yeast heir Christian Holmes; in the 1960s it was featured on the trailer for the t.v. show, "Gilligan's Island." As I looked around, two gangly coconut trees on the other side of the highway framed the image.

The image brought about a strange feeling. I had fallen into an "iconic" landscape, a scene photographed and reproduced so many times that it had become both mythical and cliché. The actors in iconic scenes seem liberated from the mudane world, being momentarily transformed into a higher realm. Perhaps the pleasure derived by tourists "seeing the sights" is an easy form of liberating detachment. The *topos* of the Bay and Coconut Island before me, then, produced a stereotypical Hawai`i. It existed for a fleeting momemnt at this bus stop. Here, the dream and the reality were not far apart. That morning when I eventually arrived at my office and wrote about the Tibet of blood and war and the Tibet of Shangri-La, I realized that the real and the ideal are, in fact, dependent one upon another.

I raced to finish the thesis that summer, copies of each completed chapter circulated to five, sometimes six, committee members. Revisions and wee adjustments were hammered down as I honed and inflated, pared and tweaked the manuscript. Finally in October Ethyl ushered me into a mysterious little room in Porteus Hall, an inner sanctum where only doctoral students and their proctors sat in examination. This privileged place had great glass windows overlooking the Ko`olau Range, a sisal rug, and well framed art prints on the walls. At precisely 11:00 a.m., the committee members entered, one after the other. I spent the next two hours answering endless questions, only drawn, mercifully, from the dissertation that I had just written. How does this research relate to essentialist and functional categories of identity and inclusiveness? How does this work fit within the general schema of Tibetan cultural studies? It seemed to be going well. Even Dr. Linnekin was smiling. Then the committee excused me and Ethyl reappeared, escorting me to the outer office, where I sat on a small chair in full view of fellow graduate students. My colleagues gave me the thumbs up behind the huge smoked glass windows. Through a cloud of smoke, Ethyl brought me her usual tiny styrofoam cup of weak coffee. A few minutes later my chairman appeared: "Congratulations, Dr. Falkenberg."

"That's it?" I cried.

"Yeah. Easy. No problems. Why don't you come back to the room now."

From that point on, Eric sat annointed. The thrill wasn't so much from staying in school long enough to eventually get a Ph.D., or even winning a doctorate in anthropology. For Eric, my greatest pleasure emanated from the success of aiming in the direction of Tibet, and clearing the obstacles to work with its special people. It was the only important thing.

I pushed through the paperwork to be able to go through the winter commencement ceremony, even though I had ample corrections with the manuscript. Letters of congratulations came from Moon Light and his family. All he hoped for was a chance to come to America, and all I wanted to do now was to get back to India. What fun, I thought, it would be to travel around the world for six months, and settle in India.

On December 10, five days before the end of semester finals, I received a call from someone claiming to be an official at the University of Pittsburgh's Semester-at-Sea Program. There had been a last minute cancellation in anthropology, so it seemed. Would I like to teach shipboard on the spring cruise around the world? Yeah, right. And I'm the King of Sweden. I let the guy talk, and asked him if I could call back the next day. Then I frantically set out to discover if the "dean" was legitimate. He was. I figured since the dean told me that the ship dry-docked in Asia, and that we all could stay on in Asia, it seemed to be the best way of getting back to India.

The ship would leave from Port Everglades, Florida in three weeks. No problem to dissolve my Honolulu teaching obligations, my house rental, my relationship, and my stuff. I got my friend Richard and Ethyl to shepherd my thesis corrections through the punctilious Graduate Division, and soon found myself in my old friend John Bornmann's cottage in Ft. Lauderdale. The next day he drove me to the S.S. *Universe*. Five hundred students, 40 faculty and staff members, and 120 crew and officers of the 600-foot long Taiwanese ship soon set sail across the Atlantic.

Chapter 6

The entire voyage passed as a blur. Spain, Gibraltar, Yugoslavia, Turkey, the Black Sea, Egypt... It took us nearly ten days to travel from Port Said, down through the Red Sea, past the forbidden isle of Socotra off the Arabia Peninsula, and around the viscous waters of Sri Lanka. I sent two telegrams from the ship. I sent one to the Office of the Dalai Lama in Dharamsala requesting an audience with H.H. in two months time. I carried a copy of my dissertation to deliver to him personally. The other wire went to Moon Light in McLeod Ganj, inviting him down to Madras. We would be in port for a week.

Moon Light stood waiting for me on the pier as the ship docked in the smelly city. I saw him waving and jumping up and down. I couldn't believe that he spent three grueling nights on the train from the railhead at Pathankot just to meet me down in Madras. The *Universe* hadn't even cleared customs when I ran through the corridors of the ship, dodging students and Indian officials. The remarkable Burmese junior cook, Myo Aung Myo, unofficially attended to the opening of the main passenger hatches. As I stood in the doorway, Myo Aung sympathetically motioned Moon Light to climb the walkway. I walked halfway down the gangplank with Myo Aung. There were several hundred passengers looking down on us as we three met on the ramp. Most of my onboard friends had heard the story of Moon Light. I hesitated a moment, then gave Moon Light a great hug before our audience. Myo Aung looked on with a broad smile, then I introduced him. We sat down in the middle of the walkway, watching as the officious Indian custom's agents came and went. Myo and Moon Light were the same age and build—in fact, they looked remarkably alike.

"Try to speak to each other in your own language" I volleyed. They did, splendidly well. Moon Light asked Myo about his health and the weather, and the Burmese boy responded.

"I can understand this, no problem!" Moon Light laughed heartily, exposing his infamous white teeth. And Myo nodded his head, animating his own thick shafts of glossy black hair. They were such good sports.

Eventually we all cleared customs and were allowed to leave the ship. Unfortunately, we couldn't take Myo Aung, because of the ancient rule of the sea not to fraternize with crew members. So we left him high up on the plank, as Moon Light and I plunged into the teeming crowds down the street.

Moon Light looked totally exhausted. The long rail journey had been especially tiring for him. I took him to tea, and then to a nearby decent-looking hotel. "No sheets," said one desk clerk; "Salt water showers," said another. We went from one inn to the next, and over again. Finally, I found one relatively expensive place that seemed to have everything to make him comfortable.

I gave Moon Light a great stack of rupees and dollars. "I really don't have any use for this," I said, laughing.

His eyes bulged. "Oh, that's so much!" he uttered. "Thank you, Eric." It would take care of his travel expenses and perhaps something for the immediate future. Time had passed over, I hoped. It was guilt money.

With the ship's photographer Adam and nurse Nancy, Moon Light and I chartered an ancient four-seat Indian Ambassador with driver. Everyone in the know on board the ship suggested a visit the granite temples at Mahabalipuram along the eastern coast.

After a few hours cruising south, stopping once to see a crocodile farm and again to photograph farmers planting rice, we arrived at the site. Expecting large crowds, we were particularly pleased and surprised to find a great expanse of palm-lined beach with bone white sand and only a drifting tourist or two.

The next day at breakfast I told Moon Light of my plans to present the results of my research in an audience with the Dalai Lama. He grew very excited about the idea, but still resisted telling me of his problems with the Chinese police and the villagers back home in McLeod Ganj. "You can come back to Dharamsala and I will tell you the whole story," he said repeatedly each time I brought the issue up.

After two more blissful days amid the granite elephants, the white sea foam, the spicy curries, and tiger cowries in the tide pools, we began the slow drive along the narrow asphalt road back to Madras. There I took Moon Light to one of the hundreds of local shirt factories and bought him a half-dozen plaid and striped Madras shirts in pastel pinks, yellows, and greens. The time slipped away, and soon I was standing with Myo Aung on the promenade deck waving back to him. It was so painful to leave Moon Light alone on the wharf. Following three prolonged, black belches from the yellow funnel, the S.S. *Universe* steamed out of the harbor, bound for Penang, Malaysia.

Six long weeks later Semester-at-Sea ended, and rather ungraciously at that. One by one the familiar services ended, the bar, the dining rooms, the pursers—the great white mother cocoon had split open. Instead of returning to the United States as this aging liner normally did, the ship had been scheduled for drydocking in Japan. With four months worth of shopping and luggage, the 500-odd students, faculty, and staff were dumped out at the rickety wharf at Keelung, Taiwan. The scene was a rout as students argued about their just-posted grades while faculty struggled down the stairs with their bags, laptops, sun hats, and assorted flotsam. I extricated myself from the chaos and headed for the city. From Taipei, I made haste to Hong Kong airport, where I stowed my bags in left luggage. Then I quickly found a willing Thai airliner to fly me to Kathmandu that very afternoon. I needed to learn more about Moon Light's plight from my friends in the Nepalese capital before I returned to Dharamsala.

In a few hours, I found myself brushing past the usual group of dozing adolescent boys at the Blue Diamond Hotel. I felt blissful to be off the dying ship that had confined me for nearly five months. I was invigorated to be back in Kathmandu. After a quick clean up, I jumped, breezing through the streets of the ancient Gurkha capital, finding much to amuse, fixate, and fill my senses.

After a day or two of deep relaxation, I went out to Boudanath to find Thinley. I found him easily at the *chang* bar not too far from the Khampas' apartment where Moon Light and I stayed. Thinley told me a bit about Moon Light's transit through Nepal. By the time he received my letter suggesting that Moon Light be given $100, the fleeing chap had already left for Dharamsala. So the story went—I didn't get the $100 either. I returned to Thamel. And after about a week of roses, fountains, and laughter in the black-green glades of Ratna Park, I left for Dharamsala.

Arriving in Delhi, I immediately hailed a scooter taxi and drove directly to Kashmiri Gate Union Bus terminal to await the evening ride to Dharamsala. I had missed the daylight bus, and didn't want to take an orange something touted as a "super luxury coach" to Himachal Pradesh. "Luxury" in this context meant a tinny stereo playing eardrum-splitting, over-modulated Indian pop music through cheap speakers tacked on the ceiling. Instead of this conveyance, I caught the

Chapter 6

overnight Himachal Transport bus, a glistening silver affair encrusted in vomit splatters.

For once I fell soundly asleep on an Indian bus, and stayed in that state through the smooth, gentle ascent of the Punjabi plain through slumbering Ambala and Chandigarh. Four hours of twisting and climbing in pitch darkness followed, finally arriving in lower Dharamsala at sunrise.

I staggered up the hill to McLeod Ganj with my luggage strapped to my back as usual. I walked around the rain puddles in the bus stop plaza, to the side street, and directly into the Kalimpong Café. It seemed empty, except for Moon Light's sister. Her eyes popped out and she immediately turned into the kitchen. That sent Moon Light running out, followed by Amala and the whole family, engulfing me in hugs. Big white teeth flashed everywhere. I spent the bulk of the late afternoon sitting in the tiny living room at the back of the restaurant, surrounded by three brothers, two sisters, Amala and Phala, and the "Delhi Momo-la," an old lady who was a relative of Phala's. Cosseted in pillows and heavy Tibetan rugs, a Lhasa apso underfoot, we watched round after round of Pakistani soap operas broadcast from nearby Lahore.

That night, Moon Light's family settled me over at a Tibetan guest house—a plain concrete room with a great black spider spinning in the corner. The hotel stood right next to famed Tibetan doctor, Yeshe Donden. During their morning run to the WC, hotel guests in pajamas and towels would be greeted by long lines of patients queuing up outside the doctor's office.

I returned to the Kalimpong Café at about 8:30 the next morning. The restaurant was dark. They hadn't bothered to turn on the lights for lack of business. But Moon Light planned a surprise picnic just for him and me. He packed momos, cheese, and bread, bottles of Mr. Pik and Amul biscuits.

My friend stuffed silverware and tea cups into the backpack, and rolled a medium sized carpet to take along. We headed for the area simply known as "the Park," a grassy area on top of a forested hill between McLeod Ganj and the Thegchen Chöling Palace. Moon Light chose this moment to tell me the full story of his problems in Tibet and his escape from the Chinese authorities. At about 9 a.m. we put the little-used restaurant under the charge of the two youngest siblings and headed out.

The Park was fairly isolated, despite a huge Indian hotel recently built over the bluff nearby. Just out of the woods stood a nunnery for young "orphan" nuns not attached to any large monastery. My old friend Patricia, who had now become Ani Karma Lekshe Tsomo-la, had established the retreat. Poor thing, the Western nun had been bitten by an Indian cobra here a couple of years ago and nearly lost her arm. Since Ani-la was now in residence, I intended to pay her a call and bring an offering for her nuns. Moon Light and I stopped at three or four shops on the way to the Park, buying large jars of Amul orange marmalade, condensed milk, sugar, candy, and any other relatively pure, clean, *sattvic* thing I could think of.

In about ten minutes we arrived at the nunnery in the glen. I knocked on the door and waited. Again I knocked on the door. No one appeared, which was fine because I was dying to finally hear Moon Light's story. We left the groceries at the doorstep, and after a short climb we arrived at the soft little meadow on top of the hill.

Moon Light spread out a somber green and blue rug over a dry patch of grass. We both said nothing for endless minutes, moments that drifted off into a tidy mid-morning nap. The sun inched up through the pine boughs, throwing golden beams along the dappled leaf littered lawn. I kept a subtle consciousness, a residue of caution. Moon Light and I woke as a cool gust from the mountains refreshed the hazy atmosphere. He sat up, and poured us each a cup of sweet milk tea from a battered thermos. Then he took out a handkerchief and wiped his face.

"So, Eric-la, this is how it happened. It was the first day of the uprisings. I had just got into town, back from a short trip to the Chang Thang with this German man. I had gone up to my room in the Banok-shol hotel when I heard a horrible commotion. People were shouting on the streets—there were sirens and police cars running everywhere. All the *injis* came out of their rooms and went downstairs. The hotel owner told them loudly, 'Don't go out there, don't go out there'. But out they went. I went over and asked the manager what was happening, and he said he thought it was a freedom demonstration by monks. Many, many other people joined, including a lot of young *injis*. The manager told me it was dangerous, and to go back to my room."

I took another sip of tea. By now two crows had alighted on top of an adjacent pine tree and looked down at us.

"So I went back to my room. I didn't even go out for dinner. At about 7:00 a police car drove up to the hotel. It parked in front, by the door. Three policemen got out. In a second there was loud booming on my door. The police opened the door with the key they took from the manager. Immediately they grabbed me and put my hands behind my back and bound them together. Then another began to go through my bags and dresser drawers. In no time they found all the money I had saved, nearly ¥10,000. One put the money in a big brown envelope. Eric, then they started asking me angry questions, like 'Where did you steal this money?' and 'Are you a splittist, too?' When one asked me if I had any Dalai Lama photographs, I told them just the one I have for prayer. He didn't believe me, and kept screaming about where the others were. Then they pushed me out of the room and forced me to go into the car with them. I was really scared. I remember the hotel manager looking shocked as I was escorted out the front door."

"So you were arrested? Moon Light? Jeeze, how can they do that?"

"They took me to a police station on the other end of town, and put me in a dark room with a couple of chairs and a table. They asked me hundreds of questions, few of which did I have any answer. I told them I wasn't interested in politics. I had just come to Tibet to see my homeland, and make a little money as a tour guide for foreigners. They kept telling me that I didn't have a permit to do that—this is illegal. They kept saying that it was illegal for Chinese citizens to tell foreigners that Tibet is separate."

I looked at Moon Light and knew that his ordeal had been far worse than his polite manner would permit—a lamb destroyed by a pack of dogs. I put on my jacket.

"I didn't know what they were going to do with me. But after awhile they led me through a long corridor and put me in a cell with several other Tibetans. Some were bleeding or swollen, all were dirty. After awhile I told one of them who I was, and asked quietly what happened out on the streets earlier that day. This guy told me about the monks' demonstration at the Jokhang. These men had been watching the monks call for independence and were taken away by the police. The next morning the officer called me into the office again, and asked me the same questions and told me that I had broken major state laws. They said I was in big trouble. When I told them that I was from India, he said 'No! You're a Chinese National. They gave you a Chinese National permit to visit here. That means you are Chinese. Don't believe in those silly Dalai government lies!' he screamed. Then I was led back to the cell."

"Later that afternoon, I was called again from the room. This time they bound my hands again behind my back and drove me away. In about twenty minutes we arrived at the military camp under the Chakpo-ri with the broadcasting tower on top. I was brought into a studio. A woman appeared who abruptly combed my hair and wiped my face. Then they sat me down in a studio in front of a television camera and handed me a script."

"Script?" I said.

"Yeah. Eric, it was in English, too. They wanted me to read it for the television! It simply said that foreigners were not permitted to take part in, watch, or take pictures of the demonstrations. I asked them questions, and found out that there had been even a larger demonstration today, and many people got hurt or arrested. They told me that I had to read this script to prevent the foreigners from getting hurt. It was for public safety. I also got a clear message that if I didn't cooperate I would be beaten and sent to prison. I didn't think that there was too much problem in this speech, if it could save some people. So I read through it once aloud. They then asked me if I was ready. I nodded. The camera light went on and I began to read the speech."

"I can't believe they forced you to do that! What did you say?"

"I didn't say anything bad. I didn't denounce the Dalai Lama."

"Denounce the Dalai Lama? Who would have thought of that? Who's thinking of that?"

"I didn't even mention him. I just read the script that the *injis* should not take pictures of the demonstrations or even watch them. It was internal affair. I told them that if they took any photographs they would violate state law and their cameras and film would be taken. Also I said that it was very dangerous to their safety to be in Lhasa or the Tibet Autonomous Region, and that all foreigners had to leave Tibet within three days. The paper said that anyone caught after that time would be subject to arrest and deportation. When I read these words the first time, I became very frightened what the Chinese were planning to do with us after the *injis* were gone. I thought after the *injis* were gone, they would take me out and shoot me. I thought they would destroy everything."

"Did you ever think about refusing to speak on television?"

"No. I thought it might help save lives. And I was forced."

"Even if it meant the *injis* were gone and there were no witnesses?"

"It didn't matter because they could have made all the *injis* go away anytime anyway."

"Moon Light. Do you think they used you to show a refugee who cooperated with the government? Like someone who had returned voluntarily?"

"But I said nothing bad about anyone, especially nothing about His Holiness or his government. You know I'm not interested in politics."

"Did you keep your job with the hotel afterwards?"

"Yes. That seemed the end of it. After the broadcast they drove me back to the Banok-shol. But my money and valuables were gone. I never saw them again. Next day I went back to my job. The police called my boss in the morning and they talked a long time. Nothing more was said about it."

Götterdämmerung

I opened the back pack and set out our lunch. First I opened a bag of chips, then the cookies. I poured Moon Light another cup of tea.

"Please drink this," I said, handing him a little silver cup. "How much longer did you work?"

"Well, oh, I wanted to leave right away, but they had taken all my money. So I had to work awhile."

"But I thought you said all the *injis* were leaving?" I continued, feeling a bit like a papal inquisitor.

"There still were escorted tour bookings that had to continue for the season."

"So you left after the season in December?"

"No, I left when I thought I had enough money."

"So you must have had very little funds when you arrived in Kathmandu. All of that, you say, it must have been 10,000 *remenbei*. That's enough to live a year in China, or a round-trip plane ticket to anyplace on earth"

"Very little money in Kathmandu," Moon Light said quietly.

"What did you do in Kathmandu for money? You know I sent Thinley out with $100 but you couldn't be found."

"Oh, I stayed here and there with new friends that I made."

I remembered the disturbing letter that Thinley had sent me. "*Inji* friends?" I asked. Moon Light nodded. "Why didn't you stay with Momo-la and the Khampa family out in Bodhanath? They would have taken care of you until I could help."

"Oh no they wouldn't have!"

I looked at Moon Light, "Why not? I thought they liked you."

"I don't think they were around."

"Not around? So you were in Kathmandu about one month, then went back to Dharamsala?"

"Yeah, Eric. But it was very bad."

"I don't get it. Weren't you happy to be home?"

"Sure, my family was. But that is all. You don't understand the gossipy people here. Tibetan people told stories from someone who saw the broadcast in Lhasa. Word got out all the way over to Dharamsala, but they weren't accurate words. They said I had denounced the Dalai Lama. It was horrible. Sonam Tenzin just stood in the middle of the bus stand and pointed us out, screaming 'Traitor! Traitor!' and 'Kalimpong family are Chinese spies!'"

"Oh God, Moon Light. Why didn't you tell me this before? I sat there horrified that this could happen to him. The Tibetan security office and other bureaucrats did nothing to help resolve the truth. They said they believed Moon Light, because they had the intelligence reports. They knew he did not denounce the Dalai Lama.

"I waited to tell you until I knew you would be here, otherwise the problem might keep you away. And you had to have your book to prove I had been your assistant. And then you could make audience with His Holiness."

"You want to tell him your story?"

"Yes. He's the only one who would understand. The only one who could save my life. We poor Tibetan refugees cannot make audience with Dalai Lama. Only great foreigners can, especially ones who have written books about Tibet."

Chapter 6

"But I have some difficulty," I responded. "I don't have a confirmed appointment. I'll go to the security office today and see what has happened to my telegram. I asked them to confirm the audience while I was on the ship, but never heard anything."

It seemed imperative for Moon Light's sake, and the sake of his family, to draw this matter to the Dalai Lama's attention. He still had absolute power over his followers. I had visited him many times, it should be no problem. Leaving Moon Light, I went back to the hotel with the big black spider in the corner to sleep and relax and prepare myself for a visit to Thegchen Chöling Palace in the morning.

I felt jubilant as I walked in the easterly sunshine filtering through the rhododendron trees on my way to the Dalai Lama's security office. As in the times before, all foreign visitors to Lhasa were required by good manners to pay a call on the sovereign, a polite way of informing the government of one's whereabouts. I also needed to let the officials know that I was in Dharamsala and anticipated my scheduled audience during the first week in May. I walked into an empty reception room and sat down on a short upholstered couch. A few minutes passed, and still no one arrived. Finally I heard sounds coming from an adjacent store room.

"Hello? Anyone there?" I called.

"I'll be there in a minute," answered the voice of a rather flustered young man.

A few moments later a pimply-faced youth in a v-neck sweater and sneakers appeared carrying a large box of dusty documents. He placed the box under a desk and asked in an Indian accent, "What is it that you require?"

"You are the appointments clerk?"

"Yes, I am in charge."

I raised an eyebrow, "I wanted to report that I have arrived in Dharamsala for my audience with Kündün on Thursday," I said with a smile. "My name is Dr. Eric Falkenberg."

"On this Thursday?" the clerk responded with a surprised look.

"Yes...is there some problem? You did get my telegram?"

"Let me check," the boy clerk said. "His Holiness is not supposed to have any audiences this Thursday."

While he flipped through a large black schedule book, I thought of some oligarch's son put in his position to please daddy. Back and forth through the green lined pages, the clerk kept shaking his head. I felt a tingling sensation in my feet.

"Falkenberg? I'm sorry. I don't see anything here."

"But I sent you a telegram back in January," I said with increasing exasperation.

The clerk went over to the ancient metal filing cabinets, pulled out a correspondence file, and slowly read each piece of paper. "Here is something, I think, with your name on it," he intoned, "but it is not valid."

"Not valid! What do you mean? I said that I would be in Dharamsala during the week of May 2-8, and that any time during that interval would be fine."

"Oh yes," he said sarcastically, "but you didn't specify which date, so we didn't think you were serious with your plans."

"Not serious? I indicated a range of days for your own convenience!" I felt my nostrils flair and face beginning to blush. "Look. I'm not a tourist here to bother Kündün for some exotic *dharsan*. I have been working with Tibetan refugees for ten years, and I have just written a serious thesis on Tibetan nationalism. I might not be well known to you, but this will be published as a book and the Dalai Lama might wish to look at it before that time. It might be of some value to the government. That is all."

"It is impossible," the acne-garlanded troll chirped, " Kündün's schedule is booked."

"If there is anything in my manuscript that is inaccurate or not supportive of the exile movement and His Holiness's administration, I want to know about it so I can change it. I don't wish to offend the exile government accidently. Why couldn't you have contacted me earlier? I cannot guarantee that the book will be of benefit, and I have to add that I am extremely disappointed with your attitude. Do you have a supervisor with whom I could speak?"

"They are all out today, so I am in charge."

I glowered at this petulant teenage flunky, trying to set fire to his uneven eyebrows, then moved over to pick up my red covered manuscript lying on the reception desk, and finished my temper tantra.

"You all really don't care, do you?" I whispered, as I slowly backed away from the Thegchen Chöling reception desk.

Moon Light waited for me just outside the door. He took me up the hill to a sunny, grassy meadow. Torrents of tears streamed down my face.

"It's all over, Moon Light," I cried. "All over — all my work for the Tibetan government-in exile, all the chances for you...all destroyed by a little peon bureaucrat."

It had become clear to me in that moment that all this had been an illusion. I never helped Free Tibet, I never helped any single person, because some never understood how to manage the bountiful goodwill *injis* had for them. Perhaps the Chinese were right. Perhaps all this feudal gang of exiles is interested in is feathering their petty nests and ascending the shaky ladder of a formerly immense social hierarchy. I remained inconsolable for three hours. All the years of working with Tibetans towards freedom seemed a sham. I had become a blond haired robot for defeated Central Asian wannabes.

Moon Light's patience stood as a magnificent bulwark. He sat with me through it all. Eventually he led me away from the growing afternoon in the meadow back to the Kalimpong Café. Here Phala learned the story, and soon many others in the neighborhood knew of our misadventures with the Dalai Lama's receptionist. I could hardly show my face to the family. I just drank the tea they brought, and passed on dinner.

About 9:00 a.m.the next day, one of Phala's friends dropped by. Dhonyu worked as a guard at Thegchen Chöling. One of the neighbors told him my story. He promptly suggested that I write a letter addressed to H.H.'s private secretary. Dhonyu would then pass it through the appropriate people. It would not go astray, he assured. Everyday Tibetans worked hard to help assure that the Chinese propaganda about His Holiness being the thuggish fugitive "Dalai" is squelched. If the truth could prevail, the Tibetans would always be victorious.

Chapter 6

We were all elated. Moon Light and Phala jumped up and down. I wrote out a long note of introduction in English. Phala had his friend Dhonyu address the envelope in courteous cursive. Then I gave the completed letter to Dhonyu, who carried it to the guard at the gates of the Dalai Lama's palace with instructions to give it directly to the Private Secretary of His Holiness, and to no one else. And then we waited.

I drank endless cups of tea in the Kalimpong Restaurant as the afternoon slipped away. Finally, just before dinner, Phala's friend reappeared with a slip of paper. It invited us to come to the Private Secretariat tomorrow at 10:15 a.m. It was a sheer breakthrough! I could see the look of well-earned relief on Phala's face. Amala came out of the kitchen wiping her hands as she smiled and took in the news. Moon Light was elated, teeth glistening from ear to ear.

The following morning, Moon Light came over to my room. We were both nervous as we dressed in suit and tie. Over and over we rehearsed our speeches, our questions, what we would do if we were brought into audience with the Dalai Lama. Okay, we were ready!

We walked briskly through McLeod Ganj in our Sunday clothes. To the smiling and chatting villagers who saw us, it only meant one thing—we had an important meeting at the Palace. It only took a few minutes to walk along the precipitous road leading to Thegchen Chöling. We stated our business with the guard, and were shown into the outer security office. The bad peon receptionist saw us and immediately busied himself with paperwork. Another agent walked us over to the Secretariat. But instead of turning right to the row of offices built along the hill, he turned left directly towards the Dalai Lama's residence. Our hearts began beating very fast. We were escorted into the outer reception room and were invited to sit on the couch. Then the official went away.

"This is the Dalai Lama's living room!" exclaimed Moon Light.

"Look at all those statues. You're right, this can only mean one thing. But let's wait and see." I said.

"Do you have your book ready, Eric?"

"Yeah. Guess this is it."

I looked down at the magnificent Tibetan refugee carpets, at the splendid *thangka* on the walls. The room had hosted everyone from Heinrik Harrer to Richard Gere. The room seemed rather feminine, with floral designs and pastel puppy-like snow lions. We were bathed in cozy tranquility, with none of the "barbaric splendors" described by the Shangri-La literati.

But my doubts were confirmed a few moments later when the attendant returned,

"The Secretary will see you now. Please come this way."

Deflated, we were summarily marched out of the residence, down a flight of stairs, and through an outside corridor to the Office of the Private Secretary. Moon Light would have to be satisfied in making his appeal to this important official.

"Hello, I'm Tenzin Tethong," the affable man with spectacles said. "I understand you have a matter to discuss with the government? I hope that we are able to help you in some manner."

"It is a pleasure to meet you," I said. "And it is nice that the government of His Holiness has invited us today. May I introduce you to Da'od Gyatso? He has a story he wishes to present before His Holiness. Perhaps you may listen to his story and judge its merits. All I can say is that I have known Moon Light for several years, and he has always been truthful. He is suffering greatly now, and insists that only His Holiness can help him."

"I would be happy to listen. How can I help?" the Secretary said, then turned to Moon Light, who began to speak, slowly at first, carefully, in a type of polite speech designed for monastics. Methodical, Moon Light related his story directly, without interruption. He presented his soliloquy. He talked about the horrible day of the first demonstrations in Tibet. He discussed his detainment, and the television studio, about the Chinese "losing" all his money and how they would release him only if he helped get the foreigners out of Tibet. By now Moon Light spoke excitedly. He told the Secretary how he escaped the country, about the difficulties in Kathmandu. Finally, when he returned home, suspicious McLeod Ganj residents began to spread false rumors that he was a spy for the Chinese. Moon Light told him that he and his family were always loyal to His Holiness, and were good followers of the government-in-exile. The gossip scared business away from the restaurant. No one wanted to be associated with someone accused of treason and disloyalty. He wanted to tell the Dalai Lama because such a highly realized being could see the truth.

Tenzin Tethong finally took a deep breath, and said, "That's awful. I know those people you are referring to here. What they say doesn't amount to much. It is possible for us to make our own investigation, if that's what you would like to do."

"Yes, very much so," Moon Light countered. "Please look into it."

"He and his family have suffered greatly," I slipped in. "Please pardon me, but what he says is true. It is unfortunate that the Tibetan government-in-exile, for all its stong stand on Tibetan freedom, cannot prevent or arbitrate disagreements from within. Perhaps some of the older people here, those who have gone through family destruction at the hands of the Chinese, are intolerant of a young boy choosing life instead of dying by refusing to tell the *injis* to leave Tibet. Like so many other youth in your community, he was curious about his homeland. I think that what the Tibetan government-in-exile lacks is a judiciary. Not being sovereign, these matters would be up to an Indian court. This sort of thing would not interest an Indian court, especially since it might upset their neighbor China. So young people such as Moon Light make a mistake and it becomes an instrument of shopkeeper business politics. He never denounced the Dalai Lama, but he is being demonized here in order to destroy the most popular restaurant in town."

Then I handed the Secretary a copy of my thesis. "Would you be so kind as to present this copy of my doctoral dissertation to His Holiness? It is about *rang-bstan* [freedom] in history and nationalism under present circumstances. I hope it is in some way useful to him and the government."

"I will be sure to give it to him directly," the Secretary assured me. "Thank you very much for all your hard work. We appreciate your perceptions."

Moon Light looked greatly relieved. The meeting had lasted well over an hour and one-half. We shook hands with the Secretary. The attendant reappeared, and we were brought back to the steel gates of Thegchen Chöling and the Indian honor guards. We passed through the portal, and went out upon the streets of McLeod Ganj. Faces appeared at windows. Hands went in front of mouths as the gossips continued on their rounds

Chapter 6

with this latest bit of news. The demon spies were coming out of the Palace! Whatever could have happened?

Only time now would prove the effectiveness of the Private Office's efforts. My time in McLeod Ganj was coming to an end. It would have been pleasant to spend the summer with my Tibetan family, to watch the sunrises over the Pathankot hills, and follow the course of the sun around the peaks of the Western Himalayas. "Next time you come back, come back to stay, I will build a room for you and Moon Light to live in," Phala said.

I sat in the front seat of the bus at lower Dharamsala next to the driver's glassed-in bubble. The window on left side was open. Moon Light and his dark-skinned brother Kunga stood adjacent to the bus. With my right hand I held Moon Light's. In my left hand I held Kunga's. They were both very warm, as if the boys had just been practicing *tumo* meditation. We didn't say a word to each other, but casually roamed the interstitial spaces between each other's being. With our eyes and touch, exploring commonalities and difference, our three beings promised not to abandon each other. So very forgiving seemed Moon Light's family, I thought. Here I am again in the arms of my beloved Tibetans.

In a hurried instant the calm shattered by the sudden appearance of the determined driver and urgent porters, followed by 40 or 50 pushing and shoving Indian passengers. The doors of the bus slammed shut, the engine started, porters banged on the rear, and we lurched forward. My brothers' hands were wrenched apart from mine with a brutal snap, like the uncoupling of pneumatic hoses. Then all of Dharamsala disappeared.

The next 14 hours were spent in a whirl of arms and legs and being smacked on the head by protuberant luggage. I arrived in Delhi and went directly to the offices of Royal Nepal Airlines. What tremendous luck! One seat was available on the afternoon flight to Kathmandu. But I had to rush, only two hours lay between me and take off. I rushed out onto the street and hailed the first scooter taxi that approached. I flashed the Sikh driver Rs 100 and said, "You'll get this if you can get me to the airport in 45 minutes." He did.

I had expected to spend three or four hours at the airport, while various crew members and ground staff arrived and made their obligatory social calls before calling the flight. But most unusually, the Royal Nepal agent insisted that the plane would leave on time. On the jet I learned that the sister of King Birendra was on board, hence the great service.

I stayed in Kathmandu just long enough to say good-bye to all my friends in town, including Sangay Lama, the tiny muscle man, Judy, Pierre and Lulu the Canadian social workers, the guys out at Tribhuvan University, and my new friend, a splendidly tall Newari lad named Ramesh. I had a tearful parting at the airport. My friends drove away, but I didn't get farther than the ticket counter. Finding it only had 14 passengers to fill its Boeing 737, the unfriendly skies of Dragon Airlines decided to cancel their flight to Hong Kong. After an hour of noisy protest from an eight-member mountain climbing team from Germany, the airline agents finally relented and booked us on the next day's flight. In an unheard of show of concern, or fear of lawsuit, they even put us up at a decent hot el.

We were soon trundled off to the Yantra Hotel in Kathmandu, a four-star affair painted in the deepest blue with thick, voluptuous shades on the windows. I didn't bother informing my friends who had seen me off at the airport—it had been a good farewell and it would be dreadfully anticlimactic to repeat it. Instead,

Götterdämmerung

the mountain team and I discovered that our rooms' minibars were expensed to the airline. After an all-night testosterone fest strutting like roosters and chugging mini bottles of *rakshi*, the mountaineers and I eventually gathered up our belongings. We were driven to the airport and shoveled onto the morning flight to Hong Kong. As the plane climbed out of Kathmandu Valley, I could see the complex summit of Kangchenjunga marking the end of the great Tibetan plateau. The sleek 757 then ascended into the slate grey clouds of the early monsoon, its turbines glowing with blue fire. We crossed over the horizon.

7. Knave of Hearts

> Every foreigner is a messenger from a world of dreams.
> —Pico Iyer[35]

How quickly, and with such finality, these bright sparks are drawn into the endlessly insatiable void. And thus my companions disappeared one by one, irredeemable, to joys unknowable.

After a hundred airplane rides and a hundred storms, I finally arrived back in Montana, to a great void. Like Rip van Winkle, all had changed and people I had once known so easily were serious adults with serious problems. In Great Falls, at least, I could gather all my toys together in a mound, and contemplate my possession of them. Nothing of the last few years in Asia had the most remote bearing on the day-to-day life in the small town life of the intermountain West. People still shopped at Herberger's for bell bottom jeans in the 1990s; they still bought gas at CircleK®. A big night on the town was beer and pizza at Howard's. Eric seemed entirely disengaged—as if he had developed acute autism. Experiencing day after day of watching the tumbleweeds blow across 10th Avenue, what could prevent my implosion?

I wrote a book, a book on the history of Tibet and the exodus of its refugees. I built myself a little den in my mom's guest room in the basement of her house, and gathered all my notes and photographs, books and articles. What constituted the essential theme of the nation of Tibet, I thought, what brought it all together? I started working on this project, and it took me through the dark days of winter and out to the first thaw of spring. Throughout, Moon Light had been sending letters from India, not just to me but to my mother, reminding her that he was a son, too. If by some chance I should publish my book, it would serve as a catharsis. Perhaps even the officials back in Dharamsala would read it, perhaps they could even understand Moon Light. By some miracle, he might be released from this web of false accusations and even come to America.

That spring I drove to Missoula, the place where I had gone to undergraduate school and the town where Karl still lived. While walking through my old haunts, I happened upon a bright blue announcement for the "Shamar Ling Tibetan Cultural Center." How exciting, I thought—finally, Tibetan culture had made it down home. I decided to investigate.

I stopped in one evening for their weekly Tibetan dinner and lecture. The center itself was just an old yellow house on East Front Street near the downtown district of Missoula. No one answered the bell, so I just walked in. I heard voices coming from the kitchen, and found a middle aged woman, a tall young graduate student who was giving tonight's lecture on wildlife preserves in Tibet, one very young and slight Tibetan man, and three or four women of various ages. They were all making momos together. I watched for awhile, then carefully walked over to the Tibetan man. I asked his name and what these people were doing, in his

Chapter 7

native language. His large black eyes lit up. Pemba Lama was his name, and these *injis* were making their weekly community dinner.

"Stay with us!" Pemba offered.

"Ooooooh, you speak Tibetan!" chanted the middle aged woman, "Where on earth do you come from!"

"Dharamsala, via Great Falls," I responded. "My name is Eric. I am so happy to have found you all here."

"Yes. For sure. Great Falls? What a coincidence! I'm Bernice Cobalt and I run the Center. This is Frank, and Pemba, you've met I think."

"Yeah, she's the Inji Queen," laughed Pemba in our secret language.

"Frank has worked in Tibet in wildlife conservation. He's talking tonight. Would you like to stay for dinner?"

I started helping to make momos like an old pro. Our conversation turned on a hundred things about Tibet and Tibetan refugees.

"I'm just amazed, just amazed that you just walked in here! We are so remote up here," said Bernice.

Then I heard a commotion coming from a stairway behind the kitchen.

"Save some momos for me!" announced the booming voice of another older woman. I heard the jingle of ankle bracelets as she bounded down the steps. Then I saw a swoosh of violet and pink silk Pakistani pyjamas, a bulging midriff, and a palladium of gossamer green. This woman, probably in her fifties, talked and glided about like an animated teen. Something seemed very familiar about this person. Her Tammy Faye blue eye shadow was accented by harsh black mascara and eyebrow lines, her long blondish hair streaked in grey and dull brown. Yet she possessed vibrancy and self-possession, delighting in all around. She took one look at me and said, "You! I know you. Hah! You were with Moon Light. What are *you* doing here?"

"Guess who?" I said.

"You, you were in the Banok Shol Hotel with the little Tibetan guide Moon Light. Eric, right?"

"Ah, shut my mouth," I teased, "Why, you're the last person I would expect in Missoula."

"You didn't know?" Veejay chided, "My sister and I have a ranch just outside of Helena. The Feathered Drum Ranch. We hold spiritual retreats there. I take classes here at the U. Back and forth. I didn't know you were from Montana either. Did you know that Andre and Pam live here, too?"

"No. I didn't know they were your friends. That was quite some time in Tibet, eh? I first thought you were from the country club set, with a Coach bag and kid gloves." I could not believe it— here stood the woman that Moon Light thought would make him wealthy. A matronly New Ager from Connecticut, we had believed.

"Hah, no! I'm an old hippy."

Bernice grew even more astonished listening to Veejay and my conversation. Her gaunt face wrinkled and her eyes narrowed to slits as she grasped the coincidence with mystical reverence, "This is a karmic experience. There is some major karma here. It is no chance meeting, things like this." Pemba, leaning against the wall in the corner of the room, laughed to see such a sight.

Later, after dinner, Bernice brought out a huge stack of pamphlets and petitions, tracts and pro-Tibetan political tirades. She spoke of a new fund being established for destitute monks in Nepal, increased contributions to the Tibetan

Women's Association, and a charity drive for aged Sherpa guides in Namche Bazaar. She talked about her list of speakers booked to give Dharma teachings at Shamar Ling over the coming year, and of her own lecture series to local schools and the University of Montana. Bernice, it seemed, was also the local representative of the U.S. Tibet Committee, thus in effect a representative of the Tibetan government-in-exile. Maybe that's why she wore knee length yellow stockings and a maroon jumper.

It seemed incongruous to see prayer flags hanging down from clotheslines strung from the eves of the broad front porch. A typical, old Missoula framed-porch residence housed the Tibetan Center, situated across from the public library and the fire station and next to the old brick elementary school. Inside, a thick pall of incense hung over worn out college dorm couches and cracked Formica and chrome tables. About six inches of snow lay on the ground while the calendar approached Tibetan New Year, Lo Sar.

I drove a quick turn-around to Great Falls and back, about 160 miles from Missoula. There must have been 30-40 people at Shamar for the Tibetan New Year celebration, and a hundred types of foods, ranging from Chinese take-out to delicately rich Indian curries prepared by professors' wives. Pemba and his friends even managed to get a hold of *drimar*, yak butter, for making authentic salted tea. There were *kaptse* cookies and fiery chilies, *thukpa* and *thentuk* noodles, bowls of dried fruit and nuts. Dharma Center members had come from as far away as Spokane to the West, and Butte and Billings to the East.

As a highlight to the evening, Bernice presented a slide show of her treks in Nepal. She set up a slick exhibition using two fade-out projectors with synchronized Wyndham Hill music. "Imagine…" her script ran, "you are standing on top of a pure crystal mountain…" Her dialogue flowed as slippery and hypnotic as a Buddhist *sadhana*, the meditative visualization taught by Tibetan lamas. She constructed an image of Tibet as a wondrous land of auspicious bounty, where the slightest touch or glance from one of the holy teachers could bring forth myriad flowers of compassion and gilded inflorescences of virtue. Her talk bordered on the sensual but daft writings on Tibetan Buddhism by Lobsang Rampa in the 1960s.

Having spun her web, having cast her nimbus of hyacinth blue rays, Madame Cobalt sharply reminded us all of the "Program," the dozens of projects, speakers, Dharma talks, and charity get-togethers planned but located high in the clouds. Whether Rampaism or Rasputinism, hers seemed not a religious message but a call to arms.

Like some anorexic Jeanne d'Arc, Bernice admonished the audience to be ever vigilant to the true history of Tibet and its rightful ruler. I imaged her standing in a stratospheric pulpit:

"Acknowledge the messages emanated by the Office of Tibet in New York! And go out, proclaim this good news from roof top to roof top, on the streets and bike paths, at the whole-grain stores, and upon the trails."

Good God, who was this zealot? Bernice reminded me of Myrna Cole Hamm, the local news anchor and social whirligig of station KBOG when I was growing up in Great Falls. An inspired but vacuous soul, she feigned delight in every subject of conversation, and prospected for merit in all manner of folk brought before her. She had nothing to offer of herself, but just existed as a gabby facilitator.

In the next few weeks, I further found Bernice to be a tightly wound ascetic, full of iodine and knotty emotional scars. In a vicious moment, Bernice told me that her boarder Pemba was neither interested in the Dharma nor Tibetan nationalism. He hailed from one of the wealthiest families in Kathmandu, carpet moguls they were. While the family apparently had to post a great sum with the U.S. government for Pemba's student visa, not a penny had been transferred for room and board. Richie Rich, Bernice grumbled, had allegedly been dumped on the Center by the family, a family that assumed a *jin-dak* or patron-client relationship had been created. In reality, poor Pemba, a serious but fun loving student, was kept in the basement. Bernice brought him out like a lively monkey to add ethnic color to her public programs.

And it came to pass that Bernice wished to go to Dharamsala, to the Grand Inji Conference being held in the spring. The first of its kind, it was designed to bring together representatives of the hundred or so Tibetan freedom groups from around the world. She needed someone to manage the center, keep the Program going, and the donations rolling in with the tides. Would I volunteer?

I was tempted. I had finished writing the book, and I had it circulated among publishers. Teaching jobs still had not materialized. What better platform to secure the emigration of my Tibetan friends than to build this cultural center? Missoula was a cool place—the town could support it. Within the week I had moved to this metropolis of Western Montana.

Bernice took me around on her gigs to schools and Rotary Clubs. "You must memorize these facts about Tibet," she insisted, repeatedly, like a mantra, handing me tracts from the Dalai Lama's information ministry. And she would consistently plunge deeply into the red to bring the most famous lama possible to Missoula, regardless of the cost. "I think we shall invite the Dalai Lama next year," she mused. Bernice had events from six to twelve months back that were still not paid for, nor would they ever be. Who would contribute to a botched project from the past? To save money, Bernice cut back the thermostat until frost formed on the inside of the window panes of the house. She put her car into storage, ate nothing but brown rice cakes for weeks on end. During weekends, she sold Tibetan kitsch on blankets at the downtown farmers' market next to the ancient Northern Pacific Railway depot. Every thought, every idea of Lama This-or-That seemed to have the potential of a program, a fundable program from which donations could be solicited and operating costs obtained. All this was for the advancement of Tibet, of course, and the merit of increasing the visibility of the Dharma. Buddhist teaching and the freedom of Tibet were one and the same. Enlightenment itself derived from Tibet, it seemed. Mere personal contact with a Tibetan effected a sort of spiritual liberation.

Bernice instructed me in version of the *Vinaya*, five cardinal rules of the house: 1) no killing, 2) no lying, 3) no sex, 4) no alcohol, drugs, or tobacco, and 5) no pointing of bare feet at holy objects, no rock and roll. We kept quiet hours, prostrations before teachers, and no pets—except for Bernice who sported about a schizophrenic coyote hybrid who snapped at anything with a shirt, including lamas.

After fussing and fidgeting for what had seemed an eternity, Bernice boarded the Greyhound bus bound for the Seattle/Tacoma Airport loaded with gifts for Moon Light—mostly shoes and t-shirts, photographs, and letters for the family. We watched Bernice depart—her gaunt face stretched across the scaffold of an excessively pointed chin. Veejay, Pemba, and I stood on the platform as the bus pulled away, our faces wreathed in smiles.

She left me as free as a lemon yellow finch, and now I was in charge of a real Buddhist Dharma center. Of course, I had Pemba to help me continue to present "Tibet and Its Mysteries" to the forestry jocks and ecology majors at the university. And I would help the Tibetan sophomore from Kathmandu wrap himself up in *chupa* for special occasions. I folded his pleats, and tucked in his belt. He was widely accepted as a personification of Tibet in Exile. On these public days, his wide, dark eyes would sparkle like those of a curious racoon, framed in an arched mask of dusky tan. Pemba refused, though, to wear his hat, a stove-pipe shaped *shamo tshering* native to the capital of Lhasa. He thought it made him look silly.

I gave my lectures at the university, and kept track of the donations that trickled through. I kept the archaic *Vinaya* rules of the household, as did Pemba, who lived in the basement next to the hoary old furnace. In liberal Missoula, it seemed very quaint but ironically suggestive when Pemba-la mentioned his celibacy to his classmates. "I am a student, and I am proud to have maintained my virginity."

It was a strange moment when I first sat down on the seat reserved for the Center's Dharma teacher, the central "throne" facing the congregation. Not all that uncomfortable...in fact it was very relaxing to be dressed in a white silk Tibetan shirt and maroon pants, barefoot, leading the group through routine meditative visualizations. Some sang their mantras like in a Lutheran choir. I attempted a *basso profundo* in imitation of the Namgyal Losaling monks from Dharamsala. I also had daily altar duty, consisting of ritually washing the 14 offering bowls, removing the wilted flowers, and keeping the carnation-scented oil lamp fueled. It seemed a pleasant experience, too, and made me feel like a young acolyte in attendance at some well-worn abbey.

Here in Missoula I lived in communion with many elements of the larger Mahayana community of Hmong and Lao, Vietnamese and Chinese Buddhists. Former officials from the Tibetan Government-in-Exile came to speak at Shamar functions. At these events, Tibetan national flags fluttered as cowboys in denim, fresh faced college students, Native Americans, and tightly corseted city council members listened in rapt attention as the speakers illustrated the wonders of their country and the horrors of its occupation. We always had the living exclamation point known as Pemba on hand to lend authenticity to this highly contrived relationship between Missoula and Tibet. My old professor Frank Bessac was very supportive of the Center, and even recommended me as his possible successor at the University.

Damn, Moon Light could fit right in here! A university for him, a Tibetan cultural center as his very own public relations office, with lots of people who would chase him all over for interviews, photographs, and who knows what. It was all happening now to quiet Pemba. Imagine the impact of the colorful, extroverted Moon Light upon this community!

Hybrid projects were bourgeoning. One rancher was raising yak up in Flathead Valley; elders of the Salish-Kootenay Tribe met with visiting lamas and Tibetan leaders; a sister city project was established between Missoula and Lhasa; the University Library wished to create formal relationships with the Library of Tibetan Works and Archives in Dharamsala. These and a hundred other projects,

Chapter 7

all requiring great investments of time and money, were planning and being dreamed. And money is what Bernice needed in India, too. She had left me with a huge stack of bills. I didn't even have enough reserves to meet her photocopy needs in Dharamsala, let alone save elderly Sherpas. Almost daily I received letters from her asking for money for this or that new charity she had founded, sponsorships for this or that lama, contributions for expenses related to the Grand Inji Conference, a trip for her to see her guru in Nepal. It went on endlessly and unreasonably, but I stood determined to remain loyal to the Program as long as I could.

Bernice shared much in common with her colleagues at the Grand Inji Conference. Despite the good intentions, despite the great efforts, many Western activists for the Tibetan cause were unaware of a profound imbalance between themselves and the Tibetans. Through her status in the movement, through her own self-mortification, Bernice played the unsullied martyr, pushed against the evil forces about her. Those obstacles might even include local Tibetans who were not as zealous as she. I again recalled the words of Pico Iyer:

> ...to regard ourselves as beleaguered innocents and those we meet as shameless predators...is to ignore the great asymmetry that governs every meeting between tourist and local...and that we, often courted by the government, enjoy a kind of unofficial diplomatic immunity, which gives us all the perks of authority and none of the perils of responsibility.[36]

I, however, had the responsibility of assuring Pemba, Veejay, and the others did not freeze this winter. Finally one evening I received a call from India. It was Bernice. Naturally, she was wondering why I hadn't sent any money.

"The electric bill," I said, "and we need to keep the phone on, too."

"I see." Then she added, "There's someone who'd like to talk to you."

"Hello? Hello, Eric-la?" It was Moon Light! I felt heaven blessed to hear his sonorous voice. "We all here give you big Tashi Delek from the Family."

"Moon Light! I can't believe it. It's so nice to hear your voice."

"Bernice-la was so nice to come a get me for her call to America!" Moon Light chirped.

"Yes, it... was very... *nice* of her." I added haltingly, becoming enraged at her attempted hostage-taking. "Moon Light, please be careful of people who make promises to you. Stay on the course. For myself, I am trying very hard to set up a life for you here. I don't know how long it will take. Please be patient!" I pleaded.

Bernice abruptly returned to the phone "See, he really loves you," she said in a rehearsed voice.

"I know that!" I barked.

There was a long silence. "Well, just send what you can. I will check Western Union every day."

That evening, I used the remaining $153.67 in the Shamar regular account to pay the phone bill. My own account was running low, as I received no salary from the Center. Wrong to try to earn a living from the Dharma biz? Did Free Tibet mean an empty wallet?

I learned from the many visitors to the Center that poverty was not the inevitable case. Many former Tibetan government officials were on the international lecture circuit. Lamas, dancers, and singers were all in demand in Missoula, in fact throughout the Western world. The difficulties of running this Buddhist center was no different than the experience of Greg and Tanya in Hawai`i, or others throughout America and Europe. In the West, there are no great monastic estates to provide revenue to maintain monks and nuns and to keep a religious curriculum active. Dharma center directors had to be resourceful and devoted, if not fanatic for the cause.

Among the more exotic visitors at the Center during my tenure was that of the biographer Glenn Mullin, this time without his troupe of chanting monks. Mullin normally played Buffalo Bill to a "Wild East" Show that toured the world. His Gyuto monks, from Namgyal Monastery, the Dalai Lama's private *gompa* in Dharamsala, were known for their remarkable ability to chant individually in "chords." They created striking musical overtones in their throat and nasal passages. Ironically, these great bass blasts were billed as the "Sound of *Sunyata* [Emptiness] itself."

Like Kip and I, Glenn portrayed himself as an Old Guard expatriate in Dharamsala. He stood tall, 30ish, and muscular, with a sunny yellow ponytail that fell down to his waist. He intimidated the local Tibetan studs by racing his chopped Harley up and down the narrow paths between McLeod and Dharamsala. This hell raiser, a modern day Gedun Chöphel (an early twentieth century Tibetan scholar and libertine), wrote the biographies of all 14 Dalai Lamas. Here in Missoula we scheduled him for a talk at the Center.

After I introduced him at Shamar, Glenn walked in great state from the kitchen stove to his seat in front of the living room fireplace that served as the altar, as if there were a retinue of eunuchs with censers and nimble musicians surrounding him. The stunning speaker wore a raw silk shirt in the Nehru style. He had wrapped a thick wooden *mala* around his wrist and had a small *gau* of silver and pink quartz around his neck. Even without his retinue of vocalizing monks, he seemed the image of an Inji Arhant, and radiated brilliant white energy to his many admirers.

I liked Glenn! We became friends. We understood each other's footprint and the creation of persona in Dharamsala. And now we two Old Guards were making our way through the West.

There was no such thing as routine at the Tibetan Center in Missoula. By the fact of the roles at the Center, we were considered instant experts on the subject of Tibet. People listened intently when we spoke out on the subject of human rights in that occupied country. Veejay, Pemba, and I sponsored Tibet Freedom Day with all the trimmings at the student union at University of Montana on March 10, the anniversary of the 1959 Uprising. Posters, buttons, Save Tibet! bumper stickers—it was all there. Petitions to sign, forms for Bernice's elderly Sherpas' home, brochures for Dharma resources in the U.S., and Dalai Lama photos were stacked on the table. We sat at long tables on the ground floor of the atrium, the same tables that I sat at a few years ago trying to sell my artwork. It seemed rather strange to stand on the orange crate now, touting a virtual nation, a stolen country. But here I stood, talking to professors and students, parents and townsfolk about the need for Tibetan national recognition. Pemba positioned himself, smiling sweetly.

The Dharma Center in Missoula was cast within the spectral glow of the New Age Movement. It didn't matter what one's background was, nor what spiritual path one took as long as the philosophy followed a heritage from the traditional peoples of the land. Pemba was a popular guest and presenter at Veejay's Feather Drum Ranch in Colorado Gulch. It catered to wealthy yuppies from San Francisco and celebrities from Los Angeles. Upon flying into Helena, they would

Chapter 7

Tibetan Freedom night in Missoula. Tibetan historian Ngawang Dhondup Narkyid shares a light moment with (l to r) the Dalai Lama's youngest brother, Ngari Rinpoche, his wife Kalon Rinchen Khandro Choegyal, and Pemba Lama.

be met by Veejay and driven past the site of Mrs. Bosell's airport beanery. Eleven miles later, and deep in the forest, the guests of the elegant retreat would steep in Kundalini yoga, deep tissue massage, and shamanic healing clinics. Although an unassuming college kid majoring in Computer Science, Pemba was a living representative of the "lost pre-modern world."

On another occasion, Veejay, Pemba, and I were invited to participate in the blessing of a residential building lot in Polsen, on the banks of Flathead Lake, about one hour north of Missoula. Betty, a blue-eyed, blonde woman from the Center led the group. Surrounded by bluebells and yellow buttercups growing wild on the vacant lot, we formed a "medicine wheel" with several other White participants. Betty, dressed in natural buckskin decorated with red and green seed beads, passed around stalks of burning sweetgrass to "smudge" and purify ourselves. She appropriated an old Lakota ritual to cleanse the building site. Pemba, wearing a sweatshirt and Levis, and Veejay, with her Asian Indian bangles, lent additional Otherness to help guarantee the success of the ceremony. It was ironic that while Betty's benedictions were held on the Salish Indian Reservation territory, no real Native Americans were present. Deloria's words seemed appropriate:

> When actual Indian people did not match this primitivist ideal, object hobbyists tended to dismiss them as tragic, degraded figures, interior Others who had been rendered inauthentic through contact with modern society.[37]

The next morning, back in Missoula, I walked along the bike trail that had been the roadbed of the Milwaukee Road. Where electric orange and maroon streamliners once sped along the Clark Fork River, thistle and willow saplings now grew. I came to my secret place, a rock prominence atop a bluff, and made offerings to Hiawatha and the gods of the wind.

The Grand Inji Conference finally ended for Bernice in Dharamsala with two major resolutions. First, Professor Robert Thurman from Columbia University and his Hollywood friend Richard Gere founded Tibet House in New York and proposed the "Year of Tibet," an international celebration of Tibetan culture. Second, the Tibet-U.S. Resettlement Project was to be rushed through Congress on the back of such supporters as Rep. Thomas Lantos and Sen. Daniel Patrick Moynihan. It mandated 1,000 permanent visas to the United States for Tibetan refugees — not refugees coming directly out of the occupied country, but for members of the "settled" diaspora in India. For most practical purposes, this meant for the solid members of the exiled community built around Dharamsala. It made for a highly unusual project for Congress, in that the immigrants were not political but economic refugees. Essentially it represented a gift from a supportive Congress to the Dalai Lama, who himself wished greater opportunities for some of his subjects through American relocation. Since they all were refugees, it was logical for some to temporarily settle in the West.

The conference over, Bernice returned to Montana and settled back into management of Shamar Ling. The Center's schedule for the next year promptly doubled. I began to work hard to set up the infrastructure that would support 50 Tibetans and their families coming to Missoula for the Tibet-U.S. Resettlement project. It seemed plausible — several companies came forward with promises of jobs for the immigrants. I went to the City Council, the County Human Services Committee, and even presented the resettlement's case to H.H. the Mayor. I want-

ed to build a new life for a few Tibetans brought in through the project. Bernice said it succulently, "If you can't live with Tibetans over there, we'll just bring them here!" The resettlement project put a spotlight on me, and I fancied becoming a "secular *inji* official" while Bernice focused herself more on being the great Shamar priestess. She now took to wearing maroon jumpers and dusky red knit caps full time.   Recognition as representative or not, I would have to provide for Moon Light privately. He was *persona non grata* in Dharamsala and had no chance even to file an application to the Tibet-U.S. Resettlement Project. One had to be a bona fide Tibetan Refugee in good standing with the Dalai Lama's government, complete with Registration Certificate. Moon Light unfortunately was hardly in good stead with his exile government; as an Indian citizen, he wasn't even technically a refugee.

I seemed most fortunate to have spunky Pemba with me. A bright and energetic young fellow, everyone loved him immediately. He excelled in his computer science program at the university, and charmed every city council member and social worker that we dealt with. The chief city planner confided to me, "You know I'm a very straight guy with a wife and a new child, but every time I see Pemba I just have this urge to pick him up and hung him tightly."

So did scores of young co-eds of Pemba's age. The boy, however, continued to profess his archaic "Path of Brahma" student virginity. This, of course, made everyone want him more. He was skillfully able to deflect everyone's interest in his person to the cause of Free Tibet.

Despite the reality of nearly a total lack of funds, the various Shamar Ling programs stumbled on. For my own survival, I tried to distance the resettlement project from the business of the Buddhist Center, but practical matters such as shared office space and telephone made a clear separation impossible. Slowly, however, I made progress towards the day when 50 sturdy Tibetan forerunners, in good standing, would win their places into the Montana settlement cluster. But it created a bitter, black pill for me, feeling Moon Light languishing away in a Himalayan fastness. He could never be made eligible. He was too old to adopt. He didn't have much aptitude nor desire for higher education. The greatest sacrifices could be made to no avail, for he had ceased being a Tibetan refugee. It was impossible. This I had to tell him. I wrote a long and carefully worded letter. I struggled through a presentation of obstacles that had occluded his life, and presented myself stripped down to a skeleton in anguish over my efforts to secure himself in a safe place with ample opportunities. "Hold on, Moon Light, please hold on!" I wrote. Then I sealed the envelope, and walked slowly a half-mile to the post office.

A few weeks later, I received not a thanks for the effort, but an angry blue aerogramme ultimatum: "Please, I don't think I can wait too much longer. You should try to make the move now to get me to Montana, or I will have to choose another option."

Another option?! The words struck as an icy white jolt of fear that shot down my spine. I gasped involuntarily. Inky pools of blackness began to fill my head, and I soon could only see the great Indo-Tibetan God of Time, Mahakala, rise up in my consciousness. Like Shiva under the bright moonlight, he stood there ominously, darkest blue, laughing and snarling. "Grasp time! *Be* time!" he commanded, stomping his fiery trident.   I remembered the assembly of *Dharmapala*, the protector gods, and their great retinues. These gods had taught me how to raise the blood to my head, to transform anger, to focus and channel wrathful energy towards clarity of purpose and will to destroy obstacles. G. Gordon Liddy could do no better, I thought.

I looked around at the 50-something women I had been associating with for the last year. Veejay had been a blast in a jangling leonine sort of way. She left clouds of lilac as she walked through a room, and rained trails of bobby pins in her wake. And there was Marge, too, a kind soul with jet black dyed hair and heavily framed glasses. She planned to head out to volunteer with the Peace Corps in Africa. The gaunt, ascetic Bernice, and dozens of others had formed this cohort, many of them single mothers. All these Dharma people and Pemba, the 100% live mascot of the Tibetan liberation movement, had formed the Center—their faces now swirled around me like the opening credits of "The Brady Bunch." I steeled my resolved for the sake of Moon Light. This dysfunctional ascetic life had to go. And like an eye-twitching REM dream, the celestial mansions vanished.

I accepted a relatively high-paying job as an anthropologist at the state museum back in Hawai`i and proceeded to work my tail off. I put in hundreds of hours of overtime. I also quickly signed a contract for the publication of my book, so I could dedicate it to Moon Light. I remembered Mary Renault's tale of Alexander the Great and his Persian boy, Bagoas.

And I continued to work my tail off. Several months came and went as quickly as mercury cascading down a gigantic pile of jagged boulders. My coffers were finally swelling, but alarmingly no word arrived from Moon Light. Airless days were spent and I caught myself staring off to space quite frequently. The nights seemed especially dark; the only sound I could hear was my own heartbeat.

Finally, one day, after concentrating my thoughts on the mailbox for endless hours, a thin blue letter materialized from Dharamsala. But then I sat with the envelope on the table, unopened, just looking at it in front of me, knowing how the "ultimatum" had come and passed months ago. Finally I lit a candle, and opened the aerogramme with a razor sharp penknife. Slicing along its folds, it blossomed as I set it back down on the table. My eyes immediately fell upon the words:

"I am going to Germany. She is pregnant with my baby and needs me there..."

After a few hectic days in Delhi, I was off to Dharamsala, on the old ride which had become as routine for me as a camping trip in the Rockies. The same ancient grey bus fumed chokingly at the platform with the same stained windows, porters elbowing elderly Indians, bodies elongating and probing to root out assigned seats. Fortune provided me with a good aisle spot for the 14-hour nighttime ride across the northern plains of India and up into the Himalayas. Directly in front of me sat a young English upright bolt named Peter, off to fuzz the edges of his adolescence and discover himself for the first time as a man. Next to him sat an old Parhari couple, a grizzled man in beige woolens, his wife in an appropriate emesis green sari. As two places on my bench seat were still unoccupied, I prayed to have at least continent travel companions. At the last minute, an old lama and a tall, young Tibetan man politely asked pardons and joined me. The lama sat at the window, with me on the aisle and the bachelor Tartar at my right side. The layman was neatly clad in white shirt, covered by a rakish black leather jacket.

I began introductions in rusty Tibetan, and received nods from the two seatmates. I was going to Dharamsala to find my lost friend, I offered, warranting a gracious smile from lama and a compassionate look from Namgyal Wangdu ("Victorious King"). I felt an immediate, warm sense of protection and family. Indeed, I was getting closer to home. I felt heartened that the only Tibetans onboard had sat with me.

No sooner had we left the soot choked atmosphere of Old Delhi than the lama fell fast asleep. Namgyal settled into an alert relaxation as we quietly shared thoughts on each other's *dharma*, our lives' activites. Namgyal worked for one of the Dalai Lama's limitless governmental offices. He was being posted from the Delhi office for training at the Dharamsala headquarters of something called "His Holiness the Dalai Lama's Charitable Trust Handicraft cum Production Import and Export Company, Ltd.," a souvenir and rug concern. A Chandigargh University education, plus a few years of on the job training, had removed him from most of his cohorts and their normative young marriage expectations. A new word became important for these young, modernizing exiles: "career." And a career for Namgyal was his main contribution to the all-important maintenance of Tibetan national identity in exile.

With the gift of the one of the worst roads in India, the bus careened through misty villages on the broad plains of the Jammuna Valley, dodging countless hay lorries, cows, and wayside pedestrians. I told Namgyal that my nearest friend was in danger of running off with a German tourist, and I had flown 10,000 kilometers for the purpose of stopping him. Whatever I had said, it seems to have stuck a resonance within Namgyal. He did not merely respond out of usual Tibetan compassion for another's grief. He sensed a mutual affiliation in our shared experiences, between abstract career dedication and intuitive passions. Perhaps to each, it seemed a broad respite from being torn to pieces by wolves.

Namgyal, it seems, had been in a similar situation with a foreigner, but had quickly sensed its danger. As he described it, a Finnish vamp on holiday to India had fallen deeply in love with him. She had insisted on bringing him back to Scandinavia, kicking, apparently, as a tall, exotic trophy to enliven the halls of some bleak flat on the Baltic. Namgyal preferred staying with his own—he loved his cultural heritage, and had dedicated his life to the service of his sacred king. I found in him an unexpected glint of spring green in my imminent Götterdämmerung—a native son uncorrupted and unseduced by my own lurid West.

Streaking light diffused across the spattered windows. The bus became silent, heads bobbed and bodies passively followed the course of gravity. The semi-desert of the eastern Punjab became cold on this moonless night. I watched tense Peter ahead, furtively attempting to build a spacial barrier between himself and gravity's gift of the deeply sleeping Parhari woman's head upon his chest. Dozing intermittently, I watched two bright-eyed Indian men, barely into their twenties, articulating unreserved affection for each other, stroking each other's arms, hugging and clearly reveling in each other's presence. They seemed to be part of a larger cohort that included the various bus drivers and porters. The gang of young men reserved the front section of the vehicle and its cab for the entire length of the trip—no outsider could approach.

Next to me, my unpretentious soul mate Namgyal was lightly sleeping. There were no barriers between us; we shared the same basic outlook, the same pain, the same point in time and space. In the chill air of the velvet dark night, through the vibration of motion, the gentle swaying, a cool, sharp edge of black leather met its counterpart. We apportioned whatever warmth we had. It flowed through and merged, the boundaries of self disappearing.

In this twilight sleep, the bus drove through countless anti-terrorist roadblocks, swirls of carbines and khaki berets, the scene as surreal and irrelevant as a bad Rambo video playing in the background of an intimate dinner party. At Chandigarh, at once the capital of Hariyana and the Punjab, the bus halted for two hours—the border with Himachal state was closed in the dead hours of night due to Sikh separatists.

Namgyal and I alighted upon the terminal platform. In the greenish white glare of food vendors booths, we kept close company—blond Eric, in black leather and dark Namgyal in black leather, moving together in counterpoint. Quietly he bought us several spicy *samosas*. Silently we smoked cigarettes and stood around in James Dean poses. We watched as cramped, sweating Punjabi tribesmen bolted from their buses, their pastel turbans askew, and headed for the food stalls. In well rehearsed routines, they boisterously hacked and spit, urinated, and frantically stuffed several dripping *samosa* in their mouths, all the while scarcely missing a syllable in animated reportage. Peter stood alone, leaning slightly on a pillar, alternating between studious indifference and glazed transfixed at these nocturnal Indian revelries.

The lama never stirred as the journey resumed, being long-departed to the realm of some deep meditation. We were climbing steadily through the mountains now, out of the plains and into Himachal Pradesh. If facing my own twilight ahead, I was protected that night, at least. Namgyal's presence seemed assurance of that. I felt a distant hope that new friends could pull me through. Waves of emotional transference began surging through. I gave little resistance to these easy feelings. I was safe in the notion that my travel partner understood. Namgyal and I shared each other's space as naturally as napping otter pups. His restless head soon locked firmly onto my chest and arm, his long hair smelling faintly of old-fashioned lilac vegetal. I gently placed his hand on my leg, his elegant fingers entwined with mine. We both fell soundly asleep.

Daybreak brought a scintillation of verdant hilltop apple orchards and clear mountain streams, following one by one. Namgyal awoke, combed his hair, and removed his shiny black jacket, heat expelling like an oven door being opened. Stiff necked Peter stared unflinchingly at the two young Indian friends near the door. In fact, they seemed to be flaunting their close affection for Peter's shocked benefit, as no one else seemed to notice. The porters, drivers, and their buddies ran the show, after all.

At high noon the bus creaked into lower Dharamsala. Namgyal told me of the office he would be working at—I hadn't the slightest idea where I would be staying myself. A crowd gathered at the bus stop, and Namgyal and the lama were quickly spirited off by a group of laughing Tibetan men and women. I looked in vain for Moon Light's father's taxi. Sadly, there were no familiar faces, just swarms of unknown Parhari porters and determined Sikhs, an occasional blond or red tourist head bobbing above the crush. Suddenly I was a foreigner again, consigned to stand alone with neophyte Peter and wait for the irregular bus to McLeod Ganj.

After finally motoring up the hill and reaching the Tibetan village bus stand, I sent Peter off to the Shangri-la Hotel, just past Moon Light's café. Heart pounding, I avoided glancing in that general direction. I felt and looked like a yeti or a sloth with green algae growing on my hair; I needed sleep and a bath. Since I

Chapter 7

had lightly packed, I avoided the usual porter touts and headed for Hotel Tibet on Baghsunath Road.

Once again I experienced the sleep of the dead, remaining in the deepest slumber for 14 hours. When I did awake to a brilliant yellow and sky blue day, I did so instantaneously. I sat up neither anxious nor blinded in awakening—there was a great excitement in what lay ahead. I opened the shades and looked out on the back alleys of sunrise upon McLeod Ganj. My eyes casually roamed over the iron rooftops and adobe shacks built behind the facades of the large concrete hotels. My room was, I figured, exactly ten feet directly above Amala's long-demolished hut, the "Last Chance Café," named for its location on the edge of town. Now the spot lay in the center of town. I opened the windows to the sounds of pots and pans being washed at the back of the Shambala Hotel. Next to it stood the kitchen and the private quarters of Moon Light's family. Beyond these two buildings rose the Asok Hotel that I had stayed in last time I saw Moon Light, and next to the clinic of a famous Tibetan doctor.

Suddenly I caught a glimpse of a very tan muscle boy bounding through the narrow passages and over the rocks and pipes between houses and shops. It was Kunga, Moon Light's brother! My heart pounded, and I hurriedly shaved and got dressed. Happy memories flowed in. Just possibly, maybe, Moon Light was here too! I looked back out the window. No, it wasn't Kunga, but someone else. Someone else's bright son. In fact, as I left the Hotel Tibet to visit the Kalimpong Café, no one on the street looked familiar. I passed the location of Rinzin's Donut place. It had a different name and it was filled with strangers. Rinzin Donut had already left for Salt Lake City, Utah, as part of the U.S.-Tibet Resettlement project. The same story in the Kokonor and Green hotels—everyone was different. Walking around town, I finally found ancient Mr. and Mrs. Nowrojee sitting on their back porch overlooking the grand valley beneath. And to the Shambala, the old Toepa Hotel, where the reassuring matronly figure of Samden still presided. She, too, planned to leave for the United States in a few weeks.

Samden, her gold tooth glinting in an ever-present smile, brought over a large pot of tea and a slice of banana creme cake for which she was famous. She filled me till bursting with all the local gossip, save one family. So I brought it up—I asked about Moon Light's family and his problems. It quickly became evident to her that I did not know.

"Eric...Moon Light has already gone."

I took another bite of banana cake.

"Ah. He left about three weeks ago. For Germany," Samden said quietly.

"Yeah. Of course, right..." I feigned, being completely unaware of his departure.

"Oh, she's a very nice girl. Very pretty. Her name is Kristin."

"How is the rest of the family?"

"Well, Amala still works too hard. The youngest boy Nima is still here, and the girls."

"Their restaurant is not doing so well, is it" I asked.

"No. The rumors..."

I stayed a bit longer, finishing my cake and drinking my tea, but Samden could clearly see my utter disappointment. At least once in your life you should travel halfway around the world for nothing. Had it all been an illusion? What to do now, here among strangers? I decided to simply walk. To Baghsunath, to Triund, past T.I.P.A. and Cow Barn. I walked over to Thegchen Chöling, the Dalai Lama's residence, and down to the Library. I wandered through the bazaar of Dharamsala, and even out to Forsythe Ganj, where rumor had it that Da Duk had returned to this small town, and was living with his mother. But even the Powerful Tiger seemed not to be there. All the old Tibetans had left, or were leaving. All that plied the streets here were strange *inji* faces and new Tibetan arrivals escaping from over the border.

And it stuck me that this, in fact, foretold the ultimate nature of Dharamsala. It stood for a place of rest on a journey, not a destination to itself. This is, in fact, reflected in the meaning of *dharamshala* in Sanskrit. Only Nowrojees were permanent residents, and they had been here since the Zoroastrian exodus from Persia. Old as they may be, they were still here, a relic of not just the British but the Moghul raj. All the *inji* grad students and Indian tourism copy writers musing about Dharamsala as "Little Lhasa" were being foolish.

Still, the Upper and Lower Villages had a history. They were places that showed great change over the years, unpredictable change. McLeod Ganj stood on its hilltop neither Indian nor Tibetan—more an alcove of the Western imagination. Over the last 20 years, it had been terraformed not by Tibetan or even Indian regional planners, but by the international community that by now had become fed-up with the lack of basic facilities. McLeod Ganj finally got a sewer system! Tourists were no longer content with flopping on charpois in stark concrete blocks, luxury had begun to seep in through continuous tourist demand. New hotels mushroomed everywhere, built atop one another and crowding the narrow streets even more.

The town was filled with so many Western boys and girls, in their 20s, even teens. All wore light cottons and many were barefooted. It looked more like a large slumber party than a refugee village in the mountains. I suppose the Dalai Lama himself had been the agent for much of this attraction. He now had become an older, wizened man, a Grand Lama for the World who you might truly expect to be meditating in a tiny hermitage on the top of a high peak. He transformed himself into a Yoda-like Buddhist pope, one who offered compassion and humor in a field where strict dogma and inhuman prohibitions to the enjoyment were common. His over-worn celebrity throughout the world, on the other hand, had placed him in the same category as any pop superstar. I would not be surprised to someday see the Dalai Lama as a guest of Larry King in company with Ann Landers and Dr. Joyce Brothers.

Dharamsala, so packed with young tourists steeping themselves in its self-conscious, exotic ambiance, always seemed just a window into Tibet. Like Tibet itself, it was never a paradise for Westerners; it merely represented Shangri-La expectations of generations of EuroAmericans. It now constructed a Western projection created largely by market forces. Dharamsala remained an unfulfilled dream, the unrequited goal of foreign empire, just a place for Tibetan refugees to rest up before moving on to a better life. Were we, as the members of the Old Guard and Tibetan Resettlement officers, merely the temporary almsmen for the Golden Horde?

I had exhausted myself walking throughout my second home, where each tree, rock, and chai shop was engraved with the images of a naive younger self and the portraits of my departed friends.

Chapter 7

But now I had bona fide, Green Card official business to do. I made a call at the Ministry in charge of the Tibetan resettlement and was appraised of the selection process. I spent many hours with the volunteer workers and the Tibetans, working on infrastructural charts and surveys. Bernice's friend from the University of Montana arrived and we presented a report on reciprocal exchange with the Library of Tibetan Works and Archives. The entire board attended. My old friend Tashi Tsering had grown into a formidable scholar. My genial teacher, Gyatso Tsering still chaired the board.

During my furtive stay in Dharamsala, I met many people, including an Indian who had become a Karma Kagyu Tibetan Buddhist. Dibyesh was his name, and he had been a good friend of Moon Light's. His mother was a very celebrated Indian film star. The worldly monk introduced me to his friend, Annie, a Scottish anthropologist, researching her Ph.D. thesis here in McLeod Ganj. She said she had wanted to meet me for quite sometime now, and seemed surprised that I was in Dharamsala. The three of us arranged to meet for lunch at Hotel Tibet.

"I know all about you. You wrote your dissertation on the patronage system of Tibet," Annie chirped. "I'm writing about the abuses of the patronage relationship in the modern times with Western tourists. Would you care to help me in my project?"

"Sure, I don't mind. You think I'm an expert?" I realized that I had myself become a subject of anthropological study, one of her "cases." Cool.

Dibyesh told me a story of Moon Light visiting the Tai Situ Rinpoche, and spending the night in the guest house with his girlfriend *du jour*.

"That was wrong," the monk said. "Even though I am a young man, too, and have spent most of my life as a worldly man, it is wrong to bring all of that up to a *gompa*. It doesn't belong there. It's something that Rinpoche shouldn't have to deal with."

"What do you think is the problem with him?" I asked.

"Oh, well, he thinks of himself as the 'Naughty Rinpoche', someone for whom the rules do not apply. Moon Light will have severe problems in Germany, and anywhere else he goes."

"You're being too hard."

"I know him well," Dibyesh suggested.

"Everyone in Dharamsala knows of Moon Light and his reputation." Annie added. "What we have with this situation with you is clearly a case of *jindak* abuse. All the Tibetans know about it, but they won't tell you out of modesty and their own embarrassment."

"Guess you're right. But I just couldn't walk away from what I think are my responsibilities."

"What do you mean?" Dibyesh argued, "You couldn't do anything for him. You just fooled yourself. What were you going to do, free Tibet for him?"

"He would have gone where ever the winds had blown him, and with whomever he could charm. When I interviewed him, he seemed to be sexually naive, not knowing the impact or consequences of his actions with people," Annie reported.

"He's just a boy." I protested.

"Yet he's made a foreign girl pregnant, and now he's running off to Germany to get away as much as to be with her," Dibyesh countered.

The monk and the stout Scottish woman lecturing me about the haloed one! They seemed like characters from the *Canterbury Tales*, the scolding clerics on the pilgrimage road. But I listened to them, listened intently. Why were they so intently interested in me?

Over the course of the next few days, and over innumerable plates of momos and pots of tea, we discussed the personality of Moon Light. We teased and tore up his complex character, as if he was an alien from Roswell. Was he a unique soul, or was he typical of the thousands of Tibetan refugees in India, ill-at-ease with the acute impermanence of their situation? We had no conclusions to our volumes and deliberations; Moon Light's life seemed a paradox.

Except for the woman and the monk, the sociologist and the cleric, all other faces I encountered were of featureless strangers or of images quickly receding into ghostly memory. The few icons still in McLeod Ganj were like faded billboards painted on old brick buildings. My work here had finished. The temperamental German-American had showed the Tibetan exile boy his homeland. But instead of learning to be a Tibetan, he had left for Germany instead. Thus, I bid goodbye to Dibyesh and Annie, and the hangers-on in Dharamsala. I returned home.

Detroit! It was sometime around March 8, just long enough after the Indian misadventure to have accrued some vacation time and extra cash. Good morning... as I stumbled wilted from the Northwest redeye from Honolulu and past the reeking Cinn-a-bun™ in the concourse. Finally, all the this-and-thats were done and I heeled hard on my way at last to Europe to visit Moon Light. Well, I wrote a whole book this month—true, but it stood tangential to my primary interest. But I am on my way to Europe, a voyage to the past and to the future. To times never-to-be. And I will take the TGV to where buckskin breeches and sew-on leather vests were tailored with bone awls 10,000 years ago, and golden hair arose through the passage of the generations rather than the peroxide bottle.

Half a day ago I floated, luxuriating in Patty Hearst's travertine marble bathroom with the clever skylights—that dripping world of raging surfs on O`ahu's North Shore. And their greatly stuffed couches, cool to overexposed skin. Now I find myself in the transit wing of the Detroit Metro Airport, with the glories of buzzing fluorescent tubes and too many shoeshine men. Airline "hub and spoke" systems are the catherine wheels of the modern age. The assaulted and insulted by the thousand are dumped here, with no recourse except to shrink into themselves. Here is the hell of the smokers' lounge where pent up stresses erupt into noxious clouds of sulfides and monoxides. Like bones sticking out of the sand of some forlorn beach, cigarette butts grew out of ashcans. Coal tar lipstick lay on burnt white stubs while old women clutched Kleenex to their shriveled bosoms.

The cranky old plane with the angry red tail finally landed at Charles DeGaulle Airport, sometime in the mid-morning. Then the Regional Express paced a slow blur to my hotel near the Bastille. Check-in and oblivion on worn cotton sheets.

The experience of mega-sleeping, this time 16 hours straight, was still completely satisfying—waking up slightly, grabbing the covers, turning over and out for a few more hours. The saga dreams. I dreamt of a nun, a great nun-authoress, who was signing books in a large hall. As I approached the table, she looked at me, then refused to sign the book I held. She called for her aide. My

Chapter 7

presence seemed an outrage. "Tsk, tsk, tsk" I heard all 'round. The news spread like the plague, and my friends dropped away, a pariah. When the predacious birds got stuck in my hair, I awoke.

It was 3:30 a.m., and I was hard pressed to estimate the day of the week. Breakfast wouldn't be ready for three hours, forcing me to eat the leftover bag of airplane raisins. I let my eyes float around the half-timbered wall of the sixteenth century pension, and out across the leaden mansard roofs of the atmospheric city of Paris.

The weight of the past demanded attention in this city of children dressed in black, relieved by flashes of DayGlo orange and green phosphor. At the Louvre, I found myself staring back from the glass reflection on Dürer's "Portrait of the Artist as a Young Man." The subject held his flower so delicately. The rawboned German behind the golden curls looked contemptuously out on the thousands of tourists crammed into the glass pyramid. In the café, chocolate melted on my words.

To Moon Light's...

What are they doing here? Twin Mercedes filled with large Germans in russet leather coats imbued with AutoFresk© roared up the steep road to the castle. The *schloß* is closed, the sign read. The tourist shops with their cheap decaled plates and bicycle stickers were marginally committed to being open. The village seemed to be slowly awakening from a winter hibernation. The lake was still nearly dried up; the boats were run aground, lying on the pebbly sand like mummified seals. Last winter's leaves covered the frosty ground where boars plowed and ruddy hunters in dark green velvet tramped. The aroma of raw potatoes suffused the air from just plowed fields.

To the village, or to the castle? With the tourist path still uncovered, the usual clues to either were missing. No peasants in their fields, no butcher or cobbler, and most unsettling, no obvious sign of "family." Oddly, there were no large mansions in Waldeck that might indicate continuing interest by or even existence of the princely clan.

The day was suffused by an eerie sensation of things I hoped would be familiar. Instead, faces and landscapes were blocked by great grey, frustrating voids of ignorance. I drew in, yet still felt disconnected—so much seemed missing. I felt like the Grand Duchess Olga visiting the Anastasia imposter Anna Andersen: "All the same, my niece's features could not possibly have altered out of all recognition. The nose, the mouth, the eyes were all different."[38]

I bought a post card, a decal, and an enameled pin with the crest of Waldeck. World War I left the burghers here with this and little more. A castle remained, which would soon be filled only with mummery and pageantry and hotel staff in medieval costume. Flag throwers, fresh from college classes in Marburg would grace boar's head banquets thrown for bus loads of tourists from Brighton and Leeds in a week hence.

But the outer courtyard flew open before us. Crenulated walls overlooked the river and lake far below. The village stood on the north side of the walls, and the low hills of brown plowed fields stretched to the east. I straddled a large cannon that pointed at Moon Light.

"Do you know the secret? It's a great coincidence," I asked from my perch.

It was all ancient brown earth, smelling of potatoes, with the village on one hill and the castle on the other.

"No... No, what is this all about?"

"I had brought you to Tibet, to your homeland. We visited Lhasa, Gyantse, and the towns and fields of your ancestors. I stood with you as you saw yourself for the first time. Your people...Tibet."

"Yeah, it was pretty amazing. Thanks for that." Moon Light smiled.

"Now, it is the same thing, only the roles have reversed. It's not because I am a tourist just wishing to see a German castle that I brought you up here. We are only 50 kilometers from where you have settled to live your life, Moon Light. You have brought me to this place, and this will shock you. My ancestors are from this *schloß*" I thought of my mysterious great grandmother, Pauline. Her life and that of her daughter were making sense now!

"My family ruled this place. Once, when they were independent princes of a tiny country. I am from the Waldeck family, Moon Light, but have never been here before. It has been a great unknown all my life. This is a wonderful legacy that I have found, a sense of belonging to a place over 1,200 years old. It seems my great fortune for you to bring me here."

"Ah, Eric-la! How do you feel?"

"A bit strange. I feel unsettled. Am I supposed to be happy, or recognize everything and myself in everyone? Yet I am a part of this soil, the air. This is my sunshine. And of course, you brought me here!"

I got off my cannon and walked over to my friends. Both Kristin and Moon Light looked incredulous. The three of us remained silent throughout the drive back to Marburg. Moon Light knew well the meaning of deep coincidences. They confirmed elements of his own past life.

Thomas served as Moon Light's martial arts instructor, and somewhat of a Tibetologist, if I gathered correctly from him. I met him the day after the Waldeck Schloß visit, and was happy to get back to things Tibetan. Thomas came over for dinner, and brought a new book on Tibetan refugees written by yet again another Western traveler. Jigme, the child who had been holding so hard to my right leg, began to cry loudly. Normally a studious and patient child, Moon Light and Kristin's baby had to see the photos in the book first. So I hoisted him up to the table, and flipped through the pages. There were 30 or 40 images of refugees in the book, mostly of shop owners or elderly monks in McLeod Ganj. Many were my friends, who always got a kick out of being depicted as an exotic indigent in some Western publication.

Thomas was working on his dissertation thesis about Tibetan refugees, and had been anxious to meet me, according to Moon Light. He had recently written a book on Kung Fu, and now had begun a serious study of demographic shifts in Tibet populations in South Asia—very precise, Germanic stuff. The paper that he handed me was a jewel of pointless lucubration.

Thomas Methfessel is a tall man, well over 6'3". He has the same wide jaw and small chin as the great artist Dürer. Long blond hair and grey eyes, with a slightly upturned nose, thin red lips, heavy bones, little flesh. His head was round, like the ancient people of Alpine stock. How great to meet someone else who is studying my topic, especially someone who is now Moon Light's good friend.

A native of this region, Thomas's ancestors have probably lived here since the end of the Pleistocene. The fact that Thomas professed Buddhism simply made him a normal part of the Central Germany Green Party-New Age set that was serious about their brand of neo-orientalism. His New Age lifestyle was representative of a rather lymphatic Hessian ambivalence towards the world. Thomas felt familiar to me. He looked familiar. In fact, his large, pointed face very much resembled that of late Aunt Mamie (the same aunt a friend once described as a close match to Agnes Moorehead on *Bewitched*). He even seemed to have some of the same hard-headed attitudes.

"So, then, what did you do yesterday?" Thomas inquired.

"We took a drive up to Schloß Waldeck," Kristin piped.

"What did you think of it?"

"It was closed—the hotel, but the courtyard was open. It's a great place. Very beautiful," I added.

"My family is from there. It's quite incredible that you went there. My mother is a Waldeck. They didn't have the "von" before the name because they had gotten away from the ruling line. I went up to the capital at Arolsen and found the genealogical papers."

My face flushed. Kristin and Moon Light immediately turned to me in great anticipation. "Then I should call you cousin," I stated. Often in the last few months I had thought what might happen if I sought out a member of the Waldeck family and arranged a meeting. Here then is the reality of parallel universes!

There are only about 300 Tibetologists in the whole world. How many are working on the subject of Tibetan refugees in South Asia? Of those, how many are close friends with Da'od Gyatso, and of those, how many are blood-related without knowledge of it?

Thomas and I looked intensely at each other, peeling each other down to the skin, to the bone. I saw in his features those of my grandmother, the one whose tales no one believed. Elisabeth Fjeld, born in Sweden, was the daughter of Pauline, daughter of Friedrich Christian, Prince of Waldeck und Pyrmont, by a certain Norwegian named Bratlund. The Waldeck family's chief claim to fame, other than the fact that they saved their independence by allying themselves with Prussia during the Austro-Prussian war of 1859, was that Prince Friedrich Christian produced another daughter. Instead of running off with a Norwegian sailor, Princess Emma von Waldeck und Pyrmont was married off to the childless King William III of the Netherlands. Plump and healthy, Queen Emma wasted no time in producing an heir, Wilhelmina, and a line of Dutch queens extending to the present day. As for the princes of Waldeck and Pyrmont, they lost the sovereignty of their 600 square-miles with the other German rulers in 1918. Fortunately, they kept their baroque palace, the Residenz in Arolsen. The more ancient Schloß Waldeck, south of Arolsen, had been given over to the tax man at the beginning of the twentieth century, and the State of Hesse remodeled it into a hotel.

Moon Light and I were awestruck; my grandmother vindicated. Baby Jigme held on to me in a tighter grip. Kristin served tiramisu.

From that day on, the Tibetan language was rarely spoken by Moon Light and me. English was primarily the medium, but with Kristin's patient help, I learned German daily, as did Moon Light. Little blond Jigme spoke only German.

In a glance to Kristin I resigned my fate. At my departure at Marburg station, the early spring sun began to set. And indeed, I was leaving, not her. Had she been a gorgon or a sea hag, I would have mounted a challenge. Yet she seemed faultless in heart and of form, which provided no cause for doubt. Her father, a medical doctor like mine, was very wealthy. This fact had an eyebrow or two raised back in Dharamsala. Moon Light had simply blundered into the Western paradise? Whatever the motivation, this formed his basic nature.

So in that instant, I gave her my acceptance, indeed my thanks, and my regrets for leaving. Then the white face of the electric locomotive appeared silently, down the rails shining red in the last rays of the afternoon. I kissed the child, grown sullen and entirely silent. My arms encircled mother and son, perhaps imparting some benefaction, perhaps being slightly ludicrous. I stood as a celibate hierophant blessing the gamboling line of fleshy rebirth. The red metal coaches drew past us and stopped. In the moment, I sensed Moon Light's increasing agitation, rocking and pacing from side to side and thinking, "me! me!" So I pulled his head to mine, and kissed him like a feather brushing softly on his apple cheek.

But now it was a hollow charade. I climbed the stairs of the coach, and settled into a first class compartment with my German books. I didn't look back as the train gathered speed, passing the University of Marburg dorms and classroom, southwards towards Gleisen and Hess-Darmstadt. After awhile, I saw the first dustings of snow on the ramparts of the old city of Rothenburg. The bakers in the ancient capital, whose town was tucked in a fold of the Main River valley, had been working hard sprinkling sugar on great cakes of toasted almonds. In the ancient Duchy of Franconia, just southeast of Waldeck, the Christmas season had begun. The dark green pines were festooned with strings of little pressed glass lights, brightly colored and glowing softly.

* * *

Notes

1. Jean Gering, "Fear and Loving in the West Indies," in Don Kulick and Margaret Wilson (eds.) *Taboo* (New York and London: Routledge, 1995), pp.186-187.
2. Margaret Wilson, "Afterword," *Taboo,* p. 252.
3. Kirsten Hastrup, "Writing Ethnography: The State of the Art," in Judith Okley and Helen Callaway (eds.) *Anthropology and Autobiography* (London and New York: Routledge, 1992).
4. Friar John, "The Journey of Friar John of Pian de Carpinin to the Court of Kuyuk Khan, 1245-1247," in Manuel Komroff (ed.) *Contemporaries of Marco Polo* (New York: Liveright Publishing, 1928), p. 7.
5. August Waddell, *Lhasa and Its Mysteries* (New York: Dover Publications, 1905), pp. 447-478.
6. Friar William, "The Journal of Friar William," in *Contemporaries,* p. 117.
7. Friar Odoric, "The Journal of Friar Odoric," in *Contemporaries,* pp. 244-245.
8. Robert Bly, *Iron John* (Reading, MA: Addison-Wesley, 1990).
9. Christine Dowling, *Myths and Mysteries of Same-Sex Love* (New York: Continuum,1989), p.154.
10. Ibid.
11. Matthaeis Parisiensis, *Chronica Major,* cited in Komroff, pp. xii-xiii.
12. Abbé Huc and Gabet, *Travels in Tartary, Thibet and China, 1844-1846.* Volume 2. (London: Routledge, 1928), p. 173.
13. Ibid, p.175.
14. Marshal Sahlins, *Historical Metaphors and Mythical Realities* (Chicago: University of Chicago Press, 1981), p. 25.
15. Bly, p. 107-108.
16. Pico Iyer, *Video Nights in Kathmandu* (New York: Alfred Knopf, 1989), pp. 21-22.
17. *National Geographic Explorer*, May/June 1992, p.16.
18. See Michel Foucault's discussion of "memory traces" in *The Archaeology of Knowledge* (New York: Pantheon, 1982).
19. See James Clifford and George E. Marcus, *Writing Culture* (Berkeley, CA: University of California Press, 1986), pp. 35-43.
20. Peter Gold, *Tibetan Reflections* (London: Wisdom Publications, 1984), p. 9.
21. Ghislain de Diesbach, *Secrets of the Gotha* (New York: Barnes and Noble, 1993), p. 262.
22. Joseph Campbell, *Historical Atlas of World Mythology,* Vol. 1(2). "The Way of the Animal Powers" (New York: Harper and Row, 1972), p. 25.
23. Richard A. Sweder, "Aspects of Cognition in Zinacanteco Shamans: Experimental Results" in William A. Lessa and Evon Z. Vogt (eds.) *Reader in Comparative Religion: An Anthropological Approach* (New York: Harper and Row 1972), p. 25.

24. Campbell, p. 171.

25. Henry Purcell (1658-1695), "See Nature, rejoicing" in "Music for Queen Mary."

26. Zhang Hanian, cited in Bert Hinsch, *Passions of the Cut Sleeve* (Berkeley: University of California Press, 1990) p. 71.

27. Iyer, p. 15.

28. Robert Bolton, "Tricks, friends, and lovers: erotic encounters in the field," in *Taboo*, p. 150.

29. Alexandra David-Neel, *Journey to Lhasa* (New Delhi: Book Emporium, 1982).

30. Henry Purcell, No. 24, Act III, "The Indian Queen."

31. David-Neel, p. 35.

32. Austine Waddell, *Buddhism and Lamaism of Tibet* (New Delhi: Heritage Publishers, 1979 [1895]), p 524.

33. Jampel Tsering, cited in Steve Lehman's *The Tibetans* (New York: Umbrage Editions, 1998) pp. 20-21.

34. Steve Lehman, *The Tibetans*, pp. 31-43.

35. Iyer, p. 16.

36. Ibid, p. 15.

37. Philip J. Deloria, *Playing Indian* (New Haven, Yale University, 1998) p. 137.

38. Grand Duchess Olga Alexandrovna, cited in Ian Vorres, *The Last Grand Duchess* (New York: Scribner's Sons) p. 176.

Acknowledgements

So many people have contributed to the making of this book. In my excitement in getting it into production, please forgive me if I have temporarily forgotten you. It was not intentional.

I was most fortunate to have the prolific author and scholar, William Hoffman, as an efficient and encouraging editor. Your acerbity *was* truly appreciated. Thank you! I also thank Dr. Keila Diehl for her insightful and common-sense reading of the manuscript. In the spirit of Tibet-o-Rama, I was blessed to have the photographic contributions of my great friend Dong Lin, whose sensitive portraits of people not only inspire but celebrate the richness of the human condition. Thanks to all the decent folk at Green Arrow Press and Hignell Book Publishing for their dedication to professional production and printing. Thanks John Zane instilling in me a 'kerning angst'. I appreciate the encouragement of Dibyesh Anand, a young firebrand of a Tibet scholar, and Stephen C., who provides a voice as subtle as the prophet's arrow. And acknowledgements go to scholars Drs. Donald Lopez and Claire Harris for sharing, over precious time, their wonderful clarity on modern Tibetan life. Thank you Glenn Mullin and Dr. Toni Huber; I sometimes get the two of your confused. Jan Magnusson, a.k.a. Rocko, thanks for lightening up the tone of my work by conjuring its title, thus making it 'fluffy not stuffy'. Veejay and Pemba, if you're still out there, you know how kindly I think of you.

How could anyone forget Samden, who made breakfast for me everyday at her restaurant in Dharamsala and continues with dinners at the Tibet Cafe in Berkeley, or Rinchen Wangmo, who was everyone's sister and filled us all with donuts in McLeod Ganj. Thanks also to "Last Chance" Amala. Throughout a generation, Gyatso Tshering, Director of the Library of Tibetan Works and Archives was a respected teacher friend to many including myself. He was astute in pointing out my errors yet encouraging me to keep my eyes wide open. I am appreciative of the gentle knowledge and instruction from Nechung Drayang Ling, Kargyu Shenpen Ling, and other *ling*s of a hundred melodious sounds. Thanks to old friends Thinley Dhondup of Kathmandu, Thupden Dawa Sangha of McLeod Ganj, and Sonam Tashi of everywhere. Cannot forget Mrs. Nowrojee and her late husband Nauser, the souls of Dharamsala.

Thanks to Dr. Carole McGranahan for her insightful thoughts on history, to Emily Yeh for her unique perspectives on Tibetanness, Dr. Charlene MacLay for her inspiring work on gender in Tibet, plus the great teachers Drs. Melvyn Goldstein, Lee Siegel, and Frank Bessac, old friends Drs. Paljor Tsarong, Laurie Hovell McMillan, Vincainne Adams, and other scholars for your thoughts and encouragement. Same to the two Tethong brothers, Tenzin N. and Tenzin G., thank you Kazur lak. A special thought goes to Dr. Fred Blake, my graduate chair, who tried to teach me about the humanistic approach to anthropology.

To my other friends in Kathmandu, thanks must also go to Ramesh Kumar Josie, Dr. Om Gurung, Harkha Lama, and Dr. Ram Chhetri. Thanks Chip Weigand, Keith Liker, Esq., Ollie, Dr. Karma Lekshe Tsomo, Lama Karma Rinchen and the late Nechung Rinpoche II. Thanks to Laura Jason, the muse in black, for her advice on the judicious use of passive construction.

Above all, I would like to express my gratitude to all the bright stars make a difference in the world and allowed me, in this particular case, to have great fun writing this book. Thank you.[*]

---

[*] And Eric will never forget Mrs. Bosell and her chihuahuas.